A History of the Protection of Regional Cultural Minorities in Europe

D1713275

Also by Antony Alcock

THE FUTURE OF CULTURAL MINORITIES (*co-editor with B. K. Taylor and J. Welton*)

HISTORY OF THE INTERNATIONAL LABOUR ORGANISATION

HISTORY OF THE SOUTH TYROL QUESTION

A SHORT HISTORY OF EUROPE

SÜDTIROL SEIT DEM PAKET

UNDERSTANDING ULSTER

A History of the Protection of Regional Cultural Minorities in Europe

From the Edict of Nantes to the Present Day

Antony Alcock
Professor of European Studies
University of Ulster
Northern Ireland

WITHDRAWN

First published in Great Britain 2000 by
MACMILLAN PRESS LTD
Houndmills, Basingstoke, Hampshire RG21 6XS and London
Companies and representatives throughout the world

A catalogue record for this book is available from the British Library.

ISBN 0–333–65261–4

First published in the United States of America 2000 by
ST. MARTIN'S PRESS, LLC,
Scholarly and Reference Division,
175 Fifth Avenue, New York, N.Y. 10010

ISBN 0–312–23556–9

Library of Congress Cataloging-in-Publication Data
Alcock, Antony Evelyn.
    A history of the protection of regional cultural minorities in Europe : from
the Edict of Nantes to the present day / Antony Alcock.
        p.   cm.
    Includes bibliographical references and index.
    ISBN 0–312–23556–9 (cloth)
        1. Europe—Ethnic relations. 2. Europe—Ethnic relations—Government
policy. 3. Minorities—Europe—History. 4. Minorities—Government policy–
–Europe—History. 5. Self-determination, National—Europe—History. 6.
Europe—History—Autonomy and independence movements. I. Title.

    D1056 .A43 2000
    305.8'0094—dc21

                                                                00–030889

This book is printed on paper suitable for recycling and made from fully managed and sustained
forest sources.

10   9   8   7   6   5   4   3   2   1
09   08   07   06   05   04   03   02   01   00

Printed and bound in Great Britain by
Antony Rowe Ltd, Chippenham, Wiltshire

Contents

List of Maps

List of Abbreviations

AERT	Autonome Europa Region Tirol (Autonomous European Region Tyrol)
ARC	Autonomous Republic of the Crimea
CD	Christian Democrats
CSCE	Conference on Security and Co-operation in Europe
CSO	Committee of Senior Officers (OSCE)
DC	Democrazia Cristiana
DL	Decreto Legge
DPR	Decreto del Presidente della Repubblica
DUP	Democratic Unionist Party (Northern Ireland)
ECHR	European Convention on Human Rights
EOKA	Ethniki Organosis Kypriakou Agonos (National Organisation of Cypriot Fighters)
ETA	Euskadi Ta Askatasuna: Euskadi & Freedom (Spain-Basque Country)
EU	European Union
FIER	Foundation on Inter-Ethnic Relations (OSCE)
FLB	Front de Libération Bretonne: Breton Liberation Front (France)
FLNC	Front de Libération Nationale de la Corse: Corsican National Liberation Front (France)
FRANCIA	Front d'Action Nouvelle Contre l'Indépendance et l'Autonomisme (France-Corsica)
FUEN	Federal Union of European Nations
FUEV	Federalistische Union der Europäischen Volker
FYROM	Former Yugoslav Republic of Macedonia
HB	Herri Batasuna: United People (Spain-Basque Country)
HCNM	High Commissioner on National Minorities (OSCE)
ICJ	International Court of Justice (United Nations)
INTEREG	International Institute for Nationality Rights and Regionalism (Munich)
IRA	Irish Republican Army
IRB	Irish Republican Brotherhood
KLA	Kossovo Liberation Army
LN	League of Nations
MRG	Minority Rights Group

MSI	Movimento Sociale Italiano (Italy – Neo-Fascists)
NATO	North Atlantic Treaty Organisation
NGO	Non-Governmental Organisation
OJ	Official Journal (of the European Community/Union)
OSCE	Organisation for Security and Co-operation in Europe
PC	Plaid Cymru (Wales)
PCIJ	Permanent Court of International Justice (League of Nations)
PIRA	Provisional Irish Republican Army
PNV	Partido Nacionalista Vasco: Basque National Party
PSF	Provisional Sinn Fein
PUP	Progressive Unionist Party (Northern Ireland)
QUANGO	Quasi-Autonomous Non-Governmental Organisation
RJ	Rassemblement Jurassien (Switzerland)
RUC	Royal Ulster Constabulary (Northern Ireland)
SDLP	Social Democratic and Labour Party (Northern Ireland)
SF	Sinn Fein (Northern Ireland)
SNP	Scottish Nationalist Party
SRBH	Serbian Republic of Bosnia-Herzegovina
SVP	Südtiroler Volkspartei: South Tyrolese People's Party (Italy)
TRNC	Turkish Republic of Northern Cyprus
UDA	Ulster Defence Association (Northern Ireland)
UDMR	Democratic Union of Hungarians in Romania
UN	United Nations
UVF	Ulster Volunteer Force (Northern Ireland)

Acknowledgements

I have spent most of my academic life involved in the problems of Europe's regional and cultural minorities and the solutions adopted or failed to be adopted to solve them. When I began in the early 1960s, with the subject of my doctoral thesis, the South Tyrol Question, the issue of minorities and their protection in Europe was more or less ignored. Now interest in European minorities is high on the agenda: we can hardly open a newspaper without reading about them somewhere – Basques and Catalans, Bretons and Corsicans, Flemish and Walloons, South Tyrolese, Turks and Greeks in Cyprus, Catholics and Protestants in Northern Ireland, and ethnic cleansing and genocide in the former Yugoslavia.

I have also been fortunate in spending a considerable part of my life in countries with culturally mixed communities – Canada, Quebec (1958–61), Switzerland (1963–71), Belgium (1972–74) and Northern Ireland (from 1974), and I am indebted to many people in those places who have helped me in my researches. It has also been a privilege for me to serve on the Advisory Council of the International Institute for Nationality Rights and Regionalism (INTEREG), Munich, and attend many of its stimulating and spirited conferences. I should like to take this opportunity to thank all those involved with the work of the Institute for their help to me at various times.

In the preparation of this book I would like to begin by thanking Dr Max van der Stoël, High Commissioner on National Minorities of the OSCE, The Hague, and his staff, particularly John Packer; Donall O'Riagain, formerly Director and now Special Adviser to the European Bureau for Lesser-Used Languages, Dublin; Hans de Belder, Plenipotentiary Representative of the Minister President for International and European Affairs of the Government of Flanders, Brussels; and Patrick Thornberry, Professor of International Law, University of Keele. I should also like to thank my colleagues at the University of Ulster for their help in providing or drawing attention to material in their areas of expertise, notably Dr Stanley Black, Dr Sean Farren, Micheal O'Murchu, Professor Tom Fraser, Dr Jan Jedrejewski, Professor Terence O'Keefe, Professor Raymond Pearson, Professor Alan Sharp, and Professor David Sturdy.

Librarians are vital for finding information, and I would like to acknowledge the help I have received from the Library staff of the Council of Europe, Strasbourg; the Graduate Institute of International Studies, Geneva; the Northern Ireland Assembly (particularly George Woodman); and the University of Ulster (particularly Frank Reynolds).

Those who have helped me in my earlier researches and writings have been thanked in the appropriate books. But there are others who have helped me, one way or another, who have not been acknowledged and I would like to take this opportunity to thank them too, notably Bert Biscoe, Cornwall County Councillor; Lazlo Labody, Chief Counsellor, Secretariat of the Council of Ministers for National and Ethnic Minorities, Budapest; David Madden, United Kingdom High Commissioner, Nicosia, Cyprus; Yvo Peeters, Flemish indefatigable international campaigner for minority rights, and civil servant, Brussels; Robert Ramsay, former Director of Research, European Parliament, Brussels; Francesco Sonis, teacher and poet from Uras, Sardinia.

Introduction

This book is about cultural relationships among the indigenous peoples of Europe at the dawn of the third millennium. Generally, it is about those who, because of conquest, secession, or the decisions of peace conferences find themselves voluntarily or involuntarily, totally or in part, an ethnic or linguistic or religious minority in their so-called 'host' state. How they came to be part of that host state usually accounts for their aspirations, which can range between some form of group and/or territorial autonomy to outright separation, and for their treatment, usually based on greater or lesser degrees of resentment, suspicion and hostility – even contempt – by the majority culture.

The history of protection of minorities in Europe can be seen in five parts. The first dates from the sixteenth century to the French Revolution when, after a century and a half of religious wars stemming from the Reformation and Counter-Reformation, the minorities to be protected were religious. It was not until the second stage, from the French Revolution to the end of the Second World War, a period associated with the rise of nationalism and social Darwinism, that language and culture came in turn to be politicised, being seen, for varying reasons, in the same hostile light as the 'wrong' religion in the previous centuries. Even so, measures of protection in the nineteenth century still concentrated on religious groups. Not until the interwar period, when nationalism was at its zenith, was the protection of linguistic minorities addressed. Under the circumstances the agreement between Sweden and Finland in 1921 to provide a territorial autonomy to the Swedish-speaking inhabitants of the Aland Islands must be seen as a measure of protection well in advance of its time, even though the monocultural composition of the islands made conditions particularly favourable and were hardly matched elsewhere.

After the Second World War, in the third stage, the emphasis changed again, to human rights for all rather than special rights for some. But this too proved unsatisfactory. Technological progress, the need for educational skills, and job mobility was making life ever more complex, and it came to be realised that for the individual members of the minority to flourish more than just 'equal rights' and non-discrimination as regards their language and religion was required. Vital elements of the social life of the individual member of the community can only be enjoyed as part of a group, and the enjoyment of minority rights therefore depends on the existence and development of the group.[1] The fight for group rights has been a vital part of the struggle for survival by minorities. In that respect the Paris Agreement of 1946 on South Tyrol was a landmark exception to the general postwar trend in that it proposed for a multicultural area a political framework for the protection of the German-speaking minority in Italy, namely political power-sharing within a territorial autonomy, as well as a number of group rights. And implementation of that Agreement would reveal that economic and social considerations were as important as legal and linguistic ones in determining the well-being of a minority.

It was not until the fourth stage, in the 1970s, with the process of western European integration well under way and the fall of dictatorship in Spain that other minorities were able, to a greater or lesser extent, to emerge from the darkness of hostility and suspicion and begin adapting the lessons that had been learned to their own circumstances.

In the fifth and present stage the wheel has turned full circle. In eastern Europe many minorities gained their independence with the fall of communism and became the dominant majority, while in western Europe many minorities have become dominant majorities in their homelands. It is disconcerting to see the same hostility being shown by these new majorities to the minority cultures of their areas in east and west as was formerly shown to them.

Before proceeding further the scope of this book must be set. What is meant by the term 'minority'? What, indeed, is Europe?

Providing a satisfactory definition of minorities has baffled politicians, academics, civil servants and international lawyers ever since a definition was needed for purposes of international legal protection. Indeed, although a few definitions exist,[2] of the many United Nations, Council of Europe and OSCE instruments which provide for an array of rights and standards for protection of minorities and their monitoring, only one contains a definition.

Recommendation 1201 (1993) of the Council of Europe defines a minority as 'a group of persons in a state who (a) reside on the territory of that state and are citizens thereof; (b) maintain longstanding, firm and lasting ties with that state; (c) display distinctive ethnic, cultural, religious or linguistic characteristics; (d) are sufficiently representative, although smaller in number than the rest of the population of that state or of a region of that state; (e) are motivated by a concern to preserve together that which constitutes their common identity, including their culture, their traditions, their religion or their language.'[3]

This book is not about the so-called 'new minorities' – migrant workers and their families, persons seeking asylum as refugees, even though the size of such communities can be considerable, and they may have been resident in their host states for two or more generations.[4]

This book is about the dark underside of European history. It is about the will to survive of cultural groups as small as 30 000 Ladins or as large as 7 million Catalans, resolved to live and prosper as they would no doubt have lived and prospered if they had been independent or part of their kin state, and of the efforts to eliminate these groups either culturally through assimilation or physically through genocide.

Genocide sees nationalism at its ugliest. After the Second World War horrified Europeans asked how it was possible to carry out programmes of extermination and ethnic cleansing, particularly of Jews and Gypsies. They are just as horrified now to realise that lessons have not been learnt, and the ethnic cleansing that followed the collapse of Yugoslavia is an awful reminder that ethnic hatred is a spirit still not exorcised.

But another ugly side of nationalism is the attempt to deny people their cultural heritage, usually on the grounds that it is of lesser worth. This has taken the form of humiliating children for speaking their mother tongue by forcing them to wear some symbol of unworthiness; humiliating parents by refusing to allow them to give ethnic given names or names that 'offend national sentiment' to their children; humiliating people by forcing them to change their names (usually simply translating them into the language of the national culture); and even humiliating the dead by having the names changed on their tombstones. But is it worthy of any nation to accuse and try people in a language they do not understand? To deny people posts not on merit, but on the grounds that the job was 'too important' for one of their group to occupy? Is it not extraordinary that in Western Europe in the 1980s it was still possible for minority cultures to be considered 'degrading of the national identity' especially when one considers the sacrifices made by these minorities in numerous wars for the country that so despised them?

The background to these events is the Europe 'from the Atlantic to the Urals' of forty-eight states, including European Russia and European Turkey. However, not all of these states play a part. Iceland, Malta and Portugal do not have any minorities within the definitions set out above. Andorra, Liechtenstein, Monaco, San Marino and the Vatican are obvious candidates for exclusion because of their size and the composition of their populations. Nor is Luxembourg included, since there are no problems with the three languages spoken there – French, German and Letzeburgisch; the latter, spoken by the entire indigenous population is a dialect of German.

However, the other thirty-nine states have all contributed in one way or another to the history of Europe's regions and peoples, few with honour. It is the hope of this author that wider knowledge and greater understanding of the issues behind protection of regional and cultural minorities will serve to develop a sensible approach to the 'unity in diversity' proposed for the process of European integration.

1
Protection of Minorities in Europe before the First World War

From the Edict of Nantes to the French Revolution

Since the days of Alexander the Great the prevailing view had been that mankind was one and, at least in western and central Europe, as Christianity advanced, this universality was postulated in the form of a universal (Catholic) church under the Papacy and a universal empire, whether Roman or Holy Roman. Below that universality feudalism ensured that authority was regionalised into a mosaic of large or small kingdoms, dukedoms, counties, bishoprics, and if people had been asked in the High Middle Ages what they were their first reply would have been a universalist one – that they were Christians (although they would not say that if they were Jews). They would then say that they were the subjects of this or that King or Lord. And only in third place would they have given an answer based on language or culture.[1] Even in Eastern Europe as the Byzantine empire collapsed and the Turks conquered the Balkans the Sultan would perceive his subjects as first Christians and then according to their culture.

Fine in theory, the idea of a European empire was ineffective in practice. Unlike the Papacy, the Holy Roman Empire, which was overwhelmingly Germanic, had neither capital nor treasury, nor a standing army. The Emperors were elected from the feudal territorial nobility and were thus dependent on their own resources to carry out their policies. Support usually had to be bought by granting ever more rights to the territorial nobility – to build castles, control justice, maintain troops, coin money, and tax. The price to be paid was the disunity of the Germanic world. Furthermore, neither the British Isles, nor France, nor Spain were part of this empire.

The process of disintegration of the universal empire and the rise of the regions within to something akin to states as we know them today was hastened by the religious wars which destroyed the unity of western and central Europe's Christian congregation.

From the moment Martin Luther pinned his ninety-five theses to the door of the castle church at Wittenberg in 1517 until the last shot was fired in the wars of Louis XIV against the Dutch in 1713 western and central Europe was wracked by war, civil and international, waged directly or indirectly in the name of religion.

It is thus not surprising that the first instruments of minority protection should relate to religion.

From 1562 to 1598 France was involved in religious civil war between Catholics and so-called Huguenots,[2] Protestants of the Calvinist persuasion. In its later stages it became known as the 'War of the Three Henrys' because of the identity of the chief protagonists, the nominally Catholic King Henri III (1574–89), the fanatic Catholic Henri duc de Guise, and the Calvinist Henri de Bourbon, King of Navarre, later Henri IV of France (1589–1610).

Several short-lived attempts were made during the war to provide protection for the Huguenots, some 10 per cent of the population of France. Indeed the war had actually broken out because of the violation by the Guises of the January Edict of 1562 under which the Huguenots had been granted freedom to worship in public outside towns and in private within them. They were allowed to hold synods and their pastors were officially recognised as long as they took an oath of loyalty to the state.[3] Fourteen years later with the Edict of Beaulieu, 1576, Huguenots were granted full public worship in all towns except Paris, the right to eight fortified towns as places of refuge,[4] and admission to all public offices including seats in the nation's *parlements*. The following year, after hostilities had resumed, the Edict of Poitiers restricted Protestant worship to the suburbs of one town in every *bailliage* and then only to towns where it had been practised before the latest resumption of the war.

The famous Edict of Nantes, issued by King Henri IV on 30 April 1598 after victory in the Civil War, slightly improved on the Edict of Poitiers. Two places in every *bailliage* could now be used for public worship by Huguenots; the Huguenots were allowed to keep control of the 200 towns in their possession, including their existing and new fortified ones; and they could enjoy full civil rights including admission into public office and into colleges and universities. Religious synods and political assemblies could be held with royal permission.

Special chambers were established in the *parlements* to try cases involving Huguenots.[5]

The guarantees for the Huguenots were thus not merely personal but territorial, and on the latter grounds at least were seen by the majority Catholic population as a state within a state, a threat to the integrity of the kingdom.[6] For ever after this would be a main cause of complaint against measures of protection for minorities anywhere. Even so, the Edict did not make the two religions equal: Roman Catholics could worship everywhere, including Henry IV's Béarn, whereas freedom of worship for Protestants was limited to a certain number of places.[7]

Nor did the clauses of the Edict of Nantes last long. The perceived threat to the integrity of the state led Henry IV's successor, Louis XIII and his famous chief minister Cardinal Richelieu to resume hostilities against the Protestants. After 1629 with the capture of Alès the peace of that name led to the Protestants ceasing to be a separate political body in the state and losing their strongholds. The liberty of conscience granted by the Edict of Nantes was, however, confirmed. Even so, thereafter the Huguenots faced a continuing battle to have the rest of the Edict implemented, especially free access to public office and unhindered operation of their schools, and from the late 1650s it was smothered with restrictions.[8] Finally, in 1685 Louis XIV revoked the Edict altogether, thus provoking a massive emigration of up to 500 000 Protestants, particularly – and damagingly to the French economy – of the skilled working class.

It was in the next stage of European history, after the Thirty Years War, that cession of territory began to be accompanied by clauses protecting parts of the local population from religious discrimination. Thus in 1660 The Treaty of Oliva (near Danzig) marked an important stage in the so-called Northern War. Sweden was confirmed in possession of Livonia, seized from Poland in 1621, giving undertakings that the Roman Catholic population would be granted liberty of conscience.[9]

By the Treaty of Nijmegen, 1678, the area round Maastricht was restored by Louis XIV of France to the United Provinces with the proviso that the Roman Catholic faith be preserved there.[10] Louis's Catholic fanaticism, which saw the revocation of the Edict of Nantes seven years after Nijmegen, was visible again in 1697. Under clause IV of the Treaty of Ryswick, Louis obtained that in the lands outside Alsace which France was to surrender to the Holy Roman Empire the Roman Catholic religion was to remain in the state in which it was at the time of the Treaty. This was over the objection of the Protestants of the Empire, particularly in regard to the Palatinate which had been forcibly converted to Catholicism, sometimes by French troops.[11]

However it was the French Revolution that would change decisively the focus on minorities, away from religion and towards culture and its main (although not exclusive) manifestation, language. And the person most responsible for this development was the German philosopher Johann Gottfried Herder (1744–1803), since 1776 Superintendent of Schools, Chief Pastor and Court Preacher at the court of Karl August, Duke of Weimar.[12] Herder was interested in social relations, and particularly how to achieve good relations between ruler and ruled, how states could emerge and develop continuously without the coercive power of government.

Among the influences affecting Herder were German pietism, which rejected the emphasis on reason that had dominated the continent since the end of the wars of religion in favour of an emotional religiosity;[13] German romanticism of the *Sturm und Drang* movement with its search for spontaneity which rejected foreign (and particularly French) influences in art, literature and science, and calling for German linguistic self-assertion;[14] and the political theories of Christian Wolff, namely, that the function of the state was to provide security and liberty in order to enable people to express the essence of their humanity.[15] It was Herder who established the link between these forces: the principle that language was the most natural and hence indispensable basis of socio-political association; that it was language which provided the cohesion for creating a *Volk*, (or nation defined in cultural terms), rather than the state, a collection of transient political institutions.[16]

Crucially 'language is the medium through which man becomes conscious of his inner self, and at the same time it is the key to the understanding of his outer relationships. It unites him with, but it also differentiates him from, others. Imperceptibly it also links him with the past by revealing to him the thoughts, feelings and prejudices of past generations ... He, in turn, again by means of language, perpetuates and enriches these for the benefit of posterity.'[17]

Language is therefore the means of identity of a group. For Herder, a *Volk* without its language was nonsense. 'For neither blood and soil, nor conquest and political fiat can engender that unique consciousness which alone sustains the existence and continuity of a social entity. For even if a *Volk*'s state perishes, the nation remains intact, provided it maintains its distinctive linguistic traditions.'[18]

A *Volk* was a natural division of the human race, 'endowed with its own language, which it must preserve as its most distinctive and sacred possession. By forsaking it a *Volk* destroys its "self".' Herder concluded, therefore, that 'intermixture with other nationalities' was to be avoided.[19]

For Herder a human being could only realise his potential fully as a member of a *Volk*. The most natural state was 'a community with its own national character' i.e. the nation-state. He therefore had no time for Europe's multi-cultural empires which he saw as being held together by coercion rather than by laws which had grown out of community traditions.[20]

Unlike certain philosophers of the following centuries Herder did not believe in a hierarchy of cultures. All cultures had equal value and should be allowed to develop. Herder particularly admired the Jews. He was no racist: it was not the mingling of blood but of language that was considered inadvisable; mankind was one and the same human species, and he could see no cause for employing the term 'race'.[21] There were, of course, a number of problems with this analysis, as Herder himself was aware. If states should be linguistically homogenous, what about areas of mixed speech which could threaten nation-state unity? Would linguistic minorities be tolerated by the dominant nationality or would, in fact, they find better treatment in a multinational rather than a national framework? What about those who regarded themselves as a nation but had no distinctive language of their own, such as the Austrians, or those who regarded themselves as a nation but spoke several languages, such as the Swiss? Then again there were ethnic groups of which only a minority spoke their putative language, such as the various Celtic groups. Herder said that each nation should be considered on its own merits, based on its situation and distinctive features and, basing himself on Jewish nationhood, he adduced four further factors – land (in the sense of *homeland*), the laws of the group freely agreed and developed over time, and the view of the group as a family or clan, perpetuated by, fourth, reverence for forefathers.[22]

However, as Barnard points out, Herder's view that the linguistic element was the decisive factor had immense political consequences. Not only did it provide the ideological foundation of nationalism. In the future 'the belief gained ground that political boundaries should be the result of linguistic enquiries and that, therefore, the assistance of professors of philology and collectors of folklore ought to be enlisted to aid, if not to replace, the modern statesman.'[23] Indeed Herder held the view that without a folk-song tradition there could not really be a nation.[24]

At the time Herder was developing his ideas the dominant figure on both the German cultural scene and the French politico-cultural scene was the philosopher Jean-Jacques Rousseau (1712–78), French-speaking but born in Geneva, a city-state associated with Switzerland but not yet part of the Confederation. Rousseau maintained that society was not a community dominated by a few kings ruling by Divine Right, appointed by God and responsible to no one except Him, but one to which everyone spontaneously adhered and in which everyone participated. Inspired perhaps by the examples of the Greek city-states or even his own Geneva, he believed in direct democracy exercised by the 'General Will' of the persons making up that society, rather than a representative democracy, and that this 'General Will' should be stronger than the will of any individual, who should give up his or her private capricious interests to that of society as a whole. The identity of that society should be based on customs and traditions. Rousseau's works, *Discourse on the Origins of Inequality* (1755) and *The Social Contract* (1762) with its opening 'Man is born free but is everywhere in chains', identified him as one of the leading critics of the world of privilege and class rigidity, particularly in France. Unsurprising, therefore, that during the run up to the French Revolution of 1789 and for some years beyond no philosopher was more respected for his stand on liberty and equality.

His basic idea, therefore – revolutionary at the time – was that a group of equal individuals had a right to reject a state held together on the basis of loyalty to the king and to choose their own constitution and their own government. This democratic ideal was the first implication of the French Revolution. But there was a further implication: that if a people had a right to decide new loyalties, they could decide whether to liberate themselves from an existing state or governmental authority and either attach themselves to another state or form an independent state. Choice was the important factor. The result was the birth of the principle of self-determination.[25]

But on what basis would a choice be made? The answer was culture, or rather its most obvious characteristic, language. The result would be that the application of the principle of self-determination based on culture would take different forms depending whether one was in western, central or eastern Europe, although the aim would be the same – monocultural states.

From the French Revolution to the First World War

Western Europe

(a) France

In France, since the country was neither occupied nor ruled by a foreign state or culture, and therefore did not need to be liberated, it was the democratic aspect of national self-determination that was stressed.[26] The decline of the minority languages in France – Breton in the north-west, Basque, Catalan and Occitan in the south – had already been well underway by the beginning of the modern period.

Under Francis I in 1532 Brittany was joined to France in a perpetual union but the ensuing francisation of the Breton élites was in reality the end of a centuries-old trend rather than the beginning.[27] Similarly the Edict of Villers-Cotterêts, 1539, which required all legal and administrative acts to be in French, set the seal on French penetration in the south rather than signalling its point of departure.[28] Nevertheless, if the élites abandoned their regional loyalties, with the nobility often to be found at the Court at Versailles, the broad mass of these communities, and particularly the peasantry, continued to use their regional languages cheerfully. In 1790 a nation-wide enquiry revealed that only one fifth could speak French confidently, under two-thirds understood it and one-third knew no French at all.[29] What the French Revolution did was to promote an identity between the State, the collection of political institutions, and the Nation, in the terms of the dominant culture.

Three factors were involved in this fusion of state and nation. The first was the implementation of Rousseau's vision of absolute power to the democratic majority, this democratic majority being seen in merely numerical terms. The second was the triumph of the Jacobin faction with its centralist philosophy over the regionalist Girondins in the conduct of the Revolution. What set in, the idea of the equality of all, and therefore the equality of treatment for all without distinction and administered uniformly from the centre, would decisively affect all future French systems of government.

The third factor was war. France and its revolution had to be defended against the foreign reactionaries invading the country to restore the monarchy. And soon attack was seen as the best method of defence. What better way to defeat the foreign reactionaries than to export to their countries by force of arms the doctrines of the Revolution, inviting peoples to throw off foreign tyrants and choose their own forms of government? For twenty-five years Revolutionary and Napoleonic France was at war with Europe. French armies marched from Lisbon to Moscow, from Naples to Copenhagen. In that period things changed radically for France's regional cultures – and for the worse.

The need to draw upon the capacities of the whole people for war, the need to develop a national consciousness, meant that the language of the democratic numerical majority became a vital instrument for promoting the cohesion and solidarity of all the citizens of the French state, and it thereby acquired an additional standing and prestige. However, if a language is either a means of solidarity or a symbol of prestige other languages stand out as elements which threaten that solidarity and can come to be considered of lesser worth, arousing contempt in the minds of those members of the dominant cultural majority towards those from minority cultures.

Thus, from the beginning, revolutionary and imperial France sought to eliminate Basque, Breton, Catalan and Occitan because it saw in them elements dividing *La Nation une et indivisible.* Priest- and aristocracy-ridden Brittany, where 80 per cent spoke Breton, was a prime target because of its suspect loyalty to revolutionary values. Typical sentiments expressed by French revolutionary leaders were that 'federalism and superstition speak Breton', that the Breton language was 'a reflection of the barbarism of past centuries.' The Abbé Henri Gregoire (1750–1831) prepared a report on the need to 'annihilate *patois* and universalise the use of the French language.'[30] And the Jacobins called for a 'sacred competition' to banish from all parts of France 'these jargons which are the remains of feudalism and the monuments of slavery.'[31] Then the Napoleonic education system was established which, largely in existence to this day, continued the hostility to regional languages until after the Second World War.

Nineteenth-century France would see minority cultures disparaged and the economic backwardness of their regions blamed on those cultures. Teachers teaching Breton to their pupils were imprisoned and fined. Basques, Catalans and Occitans were mocked and punished by having to wear the *'symbole'* (a piece of wood) round their necks. Typical was the instruction given by a Sub-Prefect in 1845 to teachers departing for Brittany: 'Remember, you are being sent to Brittany to kill the Breton language.'[32]

Not only the language, but also given names were the object of hostility. Laws passed at the time of the Revolution and renewed in one way or another as late as 1966 only allowed some names from regional cultures. Much depended for their acceptance on the local Registrar.[33] Likewise, regional history was eliminated from the curriculum, thus attempting to hide the fact that many different peoples made up the population of the *hexagone*.

It was made absolutely clear that those who wished to get on in public or professional life would have to demonstrate their prior loyalty to the French language. French government action towards minority cultures in the nineteenth century was deliberately and explicitly hostile. Nevertheless it failed to exterminate them, due either to literary circles imbued by the Romantic Movement which took up their study, including dealing with varieties of spelling and dialects[34] or to the remoteness of the cultures concerned.

One place where remoteness was a saviour was the island of Corsica, which the French had obtained from Genoa in 1768 and which became an integral part of France by decree of the Constituent Assembly on 30 November 1789. Prior to the arrival of the French the Corsicans had lived under Genoa for four centuries but they had never lost their identity and managed – because of the mountainous nature of the island – to retain a large measure of control over their internal affairs. Harsh Genoese rule made the Corsicans determined never to be 'Italian', even though the Corsican language was close enough to northern Italian for there to be a debate as to whether it was a language in its own right or merely a dialect of Italian.[35]

In fact integration into France amongst the 150 000 population[36] was not unwelcome, and there is no doubt that the exploits of the most famous Corsican of all, Napoleon Bonaparte, made it easier for the Corsicans to be proud to be French and to accept the idea of having the island institutionally and administratively as similar as possible to other parts of France. The result was that on the one hand the union with France was not challenged either on the island or on the mainland. French became the language of the administration, education, commerce and politics. On the other hand, Corsican individuality continued, even though the language was relegated to family and rural life.[37] Thus the French presence was really only to be found in towns along the coast, with officials tending to be temporary,[38] and the Corsicans were never subject before the First World War to the penetration of their homeland and to the degree of humiliation suffered by the minorities of the *hexagone*. The islanders' ideals of independence and resistance might be dormant; they were not forgotten.

Nor was the disastrous legacy of French cultural imperialism limited to France. When exporting the Revolution to today's Belgium, then the Austrian Netherlands, and incorporating it into France, the French sought to eliminate Dutch from the army and administration, even though the Dutch speakers were the majority in the area. After the defeat of Napoleon the area was given to the Netherlands as a barrier against future French expansion. However, the Catholic population of 'Belgium' resented the domination of Dutch protestantism, and the French-speaking Belgians (Walloons) resented the imposition of Dutch as the official language. In 1830, following a popular revolt in Brussels supported by French funds, an independent Belgium was set up, but was completely dominated by its French-speaking bourgeois élite. French was the language of the administration, education, the courts and the army. With the arrival of the industrial revolution French-speaking southern Belgium became rich but Flanders remained poor and rural, its people a socio-political minority, the language kept alive, as in so many other places, by a literary movement, the *Heilig Verbond*. Dutch speakers who wanted to get on in life moved to Wallonia and abandoned their language.

This situation had its dangers only too familiar to persons who spoke a minority language. In 1866 two Flemish farm workers were executed for a murder they had almost certainly not committed after a trial conducted entirely in French. In fact the reaction led to a number of improvements. Dutch could be used in the lower courts in Flanders, in secondary schools and public inscriptions. Finally, in 1898, under the Equality Law Dutch was accepted as the second language of Belgium. Nevertheless, it was a long time before all civil servants, even in Flanders, spoke Dutch, and on the eve of the First World War only some 100 of Belgium's 8 000 officers spoke Dutch, even though the Flemish community provided two-thirds of the army.[39] As in France with Breton-only speaking troops the resulting confusion led to disasters in the field, and even injustice.[40]

Perhaps the most serious legacy of French cultural imperialism – in France and elsewhere – was its arrogant contempt for other languages. Even today Dutch-speakers accuse their Walloon co-nationals of never wanting to make any effort to learn their language. But there was another side. What affected France above all other countries in Europe, and especially after defeat in the 1870 Franco-Prussian war, was the idea of Social Darwinism, the extension of the principle of the survival of the fittest from the biological to the political and cultural spheres. France saw itself diminished, politically surrounded and culturally threatened by the British Empire and Imperial Germany. For the inheritors of the revolutionary tradition France – and the world – would be a poorer place if the country was reduced to the level of Switzerland. Hence the *mission civilisatrice* which spurred the French to attempt abroad to establish similar political, linguistic and administrative values in Africa and Asia. Obviously threats to the political and cultural integrity of France would not, could not, be tolerated at home.[41]

In the western European countries on either side of France – Spain and Britain (including Ireland) – there may not have been a revolution as in France but the same pattern of decline of regional cultures in the seventeenth, eighteenth and nineteenth centuries followed by an intellectual revival towards the end of the latter can be seen, but for different reasons.

(b)   Spain

In Spain the three main regional languages, Basque, Catalan and Galician (Gallego) had been powerful in the Middle Ages. Indeed it was from its Galician roots that Portuguese evolved.[42] And Basque and Catalan were spoken on the other side of the Pyrenees, the latter also in Andorra, Valencia, the Balearic Islands and in Sardinia. The homelands of all three languages had enjoyed at one time or another varying degrees of independence or autonomous government. For all three what would be decisive would be their relationship with Castile, the most important state in the Iberian peninsula, the one that had spearheaded the *reconquista* crusade against the Moors, and the one that would thereafter dominate the new Spain, unified by the marriage of Isabella of Castile with Ferdinand of Aragon in 1469 and the union of their crowns in 1479. In the sixteenth century the language of Castile, Castilian, drew its prestige and political superiority as the language of the Court, the government, and the expanding Empire, as well as that of Spain's Golden Age in literature. In the seventeenth century the First Minister of King Philip IV, Olivares, sought to bring political and administrative centralisation and uniformity to Spain and clearly an obstacle would be the different languages. And then in the eighteenth century the position of Castilian was strengthened by its use in a very centralised Catholic Church, the use of Castilian in the education system, and the introduction of universal male conscription into a Castilian-speaking army.[43]

The decline of minority languages was actually first seen in Galicia before Spanish unification. Very early on the Church and administration had preferred Latin to Galician and then in the fifteenth and sixteenth centuries there was the switch to Castilian, also because Galicia had supported Isabella's rival, her half-sister Juana la Beltraneja, to the throne of Castile. The severest decline was in the cities among the middle classes so that by the beginning of the nineteenth century if the language was still spoken by most Galicians it was the peasantry that spoke it.

A flourishing economy, culture and autonomy were the hallmarks of Catalonia at the end of the fifteenth century, part of the domain of Ferdinand of Aragon. Although Castilian was on the rise, the real disaster for Catalonian occurred at the beginning of the eighteenth century when Catalans chose the wrong side in the War of the Spanish Succession. In 1700 Charles II of Spain died childless. The two chief rivals for the Crown were the grandson of Louis XIV of France, Philip of Anjou, and the Archduke Charles, the second son of the Austrian Habsburg Holy Roman Emperor, Joseph I. On his deathbed Charles II nominated Philip but Britain and the Netherlands were hostile to the aggrandisement of the Bourbon dynasty. In 1705 Catalonia proclaimed the Archduke Charles as Charles III of Spain and received help from England (thus ensuring that an international war would become a civil war). But when England pulled out of the war and signed the Treaty of Utrecht with France in 1713 the Catalans were abandoned and Philip (now Philip V of Spain) had his revenge.

Catalonia's capital, Barcelona, was captured in 1714. Catalan autonomous institutions were abolished and the land was castilianised.[44] The language lost its prestige and became largely a spoken one,[45] and spoken only by the peasantry.

In the Middle Ages the Basque people inhabited three provinces of Spain – Alava, Viscaya and Guipuzcoa – and the Kingdom of Navarre, which included an area in France today the three *départements* of Labourd, Basse-Navarre and Soule. By the end of the fourteenth century Castile had acquired control of the three Spanish provinces. Navarre remained independent until 1512 when it was annexed by Ferdinand of Aragon and Regent of Castile, but by 1530 had relinquished Navarrese territory on the French side of the Pyrenees. However, in return for retaining their autonomous rights the Basques accepted Castilian and because of this were able to maintain a separate but subordinate identity, including continued use of the language. But as in the rest of Spain the minority language was more or less abandoned by the urban middle class.[46]

But the problem of Spanish centralisation and castilianisation was that it occurred when Castile's economic hegemony was over. 'Instead, a centralist government was arbitrarily imposed on the wealthier peripheral regions, to be held there by force – the force of an economically retarded Castile. The result was a tragically artificial structure which constantly hampered Spain's political development, for during the next two centuries economic and political power were perpetually divorced. Centre and circumference remained mutually antagonistic, and the old regional conflicts stubbornly refused to die away.'[47]

In 1807 Napoleon obtained the right to establish garrisons in Spain and march through the country in order to occupy Portugal, which was allied with and trading with Britain. The following year, in order to protect French interests, the Emperor intervened in a Bourbon family quarrel to force both King Charles IV and his brother to abdicate in favour of his own brother Joseph.

Although it was claimed that the French intervention was no threat to the Spanish state, merely a change of dynasty, and there were not a few who welcomed the potential benefits of liberalism and modernisation, the war that followed was soon portrayed as one of national liberty and independence, in which 'the people' saved the nation after the élites had abandoned it.[48] This affected nineteenth-century Spain in two ways. One was to reopen the debate between centralism and regionalism, with the latter supported by the traditionalists and some progressive liberals seeking federalism, calling for a return to the medieval rights enjoyed in the various areas. However, at the end of the second Carlist War in 1876 it seemed that the centralists and uniformists had won. The rights of the three Basque provinces, although not those of Navarre, were abolished. The second way in which Spain was affected was by a rise in Spanish Romanticism and belief in the *Volksgeist* similar to that occurring elsewhere in Europe.

The result was that in the second half of the nineteenth century political centralism was accompanied by a revival among the three minority cultures. Under the influence of Romanticism the past was exalted, as was lyric poetry. This was particularly strong in Catalonia which emphasised the language. The first work in Galician was produced in 1863, and later grammars and dictionaries were produced.[49] As for the Basques, with much less of a literary tradition, the father of

Basque nationalism, Sabino Arana, stressed race and in particular, blood.[50] And it was these cultural revivals that would reawaken the national consciousness of the three groups, preparing them for the struggle for political autonomy (or more) in the following century, posing a challenge to the centralist nature of the Spanish state.

(c)   The British Isles

In the British Isles the pattern of political events driving down minority languages, their abandonment by the élites and the middle class, and then a cultural revival preparing the ground for a return to political standing was generally repeated.

Edward I of England may have conquered Wales in 1282 but the country remained only very loosely attached to England until the 1536 Act of Union passed by Henry VIII whose Tudor dynasty was Welsh. During the intervening years the Welsh language 'held its own' not only in domestic and literary usage but in legal matters.[51] One result of the Act was that English was declared the only official language. With a Welsh Tudor dynasty in London it was not surprising that the Welsh élite would, like that of the Scots three-quarters of a century later, take the high road to London. Nevertheless the Welsh language continued to flourish, thanks to religion. To obtain Welsh support for the Anglican Reformed Church and to ensure Welsh loyalty in a potential war with Catholic Spain, Queen Elizabeth I ordered the Bible to be translated into Welsh, and 'thus the pragmatic Elizabeth gave back for religious purposes what her father had taken away for the purposes of state.'[52] The same thing happened two and a half centuries later. On the one hand the early nineteenth century saw the growth of Nonconformist sects – Methodists, Baptists, Congregationalists. By mid-century while the cities remained true to Anglicanism three-quarters of the Welsh population was going to Chapel rather than Church, with services in Welsh – unsurprising when between 1720 and 1870, the year when the Anglican Church of Wales was disestablished, no Welsh-speaking Anglican bishop was sent to Wales.[53] On the other hand, the 1870 Education Act ignored Welsh. Welsh was prohibited in most schools and pupils speaking it had, like in Brittany, to wear the 'Welsh Knot' around their necks.[54] But even before then Welsh had been condemned, like Breton, as a 'vast drawback to Wales and a manifold barrier to the moral progress and commercial property of the people.'[55] Only a few years before the Education Act *The Times* had declared the Welsh language was 'the curse of Wales ... its prevalence and the ignorance of the English language have excluded the Welsh from the civilisation of their English neighbours'.[56]

Nevertheless on the back of Nonconformism and thanks to Welsh exiles in London there was a literary revival and the growth of national consciousness. Even in the eighteenth century *eisteddfods* – festivals of Welsh prose and verse – had been revived. The first was held in 1789, coinciding with the Romantic Revival. The Welsh National Anthem *Hen Wlad fy Nhadau* (Old Land of my Fathers) was composed in 1856. The first newspaper in Welsh appeared in Swansea in 1814.[57] As the century developed there were calls for the establishment of a Welsh University, and eventually Aberystwyth received its Charter in 1893, and Welsh history and language could be seriously studied. There was even agitation for Home Rule and the establishment of a political party *Cymru Fydd* (Wales of the Future) but for a variety of reasons it collapsed. Nevertheless at the turn of the century, according to the 1901 census 50 per cent of the population of Wales spoke Welsh, some 930 000.[58] The language may have been in decline but this decline was hardly terminal, and if it was suffering from official neglect this neglect was at least benign in comparison with France. The absolute decline that set in with the twentieth century would be due to other causes.

Scots Gaelic was the language spoken all over Scotland and in England north of the Tyne at the beginning of the eleventh century. However, Queen Margaret, wife of King Malcolm Canmore (1058–93), saw it as her mission to eliminate the Gaelic language and culture and replace it by Anglo-Saxon, and eliminate the Celtic Church tradition and replace it by the Roman.[59] With documents in English and with the increase in trade with England and northern Europe this ensured that Gaelic ceased to be the dominant language by the thirteenth century, except in the Highlands and the Hebrides. By 1400 it was no longer spoken in southern and central Scotland.[60]

The second blow to strike Scots Gaelic was the Reformation. Gaelic was seen as synonymous with Catholicism and barbarity. Education laws banned Gaelic in use and in learning. Under the 1609 Statutes of Iona twelve Highland chiefs were pressured into agreeing to set up and support Protestant ministers in Highland parishes and to send their heirs to be educated in the Lowlands. Gaelic was linked to lack of godliness, knowledge and learning, and 'ceased to have an obvious relationship with Scottish nationality.'[61] Nevertheless, what occurred in Wales now occurred in the Highlands of Scotland: on the one hand, in order better to reach their parishioners and spread the word, Gaelic-speaking Presbyterian clergy were being recruited and sent with bibles and catechisms to the Highlands, while on the other hand teachers were being reprimanded for bringing religious books in Gaelic into their schools.[62]

The third blow was the destruction of the clan system after the failure of the 1745 Jacobite rebellion. Lands were seized; Highland dress and music were banned. And not long afterwards came the seventy year process of the Highland Clearances when sheep were preferred to men and landowners massively evicted their tenants, most of whom emigrated abroad to the New World or Australia.

In 1872 the Education Act (Scotland) was passed. The aim of schools was to 'rid society of the Gaelic nuisance'. Gaelic was therefore discouraged and schoolchildren speaking it were punished (even as late as 1930) by having to wear a stick on a cord round the neck. A Gaelic-speaking child was seen as being 'disadvantaged'. And another effect of the Act was to snuff out a Scots-Gaelic literary revival – the only area in western Europe where this occurred.[63]

According to the 1901 census, of Scotland's population aged three years and over of 4 146 733, there were 230 806 speakers of Gaelic (5.57 per cent) of which 202 700 were bilingual (4.89 per cent) and 28 106 (0.68 per cent) spoke Gaelic only. Ten years later the figures were 202 398 (4.56 per cent), 183 998 (4.14 per cent) and 18 400 (0.41 per cent) respectively.[64] These Gaelic speakers were overwhelmingly to be found on the west coast of Scotland and the Hebrides with the Presbyterian church the main instrument of the language's revival.

The English invaded and began their domination of Ireland in 1171 under Henry II. The King had been concerned about the number of his feudal subjects – and their strength – setting up in Ireland and perhaps growing too strong. But even before then Pope Adrian IV in his Bull *Laudabiliter* (1155–6) had authorised Henry to go to Ireland and extirpate once and for all the remnants of the Celtic Church. The story of that domination, particularly in the sixteenth and seventeenth centuries, is too long and complex to be told here. Suffice it to say that following the Reformation the Irish Protestant Church became the established Church. Attempts were made to colonise Ireland in order to help Britain defend itself from attack by Catholic Spain, the most notable and successful being the 1609 Plantation of Ulster by Presbyterian lowland Scots. The threat of Catholic Irish intervention on the side of King Charles I during the English Civil War led to invasion by the Parliamentary leader Oliver Cromwell and the dispersal of the Irish Catholic gentry (but not the farm labourers) to the west of the river Shannon. Then in 1688 Charles's Catholic son James II was deposed as King of England, and William of Orange, *Stadthouder* of

Holland, became King as William III. James attempted to regain his throne via Ireland but was defeated at the Battle of the Boyne (1690). This was followed by severe penal laws being introduced with the aim of destroying Catholicism (1695): Catholics were barred from the Armed Forces, the law, and all civic activity. No Catholic could vote, hold an office under the Crown, or purchase land. The religion was proscribed.[65] Nevertheless the Irish language maintained itself, and would do so well into the eighteenth century. Then suddenly, 'within the space of a century or so the language spoken by the great majority of a people became the mark of a scattered minority'.[66] Why?

First, the collapse of the Jacobite Rising in Scotland in 1746 ensured the Protestant supremacy in the British Isles. It also helped to take religion out of politics. It hastened the decay of the Penal Laws and this in turn encouraged Catholics to accept the *status quo*. Catholic Relief Acts passed in 1778 enabled Catholics to teach and inherit land and hope for advancement in their own country.[67] Second, eighteenth-century Ireland was politically quiet. The economy and trade expanded, and commerce remained as a way of advancement. A Catholic middle class developed.[68] Those who wished to get on clearly required English, so much so that the 'hedge schools' which in the seventeenth century were teaching in Irish to the Catholic rural population had turned to teaching in English. 'This was not a cause but a consequence of mass attitudes.'[69] Third, the Roman Catholic Church adapted to the situation, and accepted English as its 'language of mission' particularly after the Revolutionaries in France had not only closed its seminaries but murdered priests, whereas the British government provided funds for the establishment of a college at Maynooth.[70] Fourth, in 1831 (two years after Catholic Emancipation) a country-wide system of 'national schools' was introduced for Catholic Ireland. Managed by the Catholic Church, Irish was excluded from the curriculum. The result of all this was that Irish speakers became objects of ridicule, and schoolchildren caught speaking Irish had, as in Wales, Scotland and Brittany, to wear a tally stick round their necks.[71] Fifth, there was the Great Famine of 1845–49 which killed a million people, particularly in rural areas, and initiated an emigration that would lead to the population being halved,[72] and the disruption of community ties.

It was not surprising, therefore, that the Irish language was not an issue, whether at the time of the 1798 United Irishmen rebellion, or during the agitation for Catholic emancipation, or the Fenian revolt of

1867.[73] In 1799, of a total population of some 5.4 million, 2.4 million (44.4 per cent) spoke Irish, of which 1.6 million (29.6 per cent) were bilingual, and 800 000 (14.8 per cent) were only able to speak Irish. In 1851 the figures were 6 552 365, 1 524 286 (23.25 per cent) and 319 602 (4.87 per cent) were Irish only. There were no figures for bilingual speakers. In 1901 of a total population of 4 458 775 the total number of Irish speakers including speakers of Irish only numbered 641 142 (14.4 per cent), while those speaking Irish only had fallen to a mere 20 953 or 0.5 per cent.[74]

However, as subsequent history would show, most starkly of all in Ireland, even after the collapse of the Irish language national consciousness was not lost. There was, like with most of the other minority languages in western Europe, apart from Scots Gaelic, an Irish literary revival with a number of societies being founded in the last decades of the century but also ones to preserve and expand the language, notably the Gaelic League. These efforts were not unsuccessful. The teaching of Irish came to be allowed in the national schools as was bilingual primary education in Irish-speaking areas, while in 1913 the language was compulsory for entry into the National University.[75] One important area of debate was the future relationship between English and Irish, with some believing the two could exist side by side while others, notably the future first President of the Irish Free State, Douglas Hyde, believing it necessary to 'de-anglicise' Ireland if Irish life, language and traditions were to be saved.[76]

Nevertheless, in the case of Ireland there was also a strong political movement at the same time as the literary revival, the aim of which for most people was Home Rule. Three Home Rule Bills would be introduced into the British House of Commons – in 1886, 1893 and 1912 – but only the last succeeded in being adopted. In Ireland the most vehement opponents of these bills were the Protestants in Ulster, descendants of the 1609 Plantation who were a majority there and believed that Home Rule would be but the first step to an independent Catholic-dominated Ireland separate from the United Kingdom. What gave them that belief was the existence of organisations, notably the Irish Republican Brotherhood (IRB) or the Fenians, designed to end British rule in Ireland by force. The IRB was particularly good at exploiting rural grievances and the perceived slow pace of land reform.

Another language apparently on the way out was Cornish. Until the sixteenth century the population of Cornwall spoke this celtic language closely related to Breton and Welsh. But thereafter the language seemed to undergo a national decline, with the last acknowledged colloquial speaker, Dolly Pentreath, dying in 1777, although thereafter there were always some people who spoke some Cornish.

Central Europe

(a) Introduction

In France the French Revolution, through its democratic aspects, had had a negative effect on regional minority cultures. The state attempted to mould society into one culture, and the example was followed in Spain and Britain. In central and eastern Europe however, it was the nationalism aspect rather than the democratic that dominated – but the results were the same, namely, a drive to fusion of state and culture.

In central Europe the two dominant cultural areas were Germany and Italy. But if both were to a large extent culturally homogenous they were fragmented politically and some parts were ruled by foreigners. Germany on the eve of the French Revolution consisted of 294 states or 2 303 territories,[77] some large and powerful like Bavaria and Prussia, others of only a few acres or villages controlled by an Imperial Knight in his castle. Some territories were even ruled by foreigners – Hanover, for example, by the King of England, Holstein by Denmark. It was the same in Italy where, in the eighteenth century, of the dozen or so states that made up the peninsula, some large, some small, few were ruled by Italians – Savoy, Sardinia, the Papal States, Venice, Genoa and Lucca. The others were ruled, and changed hands from time to time in order to suit the balance of power according to the fortunes of war elsewhere in Europe, by Spanish Bourbon and Austrian families – Milan (Lombardy), Tuscany, Parma, Piacenza, Naples, Sicily, Trento, Modena.[78]

When in 1792 the French revolutionary armies invaded Germany and Italy, calling on the peoples of the states to throw off foreign and tyrannical rulers and create their own states on the basis of their choice, what was let loose was the process of political unification of those monocultural areas.

In Italy, following French intervention against Austria (1797–99) Savoy was annexed by France, and Milan, Genoa, the Papal States and Naples were turned into republics. Later Milan, Tuscany, Parma and the Papal States became the 'so-called' 'Italian Republic' in 1802, to become the Kingdom of Italy after Napoleon became the Emperor of the French in 1804. To that unified area was added Venice in 1806, the Marche in 1807 and Trento in 1809.[79]

In 1806 sixteen southern and western German states formed the Confederation of the Rhine, declaring themselves under French protection and seceding from the Holy Roman Empire. Shortly after, the Emperor himself, Francis II, under pressure from Napoleon, gave up the imperial crown and the Empire itself was thus brought to an end. Instead Francis became Francis I of Austria. When Prussia and Saxony, together with Russia, demanded the dissolution of the Confederation the French defeated the Prussians at Jena, occupied Prussia and forced Saxony to join the Confederation.[80]

After Napoleon's defeat at Waterloo in 1815 the map of Germany was again redrawn, this time into a Germanic Confederation of thirty-nine states, including German Austria and a Prussia enlarged by the addition of Westphalia and part of Saxony. Italy, on the other hand, reverted to its pre-French Revolution divisions and rulers, with Austria receiving Lombardy and Venice as compensation for the loss of the Austrian Netherlands (Belgium) which was given to the Kingdom of the Netherlands in order to bolster the latter against France in the new balance of power.[81]

(b)   Germany

But more than in just rationalising the political situation in Germany was France responsible for the process of German unification. It was true that in the areas under French influence or under French direct administration feudalism and privilege were swept away, careers were opened to men of talent, internal markets were liberated from restrictive tolls, which all helped to expand trade and promote the growth and raise the social status of the middle class. However, Napoleonic imperialism had to be paid for – and was paid for – by plunder. The occupying French administrations seized national treasuries; French armies were quartered on satellite states and these states were also required to provide and pay for troops to further the Emperor's ambitions. Heavy taxes were levied. And some states with old trading links with Britain, now France's main enemy, had to break them off. The result in Germany – as in Spain – was a backlash that would set the German people on the road to a virulent form of national unification that would not be spent until 1945.

But the division of the German people into thirty-nine states after Waterloo was not nearly good enough for the Romanticists who dominated the German intellectual class and who perceived well the consequences of German disunity. Friedrich Schlegel (1772–1829) argued that a nation was a closely knit family held together not only by ties of language, but also by ties of blood and a common past – in this case the Germany of the Middle Ages, the Knights, the Guilds, the *minnesänger*. The nation was the source of all aesthetic, political and ethical creativity; an object of love and devotion; a great family and the individual therefore should submit himself to it, and indeed could only fulfil himself within it and was nothing outside it.[82] Heinrich Luden (1778–1847), Professor of History at Jena, believed in the uniqueness of each nation. And he believed that only a state built on the principle of ethnicity could be a true fatherland, *that nation and state must coincide.*[83] Language, the symbol of the spiritual and intellectual independence of the nation, was the only bond linking the past to the present, and the only bond linking Germans wherever they were after the dissolution of the Holy Roman Empire, the First Reich, uniting them for a common effort.[84] Henceforward German nationalists would call for the creation of one fatherland out of all the lands where German was spoken. For some, like Friedrich Jahn (1778–1852) this would mean a 'Greater Germany' – *Gross Deutschland* – to include Switzerland, the Netherlands, Denmark and Alsace-Lorraine (*Elsass-Lothringen*).[85]

A dangerous situation had now been reached. First, as Professor Alfred Cobban put it, self-determination had become national determination. For French Revolutionaries if not French minorities, self-determination was synonymous with democracy, with choice. For German nationalists the nation (the *Volk*) was an objective rather than a subjective fact. 'National self-determination no longer implied an element of choice on the part of individuals: it was decided at birth. Strictly speaking, indeed, it ceased to be self-determination at all. The individual did not determine his nation; rather, the nation determined the individual.'[86] Put another way, a person could not escape his *Blutgemeinschaft*, his cultural community, based on the blood-tie and expressed by language.

Second, if in the France of the Revolution the state took over culture in order to consolidate itself, in Germany – and later in Italy – the culture would take over the state in order to consolidate itself. The desire for political unity so as to give political expression to the cultural nation would lead to emphasis being placed on the primacy of the state rather than the rights of individuals. Institutions safeguarding individual liberties would come to be seen as less important than those fostering national cultural unity.

This situation too was fraught with danger for cultural minorities. For if, first, the state was to be the political expression and controller of the cultural/racial nation; if, second, the individual was clearly subordinate to the state and the concept of liberty was not the liberty of the individual vis-à-vis the state but liberty for the state vis-à-vis the citizen to take whatever steps might be necessary in order to give political expression and protection to the purity of the cultural nation; and if, third, a person could not escape his or her cultural community/nation (and to try to do so could be construed as ethnic treason), then cultural minorities had no place.

- They were a threat to the unity of the nation and the state;
- the state was not there to protect their interests;
- the likely solution was elimination, either cultural elimination (assimilation), or displacement (forced or voluntary emigration) or physical elimination (genocide).

The histories of Germany and Italy in the following hundred years would see these alternatives borne out only too well.

German unification was eventually accomplished in 1871. The process had begun with the economic ground being laid by a number of customs unions between most of the states between 1818 and 1842. Then three wars were fought. In the first, against Denmark in 1864, Prussia obtained Schleswig and Austria obtained Holstein. In the second, against Austria in 1866, Prussia obtained Holstein and eliminated Austria from German affairs. However, in the Treaty of Prague Germany agreed to hold a plebiscite in North Schleswig. It was continually put off and eventually in 1878 Austria agreed to scrap it.[87] In the third, against France in 1870, Prussia obtained Alsace-Lorraine and, after concluding treaties with the states concerned, founded in 1871 the Second Reich, an imperial federation with the King of Prussia as German Emperor.

But the writing was on the wall for minorities even before unification. In Schleswig-Holstein the Prussians set out to destroy Danish culture. German was made the official language and that used in the courts.[88] Primary schools were gradually germanised. Danish private schools were closed. Prussia tried to buy farms for immigrants. One-third of Danes in the two provinces emigrated in order to avoid germanisation or were deported.

With the three Partitions of Poland (1772, 1793, 1795) Prussia acquired an ethnic minority. In Prussian Poland the Polish language was equal to German in public notices and official documents and Poles were admitted to public offices. This situation ended following the Polish revolt in Russian 'Congress' Poland in 1830. Then in 1867

Polish was excluded from the administration and the courts; schools in the Province of Posen were germanised; Polish immigrants from Russia were expelled; and Commissions were set up to purchase Polish-owned lands and to settle Germans on them.

After the seizure of Alsace-Lorraine in 1871 over fifty thousand French sympathisers, drawn mostly from the rural and urban intellectual elite, left the area, to be replaced by citizens from the Reich.[89] The University of Strasbourg was germanised and there were restrictions on French press and theatre.

(c)   Italy

With the exception of Trento and Trieste, which remained in Austrian hands until 1918, Italian unification had been accomplished by 1870, with the Austrians driven out from Lombardy and Venice together with autocratic and foreign rulers from the small principalities. But what would the new Italy's attitude be towards its linguistic minorities? United as it might be, the new state faced serious problems. They included the enormous disparity in economic standards between north and south, a disparity that would widen when the industrial revolution came to Italy. Central control of the state was the one chosen by the governments that followed unification, despite the regional traditions created by fourteen centuries of independent kingdoms, duchies and republics.

Before 1918, apart from islands of Greek, Croatian and Albanian-speaking Italians in southern Italy, there were three linguistic minorities. The smallest was the French or Franco-Provençal community of the Aosta Valley which had been cut off from its kin in French Savoy in 1860. At the time it contained some 85 000 souls.[90] There, a policy of italianisation was begun which led to the area being bilingual on the eve of the First World War, with French still spoken in the home, the church and in local culture.[91]

The second largest group, today over 500 000,[92] were the Friauls, belonging to the Rhaeto-Romansch family, and inhabiting north-eastern Italy, bounded by the Dolomite, Carnic and Julian Alps and the Adriatic. The area had enjoyed a colourful medieval past (in the tenth century as Aquileia it was a political entity with its own parliament) but its pretensions to independence ended in the fifteenth century when it came under the sphere of influence of Venice. In 1751 Aquileia was dissolved. In 1814 western Friuli became part of Austria's Kingdom of Italy (Lombardy and Venice) while the east became part of the hereditary lands of the Austrian Empire. In 1866 the whole of it became part of Italy. The language had flourished until the penetration of Venice when the élites abandoned it and it became a language for the peasantry. Nevertheless the nineteenth century saw a strong revival in literature and the theatre, with the existence of philological societies, libraries, archives and folk museums.[93]

The largest group was the 1 200 000 Sard-speaking inhabitants of Sardinia, 86 per cent of the population of the island. Sardinia had been under the rule of the Phoenicians, Romans, Vandals, the republics of Pisa and Genoa, the Kingdom of Aragon, Spain and finally it was given to Savoy in 1720. There was a considerable consciousness of Sardinian separate identity. But since coming under Savoy and in the period before the First World War the island was neglected; its mixed resources and agriculture were poor, and development was hampered by malaria. The language was regarded as the most primitive of the Romance languages, and under the Kingdom of Savoy was also neglected, with few Sardes literate and in any case with very little native literature.

Eastern Europe

In the Eastern Europe of the three multinational empires – Austria-Hungary, Russia and Turkey – the appeal to nationalism engendered by the French Revolution and Romanticism was to set in train movements of dissolution along lines of nationality so that, like in central Europe, this was the process by which cultural nations would become political states.

(a)   Turkey

Of the three empires in question in the years following the French Revolution the weakest was Turkey. From its high-water mark when it controlled south-eastern Europe up to the gates of Vienna in 1683 its decline would give rise to the so-called 'Eastern Question' – which country or countries would inherit its mantle? During the nineteenth century a number of wars and settlements involving Turkey would take place with, each time, that empire diminished until, on the outbreak of the First World War, Turkey's only European foothold was the area between Constantinople and Adrianople. Interestingly, as Turkish authority waned and new states emerged in its place the European Great Powers imposed on them a system of protection of religious minorities. The Balkans were thus the first place where a vague system of protection over a wide area could be said to have developed.

From 1821–29 the Greeks waged a war of liberation against Turkey and Greek independence was recognised at the London Conference of 1830. The Great Powers insisted on a special Protocol to the Treaty guaranteeing that independence be extended to all subjects, whatever their religion, access to public employment and public honours, as well as equality of treatment.[94]

Following the Crimean War waged between Russia on the one hand and Turkey, Britain and France on the other, the two Romanian provinces of Moldavia and Wallachia, which had been invaded by Russia, although remaining part of Turkey, became autonomous. In the Paris Convention of 19 August 1858 the Great Powers laid down that their inhabitants should be equal before the law and taxation, enjoy full property rights, and have access to public employment. Christian inhabitants should also have full political rights, and such rights could be extended to other religions.[95]

In March 1878 with the Treaty of San Stefano following the Russo-Turkish War of 1876–77, the Great Powers recognised the independence of Romania, Serbia and Montenegro and obtained an autonomy for Bulgaria. In addition, Britain obtained Cyprus *de facto* even if it still technically remained part of Turkey and Austria received the right to administer Bosnia. However, with the Treaty of Berlin of July 1878 the recognition of independence was made dependent on the acceptance of clauses stating that differences of religion should not be grounds for exclusion from civil and political rights, public employment, public honours, and the exercise of professions and industries. It was also agreed that the Great Powers could intervene individually in the case of non-fulfilment of the settlement.[96]

In 1881 Greece obtained Thessaly from Turkey. Under the Convention of Constantinople redrawing the frontier, Moslems were to receive the same political and civil rights as Greeks, recognition of existing property rights and freedom of religion and public worship and no Greek interference in the organisation and management of religious bodies. Those who wished would have three years in which to opt for Turkish nationality and move to Turkey, and even if they did so they would be able to retain their immovable property in Greece unless given compensation in exchange.[97]

(b) Russia

If Turkey was the weakest empire the most stable, whatever the level of nationalist discontent, was the Russian empire, a leading contender to take over from Turkey in the Balkans. There were four reasons for this stability. First, there was the all-embracing repressive nature of what was a police state. Second, there was its backwardness in terms of economic, social and political development as compared with the West – the absence of a middle class and mass peasant illiteracy ensured no liberal or popular nationalist movements would be likely to succeed except perhaps in the far west of the state, in the more recently acquired territories of Finland (1809) and 'Congress' Poland (1815) where society was more modern and identity more marked. Third, ethnic Russians comprised 44.3 per cent of the empire of 122.7 million. More than that, a considerable proportion of the rest of the population consisted of brother Slavs – Ukrainians 17.8 per cent, Poles 6.3 per cent and Belarussians 4.7 per cent, thus making a Slavonic block of over 73 per cent. Fourth, the Russian empire contained very few minorities related to the dominant nationalities of its eastern European rivals, Austria and Turkey, so that there was little call for liberation from abroad and Russia was therefore more or less immune from that type of external pressure.[98]

But russification became increasingly prominent on the political agenda as the nineteenth century developed. At the Congress of Vienna in 1815 Russia received 'Congress' Poland on the understanding that Polish national institutions would be respected. And indeed the Poles received a large amount of self-government, with Polish as the official language and local administration in the hands of the Poles. But these concessions were revoked following the Polish revolt of 1830.

For its part Finland, obtained from Sweden in 1809, began by retaining its traditional institutions, including a parliament, as a Grand Duchy, when it became 'associated' with rather than incorporated into Russia. Finnish culture flourished and its language, previously spoken only by the peasantry, rose in status. But this privileged position aroused resentment, while on the other hand politics in Finland became more nationalist, aimed at creating a greater Finland through obtaining Karelia. The Karelians were a northern Ugro-Finnic tribe. In the middle ages western Karelians were Roman Catholics before conversion to Lutheranism whereas eastern Karelians were Russian Orthodox. Orthodox Karelians were seen in the nineteenth century as potential Russians, so Russians wanted to resist any Lutheranisation because it was seen as weakening loyalty to Russia. It would be one of the tragedies of eastern Karelians that their language was related to Finnish but in history and religion their destiny seemed to lie with

Russia. Yet not until the early twentieth century would there be written Karelian.[99] Another aim was Ugro-Finnic solidarity with Estonians. From 1899 onwards attempts were made to incorporate the Grand Duchy into the Empire. Nevertheless, 'on the eve of the First World War all minorities were succumbing to russification'. One reason for the russification programme was the discovery in the 1897 census that Russians were not, after all, a majority in their empire.[100] This doubtless explained the hostile declaration of Count Peter Valuev, the Russian Minister of the Interior, that the Ukrainian language 'never existed, does not exist, and never shall exist'.[101]

But of all the minorities in Russia the one that was the object of most vicious persecution was the Jews, over five million persons making up four per cent of the empire's population. Most Jews were obliged to live in the 'Pale of Settlement', that part of Poland taken by the Russians in 1795 after the Third Partition, and including Lithuania.[102] Inevitably the brutality and discrimination against them, whipped up also by the Russian Orthodox Church, practically forced Jews into the ranks of those politically opposed to the state, and their participation in terrorist groups (including the one which assassinated Tsar Alexander II in 1881) provided the regime with the opportunity to carry out *pogroms* of persecution which neither emigration nor displacement to the Pale would abate.

(c) Austria-Hungary

However, the really crucial area, and the one that would eventually lead to the First World War was the Austrian Empire, Austro-Hungarian after 1867, Russia's Balkan rival. The Austrian Empire was made up of several so-called 'Historic Nations'. Besides the Germans, who dominated, there were the Hungarians and Slavonic Czechs of Bohemia who had both had states of their own in the Middle Ages. During the 1848 revolutions which affected most of Europe the Hungarians and Czechs had tried to obtain independence but had been defeated.

After Austria's defeat in the 1866 war with Prussia and Italy an agreement was reached between the Austrian government in Vienna and moderate Hungarian politicians providing for the transformation of the Austrian empire into the Dual Monarchy – the Austro-Hungarian Empire – with Hungarians enjoying equal status with the Austrians. The Austrian half of the Empire consisted of German Austria, Bohemia, Moravia, part of Ruthenia, Galicia, the Bukovina, Istria, Carniola and the Trentino. The ethnic composition was 12 million Germans,

6.5 million Czechs, 5 million Poles, 3.5 million (Ukrainian) Ruthenians, 1.5 million Slovenes, 750 000 Serbo-Croats, 750 000 Italians and 250 000 Romanians. Crucially, of the 30.25 million in the Austrian half, the Germans, although the dominant nation, totalled less than 40 per cent. In the Hungarian half – Hungary, Croatia, Dalmatia, the Voivodina, Transylvania, Slovakia and part of Ruthenia – the ethnic composition was 10 million Hungarians, 3 million Romanians, 2.75 million Serbo-Croats, 2 million Slovaks and 500 000 (Ukrainian) Ruthenians, and therefore of the total of 20.25 million the Hungarians, if the dominant nation, were nevertheless a minority, even if only just so.[103]

The Constitution of the Austro-Hungarian Empire provided that although the German and Hungarian languages were official in their respective halves, communes could choose their own language to conduct business; all private schools could impart education in the language of their choice; and if members of any nationality lived together 'in considerable numbers' in an area they had to receive education in its language.

Both halves of the Empire had their problems. In the Austrian half Czechs wanted to transform the Empire by obtaining equal status with the Germans and the Hungarians; and they also wanted the Bohemian part to have Moravia and Silesia – both traditional lands of the Bohemian Crown. The Germans in these areas were very hostile because if that happened they would be in a minority there. And in this they were supported by the Hungarians who were also very anti-Slav and did not want to lose their privileged position in the Empire. This problem was never solved. Other sources of conflict in the Austrian half of the Empire were the hostility of the Slovenes and Croats to the Italians in Istria, and the basic desire of the Italians of the Trentino for unification with their kin in the Kingdom of Italy.

In Hungary, on the other hand, the government adopted a policy of magyarisation of the non-Hungarian peoples, believing this would ultimately make them loyal to the Hungarian nation and Hungarians would be dominant not only politically but numerically. Historically, in the eighteenth century Hungary was underpopulated owing to the Turkish occupation, wars of liberation, and frequent epidemics. The original Hungarian agricultural labour force was reduced significantly, and the Royal and noble estates had to bring in foreign labourers and craftsmen – Germans, Slovaks, Serbs and Romanians. This process was not regulated – every landowner brought in what foreign labour he wished, which was why, except in Romania, the ethnic groups were scattered throughout the land rather than settled in a block. It would therefore be relatively easy to assimilate these incomers, and magyarisation was promoted. By 1910 all state appointments and over 90 per cent of all influential posts in the administration, press, literature, universities, medicine, were going to Hungarian speakers. In 1879, 1883 and 1891 Education Laws made the teaching of Hungarian compulsory in all non-Hungarian nursery, elementary and secondary schools.[104]

The real weakness of the Empire, particularly in comparison with its Russian rival for domination of the Balkans can be seen from the fact that the two dominant races in the Austro-Hungarian Empire made up only 43.5 per cent of the whole. The other 56.5 per cent was made up of 7.9 per cent Latins (Italians and Romanians) and no less than 48.6 per cent Slavs, all uncomfortable in, if not actually outright hostile to, the Empire, and ready listeners to those surrounding it who wished to aggrandise themselves at its expense, notably the Kingdoms of Italy, Romania and Serbia.[105]

Analysis of measures for the protection of minorities in Eastern Europe

Analysis of the arrangements for the protection of ethnic, linguistic and religious minorities imposed in Eastern Europe in the nineteenth century and up to the outbreak of the First World War reveal that they were partial, hypocritical and ineffective.

They were partial in that they were usually applied to religious rather than linguistic minorities, and in one sense this was not surprising. In eastern Europe there was little or no discrimination on linguistic or cultural grounds, except perhaps in Hungary. Also, most of these Treaties or political arrangements were imposed by the Great Powers, amongst whom the so-called 'western' powers, France and Britain, had great influence. These powers had ceased to discriminate against people because of their religion. Catholic emancipation in the Protestant-dominated British Isles had been instituted in 1829. In France, overwhelmingly Roman Catholic, the issue was one of whether there should be Catholic schools or Catholic teaching in state schools, as opposed to secular education. Jews in Britain and France were considered a religious, not an ethnic or cultural minority. But as has been seen these states did indulge in cultural discrimination against their regional minority languages, as did Germany.

They were hypocritical because at least some of the Great Powers imposed standards that they themselves had no intention of observing.

Russia carried out systematic discrimination and persecution of Jews; Germany under Bismarck waged a *Kulturkampf* against Catholics.

Protection was ineffective because obligations were not universal, being imposed on small, weak, eastern European states and Turkey. There was no machinery either to supervise in an ongoing way how the minorities concerned were treated or for them to voice their grievances. There was no impartial tribunal to interpret obligations laid down in the Treaties. And there was nothing specific laid down as to what sanctions should be applied to a state failing to honour its obligations.

True, the Great Powers had the right under the Congress of Berlin to intervene individually but there was nothing about collective intervention. This merely exposed a further weakness. The political rivalry of the Great Powers would make it almost impossible to carry out action to enforce obligations. One of the most shameful evasions of obligations involved Romania. The 1866 Constitution laid down that only Christians could become citizens. One disadvantage of not being a citizen was that one could not own land. At the Berlin Congress of 1878 Romania agreed to non-discrimination on religious grounds, but the authorities merely stated this was true in regard to citizens. Jews, however, could not be citizens. Following protests the offending clause in the Constitution was repealed, but Romania continued the evasion, proudly and openly admitting it. Only a handful of Jews ever succeeded in becoming citizens.[106]

All in all the overwhelming conclusion was that the political framework in which the system operated was an important reason for its failure.

Self-determination

The traditional means today of finding out what people want is the vote. The idea of asking whole areas of people what they wanted in regard to their political allegiance began, as one might expect, with the French Revolution through the technique of the plebiscite, which was seen to harness Rousseau's theory of the 'General Will' derived from John Locke's 1690 idea of government by consent of the governed.[107]

The French Revolutionaries, stressing the democratic aspect of the Revolution, organised plebiscites in a number of areas when the French revolutionary armies entered them, namely Avignon (which belonged to the Pope) in 1791, Savoy and Nice (which belonged to the King of Savoy) in 1792, and in Liège and some enclaves in Alsace and the Rhineland in 1793. The populations were asked if they wanted to become part of France, and doubtless most of them did so wish, although the presence of French armies might have helped to encourage the 'Yes' votes. But in any case most of these areas were populated by French speakers.

But after the defeat of Napoleon in 1815 the organisers of the peace, meeting at the Congress of Vienna, returned to the principle that land and people belonged to the sovereign, and that self-determination would be prejudicial to the so-called principle of the balance of power. It was the flamboyant Giuseppe Mazzini during the period of the Italian Risorgimento who popularised the idea originally expressed by Luden that each nation should have its state and each state should have its nation, and thus transformed the concept of self-determination into the automatic right of each nationality to have its own independent state.[108]

Prince Metternich, Chancellor of Austria, saw that if self-determination was accepted as a principle of political action then Italy and Germany might well unite, squeezing Austria in the middle; also that the Austrian Empire could well fragment into its ethnic divisions so that the Empire itself would disappear and the German-Austrians would have no meaningful destiny by themselves and so would inevitably become part of a greater Germany. The next century would see his fears well founded.

But between 1848 and 1870 the principle of self-determination flourished again – in Italy. Plebiscites held in 1860 (Lombardy, the former Papal States of Romagna, The Marche and Umbria and Naples, Sicily, Tuscany, Parma, Modena), in 1866 (Venice) and 1870 (Rome and the surrounding Papal enclave) enabled the people in all those states to vote to join the Kingdom of Piedmont and then the Kingdom of Italy.

However, the annexation of Alsace-Lorraine by Germany after the 1870 Franco-Prussian war without holding a plebiscite struck the system a severe blow, and thereafter only once before the First World War was a plebiscite used to determine political allegiance, when in 1905 Norway voted to separate from Sweden in order to become an independent state in its own right for the first time since the fourteenth century. Significantly, plebiscites were not used in the decisions of the 1878 Berlin Congress on Eastern Europe.

From 1870 to 1914 the idea of national self-determination found it difficult to flourish. One reason was the cultural imperialism of the Great Powers, already mentioned. Another was socialism, which regarded nationalism as a bourgeois trick to divert the working class from their true vocation of establishing a classless society.

But once the apparent cohesion and iron control of the Great Powers had been shaken by the experiences of the First World War minorities everywhere were encouraged. When Tsarism ended in March 1917 one of the first steps of the Russian Provisional Government was to declare that its aim was peace based on 'the right of nations to decide their own destinies'.[109] And then the dam broke as Poles, Finns, Estonians, Latvians, Lithuanians, Ukrainians, Georgians and Armenians began to go their various separate ways. A similar disintegration would take place in the Austro-Hungarian empire. As the end of the war neared Hungarians, Czechs, Poles, Slovaks, Ruthenians, Croats and Slovenes melted away from the fronts to return to their homelands. All the war-weary peoples of central and eastern Europe expected Mazzini's principles to be fulfilled and accordingly began preparing for a new Europe of monocultural states.

Effects of the Industrial Revolution

If a major reason for the decline of religious and linguistic minorities in the nineteenth century was the hostility to their cultures by their host state and its dominant culture, a parallel cause for decline were the forces unleashed by the industrial revolution. The key was the existence – or otherwise – of natural resources or raw materials in the homelands of these minorities, and, if they did exist, the ability of the minority to develop them rather than have them developed by what Professor Michael Hechter has called the core regions of the state, those regions being the headquarters of the dominant culture and the source of administrative, financial and military power.[110]

Hechter argued that historically, through the centuries, the cores extended their power to the peripheral areas of their states where the linguistic minorities were mostly to be found. What hastened their integration in their states was one of the by-products of the Industrial Revolution, namely, the revolution in transport, whether through improved roads or the arrival of railways, providing for either easier access to or easier departure from the homelands of these peripheral cultures. Another significant feature of the Industrial Revolution was rural emigration and the growth of towns, traditionally the great melting pot of cultures. And riding on the coat-tails of the Revolution came two other nation-building developments. One was the establishment of national education systems. The resulting mass-literacy enabled the core to impose its culture and values through schools and the media. And then, in the second half of the nineteenth century, with colonial expansion and rivalry, and the division of Europe into alliances came the increase in the size of Europe's armed forces, providing for yet another melting pot.

Industrial development needs three things: natural resources such as fuels, minerals, even water; capital, not only finance but land and machinery; and labour, including managers and skilled and unskilled workers.

The presence of natural resources in a minority's homeland will require their exploitation. Whether they come to be developed by the minority in its own interests, or be developed by the state in its interest will depend on whether the minority can provide the necessary capital and labour. If it cannot provide the capital then it will be provided by the state, with the corollary that it will be the state that determines policies and establishes priorities. If the minority cannot provide the required labour force then it will be provided by the state, with the corollary that 'foreigners' from the dominant culture will enter the homeland of the minority, taking the best paid and the decision-making jobs.

Two factors weakening the solidarity of the minority with its homeland are, therefore, when members of the minority do not find employment in their homeland and are forced to emigrate to the towns of the dominant culture or when the homeland is flooded by incomers from the dominant culture, not merely to take jobs but also to purchase land for second or holiday homes. Sometimes both happen together.

Thereafter the march towards cultural decline is foreseeable. The inflow of members of the dominant culture leads to mixed marriages, with the next generation drawn to the dominant rather than the local culture; the local culture ceases to be the official culture, with the language ceasing to be used on official or administrative occasions; the local culture ceases to be taught in schools, or is made optional, and finally the value-transmitting institutions of the local culture (schools, media, language, religion) are replaced by those of the dominant culture.

When the minorities of Britain, France, Spain and Italy are considered in relation to the years before the First World War, only three contained areas of economic significance in terms of natural resources – Wales (coal and steel), the Basque Country (coal and steel) and Catalonia. They were subjected to an inflow of capital and labour from their respective cores. Even so, many Welsh people were not able to find suitable jobs in the Principality and emigrated to London and the developing industrial centres of Birmingham and Manchester.[111] Elsewhere the lack of natural resources and economic opportunity meant emigration: from the Highlands of Scotland abroad to Canada, Australia or the coal and steelmills of the Lowlands or service in the armed forces; from Ireland to the United States, to the industrial mills of the midlands of England or the armed forces; from Galicia to Spanish South America and the Caribbean, the agricultural estates of Castile or as domestic servants elsewhere in Spain.[112] Bretons left their overpopulated homeland in droves for Quebec, to the colonial service, to the Paris basin or the ports of France outside Brittany, or the fields of Aquitaine,[113] whereas Corsicans preferred employment in the Marseilles area, the state bureaucracy, the army or the colonial service, particularly Algeria.[114] For the Friauls, it was the industries of the Po valley that beckoned, whereas for the French in over-populated, poor and slowly italianising Val d'Aosta the chief destination of emigrants was France itself, especially the Paris basin.[115]

And yet the threat of cultural death was not fulfilled. Instead of being assimilated as traditional sociologists might have expected, they survived, even if weakened. Hechter explained this phenomenon in terms of 'internal colonialism', namely, that the economic development of peripheral areas followed a colonial pattern, and therefore precisely because it was a cultural division of labour, with senior and specialist jobs going to the incomers of the dominant culture and the lower, menial and unskilled jobs going to the indigenous dominated culture, the latter was not assimilated.[116] Nevertheless, there were other aspects of this colonial pattern of development to give concern. The development of a specialised range of economic products making the local economy dependent on markets outside the homeland, carried the risk that if the core controlled inward investment finance and overall economic development policy, once the specialised sectors become unprofitable, then investment could cease, industries would go to the wall and since the local economy was specialised rather than diversified the result would be first unemployment and then emigration, thus weakening further the solidarity of the cultural minority. In the second half of the twentieth century some minority homelands would find the theory becoming reality.

2
Into the Night – Minorities between the Wars

The Paris Peace Conference

The Peace Settlement

In March 1918 German troops launched a massive assault in the West, designed to crush the French and the British before the Americans, who had declared war on Germany in April 1917, could come to the rescue. But the assault ground to a halt by midsummer, and with the arrival of fresh, well-armed American troops it was clear that the war could not be won. This conclusion was reinforced by news from elsewhere. Allied forces had landed in Salonika and in October forced Bulgaria out of the war. Turkey capitulated as its armies in the Middle East were defeated. Austria-Hungary was disintegrating as the by now ill-equipped starving regiments on the Italian front began to melt away to join the ethnic nations of the empire which were beginning to proclaim their independence. At home the *Soviets* of workers and soldiers had begun to foment mutiny in the armed forces and seize control in Germany's leading cities. Offers of an armistice were made to President Wilson with the proposal that the basis of the peace be his Fourteen Points, announced to Congress on 8 January 1918.

Apart from general principles such as open negotiations on problems, freedom of the seas, equality of trading conditions, disarmament 'to the lowest levels consistent with national safety' and 'impartial' adjustment of colonial claims, the Fourteen Points had called, amongst other things, for the evacuation and restoration of Belgium (Point VI); the evacuation of all Russian territory (Point VII); the restoration to France of Alsace-Lorraine (Point VIII); a 'readjustment of the frontiers of Italy … along clearly recognisable lines of nationality' (Point IX); that the peoples of Austria-Hungary … should be accorded the freest opportunity of autonomous development (Point X); the evacuation of Romania, Serbia and Montenegro, with the occupied territories restored, and Serbia accorded free and secure access to the sea (Point XI); the erection of an independent Polish state, which should also be assured a free and secure access to the sea (Point XIII); and finally, the creation of a general association of nations to guarantee the independence and integrity of states, great and small.[1]

More dramatically, in a second speech on 11 February 1918, Wilson amplified his thinking on a future peace settlement by calling for it to be based on self-determination.

> Peoples are not to be handed about from one sovereignty to another by an international conference or an understanding between rivals and belligerents. National aspirations must be respected; peoples may now be dominated and governed only by their own consent. 'Self determination' is not a mere phrase. It is an imperative principle of action ... This war had its roots in the disregard of the rights of small nations and of nationalities which lacked the union and the force to make good their claim to determine their own allegiances and their own forms of political life. Covenants must now be entered into which will render such things impossible for the future...

And Wilson went on to set out four principles for a safe settlement directly related to the Fourteen Points. The first was that each part of the final settlement had to be based on the justice of that particular case and upon such adjustments as were most likely to bring about a permanent peace. Second, that peoples and provinces were not to be bartered about from sovereignty to sovereignty in that discredited game, the Balance of Power. Third, every territorial settlement should be made in the interest and for the benefit of the populations concerned. Fourth, all well-defined national aspirations should be accorded the utmost satisfaction that can be afforded them 'without introducing new or perpetuating old elements of discord and antagonism that would be likely in time to break the peace of Europe and consequently of the world'.[2]

The problems about Wilson's pronouncements were two. First, he tended to confuse the concepts of national self-determination and popular sovereignty,[3] and this was compounded by his self-admitted ignorance of the ethnic realities in Europe.[4] Second, the world of January–February 1918 – when the Allies looked like losing – was very different by the time the President actually arrived in Paris on

14 December to begin the peace negotiations at the chateau of Versailles.

First of all, now that victory had been achieved the victorious European Allies were not interested in self-determination. The British only had to look at Ireland where the British general election of December 1918 had seen 73 out of the 105 Irish seats won by Sinn Fein, a party seeking not Home Rule but independence and ready to appeal to the Peace Conference 'for the establishment of Ireland as an independent nation'. Irish Nationalists advocating Home Rule were annihilated, being reduced from 68 seats to 6.[5] And three weeks later a Declaration of Independence was issued, with Sinn Fein establishing an Irish Republic with its own legislative Dail Eireann.[6] Moreover, it was clear that violence in Ireland would not be long delayed. In the North Unionists had won 22 of the 37 seats in 9-county Ulster, and in the territory of the future 'six counties' their dominance was even more emphatic, with 22 seats out of 29, with four going to Home Rulers and three to Sinn Fein. As the future First Minister of Northern Ireland, David Trimble, was to write, 'Nationalists regarded the 1918 election as showing a majority in Ireland which desired independence and which justified the coercion of the (i.e. Unionist) minority. However, the sharp geographical distinction in the results show instead, that there were indeed two Irelands, which had each exercised their right to self-determination in both different and irreconcilable ways.'[7]

For the French, neither the Prime Minister Georges Clemenceau nor the Commander-in-Chief of the victorious Allied armies, Marshal Ferdinand Foch, wanted anything that might restrict demands on Germany, including its reduction in size. For military reasons Foch wanted the left bank of the Rhine, and for economic reasons France needed the coal fields and steel mills of the Saar. On the other hand, equally unwelcome, a Breton delegation arrived at the Peace Conference to see President Wilson, claiming linguistic rights and the liberty of peoples.[8]

As for the Italians, application of the principle of self-determination would most certainly conflict with much of the nation's war aims and what had been promised in the secret 1915 Treaty of London – German-speaking South Tyrol north of the Salurn Gorge and the Dalmatian coast. Seeing that Point IX interfered with their plans as early as October 1918 the Italians bluntly refused to accept the Fourteen Points as the basis of the peace with Austria, even though Austria had, like Germany, asked for an armistice on their basis. Later Wilson confirmed that he realised Italy was not bound by the Fourteen

Points in making peace with Austria.[9] In order to get round the incompatibility of Point IX with self-determination the Italians at the Conference presented a Memorandum arguing that the whole territory south of the Brenner, i.e. Trento as well as South Tyrol, was *geographically* one and that since as a whole it had an Italian majority, it should rightly revert to Italy. This line, too, was swallowed by Wilson, who later admitted, 'We lack the necessary facts. It was on the basis of insufficient study that I promised Orlando (the Italian Prime Minister) the Brenner frontier'.[10]

Second, with the collapse of the Austro-Hungarian, German, Russian and Turkish empires, it was no longer a question of autonomy for the peoples of the empires but their *de facto* independence. Following the Bolshevik seizure of power in Russia on 5 December 1917 at Brest-Litovsk an independent Ukraine was acknowledged by the Central Powers and the Bolsheviks. The next day it was Finland's turn to proclaim its independence. Estonia waited until February 1918. Later in the year other outposts of the Russian empire followed suit – Azerbaijan, Armenia and Georgia. Hungary, Latvia, Lithuania and Poland declared their independence in November 1918. As for German Austria, on 12 November 1918, the day after the Emperor Charles abdicated, the parliament in Vienna voted for the new German-Austrian republic (*de facto* in being since 28 October) to join the new German republic.[11]

Representatives of all these peoples now began crowding into Paris seeking recognition, and that meant agreeing new frontiers, often in the face of incompatible claims, and sometimes accompanied by violence, as in the Caucasus, Carinthia, and eastern Hungary, to say nothing of civil war in Russia between the Bolsheviks and anti-communists including the Ukraine. But this in turn merely revealed the most important issue of all, namely, what was one going to do about Germany? What was going to be the relationship of the German people to those around them. Six countries lay, or were about to lie on Germany's border: Denmark, which had lost territory to Prussia in the war of 1864; Belgium, which had been largely occupied by Germany during the World War; Poland, one-third of which had been part of Prussia and now contained many Germans; the Bohemian and Moravian provinces of the newly-proclaimed (28 October 1918) Czechoslovak State, with considerable German-speaking populations and long considered part of the Germanic sphere of influence even if latterly controlled by Austria (indeed deputies from those German-speaking areas had proclaimed these areas as part of the new German

Austria);[12] German Austria itself, whose very existence was in doubt since its own political representatives themselves acknowledged it was not economically viable and therefore wanted to let it form a free union with Germany;[13] and last but not least, France. The French may have regained Alsace Lorraine, but they knew that in terms of potential economic and military strength Germany remained the stronger of the two. The Germans were a considerably larger population, and France had suffered proportionately heavier casualties in the war. Its industrial north east had been devastated yet the only shots fired on German territory had been in the rural east; the framework of German industry was intact. Desire to punish Germany on the one hand and fear of German revenge – one day – on the other fuelled French policy and dominated the Conference.

Most of the punitive measures imposed by the Peace Conference in order to keep Germany down – the reparations bill, the so-called 'guilt' clause, the disarmament conditions which rendered the country weaker even than the small states around it – to say nothing of the humiliating conditions in which the Treaty was presented – and their effects, although important for the development of German and European history as a whole are not part of this history, which is concerned with the decisions taken on the new territorial divisions of the continent, and the results of those decisions.

Under the Treaty of Versailles Germany gave back Alsace-Lorraine to France, and plebiscites were to determine whether or to what extent the areas of Upper Silesia should go to Poland, Schleswig to Denmark, the enclave of Eupen-Malmedy to Belgium, and two small enclaves in East Prussia to the new Poland. The Province of Posen would be given to that new Poland, as well as a corridor to the sea separating East from West Prussia, headed by Danzig, an indisputably German city. The territory of Memel would be given to the Allies to administer as a port for the new Lithuania.[14]

As for Germany's former allies, under the treaty of St Germain (German) Austria had to give up Bohemia and Moravia to the new Czechoslovak state, South Tyrol, Trento, Trieste and the Istrian peninsula to Italy, and Slovenia to the new Yugoslavia. The boundary with the latter would be decided by a plebiscite in the southern part of the province of Carinthia (Article 49). Under Article 80 of the Treaty of Versailles and Article 88 of St Germain the country was forbidden to unite with Germany, except with the consent of the future League of Nations. Under the Treaty of Trianon Hungary lost no less than two-thirds of the area held under the Habsburg empire. Slovakia and

Ruthenia in the north were taken by the new Czechoslovakia. In the east Romania gained Transylvania. In the south Hungary had to surrender the Banat, part of which went to Romania but the rest, the Voivodina, went to the new Yugoslavia as well as Croatia-Slavonia. In the west a strip of land was ceded to Austria, becoming part of the latter's Province of Burgenland.

Under the Treaty of Sèvres Turkey had to give up eastern Thrace, the Aegean Islands and Smyrna (Izmir) to Greece, the Province of Antalya, Rhodes and the Dodecanese islands to Italy, Cilicia to France and Cyprus to Britain. Syria, Iraq and Palestine became Mandates of the League of Nations. Under the Treaty of Neuilly Bulgaria had to give up south-west Thrace to Greece.[15]

But for the Allies, and particularly the French, it was not just a question of reducing the size of the vanquished states. To ensure that they were kept in their place the states around them needed to be strengthened by the acquisition of territory to enable them, economically and militarily, to play the role of watchdogs. Nineteenth-century nationalism had postulated monocultural states and as the multi-national empires began to collapse this was certainly the expectation of their putative successors. But the states created, or restored, or expanded in order to fulfil their watchdog functions, found to their dismay that they contained almost as many minorities as the multi-national empires they had replaced.

Poland, for example, had a dual role: not only to watch over Germany but also to act as the part of the *cordon sanitaire* being thrown up against Bolshevik Russia. The Allies had hoped to strengthen it economically by providing access to the sea through the so-called corridor to Danzig, separating East from West Prussia. And originally it had been intended to provide Poland with the entire area of upper Silesia, rich in coal and iron ore which had provided Imperial Germany with 21 per cent of Germany's coal, second only to the Ruhr. But the Germans protested that they needed the raw materials in order to pay for reparations and Lloyd George warned against creating a new Alsace-Lorraine in the east. The decision was taken to divide the area and under Article 88 of the Versailles Treaty a plebiscite would be held on where to draw the line.

The newly resurrected state of Poland consisted of some 27 million inhabitants of which only 19 million (68.75 per cent) were Poles. There were some four million Ukrainians, two million Jews, 1.1 million Germans (in Posen – now Poznan, the Corridor, and, after the 1921 plebiscite, Upper Silesia). There were also 30 000 Czechs from the area round Teschen, as well as one million Greater and White Russians (Belarusians) and 700 000 Lithuanians.

The frontiers of the new Czechoslovakia were drawn on military grounds to watch over both Germany and Hungary. This led to large numbers of ex-Austrian Germans (30 per cent of Bohemia, 20 per cent of Moravia) being incorporated into the Czech lands, in the so-called Sudetenland. The Sudetenland consisted of a range of mountains some 200 miles long and 20–40 miles wide on the northern frontiers of Bohemia and Moravia which, together with the Bohemian Forest and Sudeten Silesia provided the Czech border with Germany, as well as southern Moravia on the Austrian frontier. The Czechs wanted their Slavonic kin, the Slovaks and Ruthenians to participate in the state so as to balance the Germans, but the Slovaks in Slovakia were not enthusiastic. They had, after all, never enjoyed an independent existence. But towards the end of the war pressure was applied to Slovak exiles in the United States, and at Pittsburg an agreement was reached that the Slovaks should have an autonomy. To the Czech and Slovak lands was added Ruthenia so that the state should have a common frontier with anti-Hungarian Romania. As with the Slovaks, agreement was reached with Ruthenian emigrés in the United States that the area would have an autonomy[16] but of this Czechoslovak state of 14.3 million only just over half, 7.2 million, were Czechs. There were 3.3 million Germans, overwhelmingly and solidly camped together in the Sudeten areas. There were only two million Slovaks, and along the Slovak border with Hungary were no less than 700 000 Hungarians. There were also 600 000 Ruthenians who, like the Slovaks, had been promised an autonomy.

The population of Romania was 16 million in 1930 of which about a quarter were not Romanian. There were 1.5 million Hungarians in Transylvania, three quarters of a million Jews, and a like number of Germans, Ukrainians/Ruthenians, and Bulgars as well as Russians, Turks, Greeks, Serbs and Poles numbering over a million.[17] Besides watching over Hungary Romania, too, was to be part of the *cordon sanitaire* against Bolshevik Russia.

The population of Yugoslavia in 1921 was 12 million, of which there were 5 million Serbs, 3.5 million Croatians, 1.1 million Slovenes, 500 000 Germans, 500 000 Hungarians (in the Voivodina), 500 000 Albanians (in the Serb province of Kossovo) and 500 000 Macedonians.

It was Napoleon who had promoted Slovene and Croatian nationalism by creating the Illyrian Republic in order to bar Austria from the Adriatic. The Yugoslavia of 1918 was created under pressure of outside threats, particularly from Italy and its claims to Istria and the Dalmatian coast. This pushed Slovenes and Croatians to go into partnership with the 'lesser' evil, Serbia, after the fall of the Austro-Hungarian Empire. But the boundaries of these Yugoslav republics were all drawn on the basis of previous power politics – the Austrian and Turkish empires and Great Power intervention, without any reference to self-determination or the ethnic situation. The new state would soon be in conflict with Italy over Istria, and with Bulgaria over Macedonia, and be apprehensive about the Hungarians of the newly acquired Voivodina.

Other states too had come into being and found themselves not monocultural. The new Estonia had a population of just over a million. 88 per cent were Estonian, with their Ugro-Finnic culture, but 8.5 per cent were Russians and 1.5 per cent Germans. Nearly three-quarters of the less than two million population of Latvia were Latvians but 12.5 per cent were Russians, 3.7 per cent were German and nearly 5 per cent Jewish. In Lithuania, if Lithuanians were 84 per cent of the population of 2.4 million, Jews were 7.6 per cent, Poles 3.2 per cent, Russians 2.7 per cent and Germans 1.4 per cent. But many Estonians and Latvians were also to be found in the new Soviet Union, and Lithuanians in Poland. Albania's estimated population of 850 000–900 000 was also only just over three-quarters Albanian, with 7.8 per cent Serbs, 6.6 per cent Romanians, 6.0 per cent Turks, as well as some 50 000 Greeks.[18] The new Finland was only 89 per cent Finnish; the other 11 per cent were Swedes established in the south-west of the mainland and in the archipelago of the Aland Islands between Finland and Sweden.

The country which became the most monocultural as a result of border changes was Hungary, with nearly 90 per cent of its 7 million population Magyar, although nearly 7 per cent was German and nearly 2 per cent Slovak. Bulgaria however was not far behind, with 86.7 per cent of the six million population Bulgar. But there was a considerable Turkish minority of nearly 10 per cent.[19]

Although by mid-1919 some boundaries still needed to be settled by plebiscites, the drawing of the new frontiers would be leaving some 30 million persons as inhabitants of states in which their culture was not that of the majority.[20] In June 1919 the victorious Allies took two steps which would affect how problems that might arise out of that situation would be faced.

The 'Minorities Treaties'

The first step of the Allies was to respond to the clearly recognisable fact that they had departed from the principles of the Fourteen Points and self-determination. Accordingly a system was set up to get protection of minorities into international treaties and declarations and to have these put under the control of the League of Nations.

In so far as Europe was concerned the system would consist of no less than nineteen instruments:

(a) Four Peace Treaties between the victorious Allies and the former Central Powers:
  (i) St Germain, with Austria, 10 September 1919, especially Articles 62–9
  (ii) Trianon, with Hungary, 4 June 1920, especially Articles 54–60
  (iii) Neuilly, with Bulgaria, 27 November 1919, especially Articles 49–57
  (iv) Sèvres, with Turkey, 10 August 1920, especially Articles 37–45, (this treaty was not ratified by Turkey).
(b) Treaties between the victorious Allies and five newly created or enlarged existing states, namely, Czechoslovakia, Greece, Poland, Romania and Yugoslavia. These were the so-called 'Minorities Treaties'.
(c) Five Declarations, not part of the Peace Settlement, but given by the states concerned at the time they variously joined the League – Finland (27 June 1921), Lithuania (12 May 1922), Latvia (7 July 1923), Estonia (17 September 1923), Albania (2 October 1921).
(d) Three special Conventions:
  (i) The Danzig–Poland Convention of 9 November 1920, Articles 33 and 39
  (ii) The German–Polish Convention of 15 May 1922 on Upper Silesia
  (iii) The Memel Convention between the Allies and Lithuania of 8 May 1924, Article 11 and Annex 1, Article 27.
(e) The Treaty of Lausanne, between Greece and Turkey, of 24 July 1923, following the 1920–2 war between them.

Of the 'Minorities Treaties' that with Poland was the first to be negotiated and signed, and thus provided a precedent for the others. Its twelve articles faced up to a number of issues in the field of citizenship, culture and education, as well as supervision of implementation of the Articles. Most of the Articles provided for so-called 'negative equality' defined as providing treatment no worse than that of the majority, whereas 'positive equality' provided for special measures for the preservation and development of the minorities' national consciousness.[21]

Under Article 2 Poland undertook to assure full and complete protection of life and liberty to all inhabitants of Poland without distinction as to birth, nationality, language, race or religion. All inhabitants would be entitled to the free exercise, in public or private, of any creed, religion or belief whose practices were not inconsistent with public order or public morals. The emphasis on *inhabitants* was important, being designed to overcome the situation whereby in Romania Jews could be discriminated against on the grounds that they were not citizens.

Article 3 provided for Polish citizenship to be granted to all German, Austrian, Hungarian or Russian nationals 'habitually resident' in Poland at the date of the coming into force of the Treaty. The Treaty did not, however, define 'habitually resident'. But under Article 91 of the Treaty of Versailles, Polish nationality was not to be given automatically to Germans who had taken up residence in the territory of the new Poland since 1 January 1908. This was introduced in order to counter prewar immigration by Germans, forced or not, which might have led to Poles being dispossessed of land or property. The same would apply to Bulgarians resident since 1 January 1913 in areas ceded to Greece and Yugoslavia.[22] Second, there was the principle that Austrians, Germans, Hungarians and Russians who did *not* want to receive Polish citizenship could opt for *any* other nationality rather than their putative one. This was in order to accommodate Russians who might not wish to return to a Russia under the control of the Bolsheviks. Third, the importance of the father as head of the family in decisions affecting members of a minority was established as a basic feature in minority protection.

Under Articles 4 and 5 Poland agreed to grant citizenship to any Austrians, Germans, Poles or Russians born in its territory of parents 'habitually resident' there, even if they themselves were not habitually resident at the time, should they wish it, i.e., Poland would not be able to exclude criminals or members of the armed forces or police, judiciary and security services of those former empires.

Article 6 provided that all persons born in Polish territory who were not born nationals of another state should *ipso facto* become Polish nationals.

Article 7 dealt with civil, political and language rights. All nationals had the right of admission to public employment, functions and honours and the exercise of professions and industries. All could use their own language in private, in commerce, religion, the press and in public meetings. However, the Article also provided for the first 'positive equality' right, that of using one's language, orally or in writing, before a public institution, namely the courts. Again, this right would only apply to Polish citizens. Under Article 7 it would also be up to the Polish government to decide whether or to what extent a minority language should in any way be official. By comparison, Article 2 of the Czecho-Slovak Language law of 29 February 1920 stated that:

In districts containing a racial minority of at least 20 per cent, the authorities are bound to transact business with any of its members in their own language and to issue all proclamations and official notices in the language of the minority as well as Czecho-Slovak. The Public Prosecutor is bound to bring his indictment in the language of the accused.

And under Article 3:

The authorities are everywhere bound to accept oral and written communications in the Czecho-Slovak language and to sanction its use at any meeting: in other languages, only where these are spoken by 20 per cent of the population of the particular district.[23]

However, these two articles raised two issues which needed to be defined. What was a district? And what guarantee was there that the authorities would not gerrymander the boundaries of 'districts' so that as few as possible would reach the 20 per cent quota? In so far as the courts in Poland were concerned, Polish implementing legislation provided for the use of the minority language orally and in writing by parties and witnesses; statements and documents had to be translated into the minority language upon request.[24]

Articles 8 and 9 dealt with the all-important issue of education, the means by which group values are transmitted from generation to generation. Under Article 8 racial, linguistic and religious minorities had the right to set up and control *private* charitable, religious and social institutions and schools, including the right to use their language therein. Again this applied only to Polish citizens. Article 9, however, provided for 'positive equality' in education. In state primary schools 'adequate facilities' would be provided in order to ensure that the children of minorities who were also citizens would be able to receive instruction in their own language in those towns and districts in which they were 'a considerable proportion'. Nevertheless, in such schools the Polish government could make the teaching of Polish obligatory. In addition, Poland would ensure that any minorities obtained an 'equitable share' in public funds for educational, religious or charitable purposes. However, the Treaty contained no definition of such phrases as 'adequate facilities', 'considerable proportion' or 'equitable share'. This raised again such issues as to whether ethnic proportions in an area should be the rule and if so, how should the area be calculated, and who should do the calculating – the state or the minority? However, Article 9 would only apply to Polish citizens of German speech in that part of Poland which was German territory at the outbreak of the war, and thus did not apply to German-speakers from ex-Austrian Poland, nor to ex-Russian Poland where German was the second language of Russians and dominant in trade and commerce.

In practice the Polish government solved the question of 'considerable proportion' by providing, in ex-German Poland, for German-speaking citizens to have primary schools or classes in municipalities where there were at least forty children from the minority of scholastic age. If there were between 15 and 39 children the German language and religious instruction in German would be taught from four to six hours per week. Ukrainian, Ruthenian and Lithuanian speaking citizens could have primary school teaching in their language if either the group was 25 per cent of the municipality or if the parents of 40 children asked for it. The Polish government would also set up secondary schools for minorities if the parents of 150 children in any town or district so requested.[25]

Of more concern to the national governments were the issues of staff, programmes and curricula in both private and public schools. In Poland private schools could be set up at any time on condition that the programme contained courses on Polish language, literature, history and geography. But who would be teaching these courses? The Polish government was aware that if under the Treaty it had to cede control of minority private schools these could be 'taken over' not necessarily by the minority but by the kin-state government which might, via the teaching staff, fill the youth of the minority with hatred of the state perceived to be occupying the homeland of the minority. On the other hand the Minorities did not want merely to be educated in their own language: they also wanted to be taught in the form and spirit they considered appropriate for their own culture and national consciousness.

Articles 10 and 11 applied specifically to the Jews, who formed some 10 per cent of the population of the new Poland. Jewish Committees at Versailles had been prominent in the demands for protection of both Jewish and other minorities in central Europe. Indeed they had raised for the first time the idea of proportional representation: that where minorities formed one per cent of the total population they should constitute an autonomous body with the right not only to establish their own religious, charitable and educational institutions but be entitled to representation proportional to their number in all state, departmental and municipal elective bodies.

In the end the idea of proportional representation in political bodies was rejected on the grounds that it would be establishing a state within a state and undermine the authority of the Polish state.[26] On the other hand, under Article 10 Jewish-appointed Education Committees would be responsible for organising and managing Jewish schools, and distributing the public funds allocated to them. The language provisions of article 9 would also apply to Jewish schools. Under Article 11 Jews were not to be compelled to perform any act held to violate the Sabbath, for example, attending the Courts or performing any legal business. They were not exempt, however, from military or national defence obligations. Furthermore Poland undertook to refrain from holding registration for elections or the elections themselves on a Saturday.

The Romanian Minorities Treaty did not contain similar articles concerning the Jews. However, under Article 7 Romania undertook to recognise as nationals *ipso facto* and without the requirement of any formality Jews inhabiting any Romanian territory who did not possess another nationality.[27]

Machinery for the supervision of the clauses of the Treaty was vital if the shortcomings of the pre-1914 era were not to be repeated. Thus, under Article 1 of the Treaty, Poland agreed to recognise Articles 2 to 8 as fundamental laws, and that no law, regulation or official action should conflict with or prevail over them, thereby ensuring that a subsequent parliament could not repeal them. This was reinforced by the first paragraph of Article 12 which stated that the Articles of the Treaty constituted obligations of international concern and were placed under the guarantee of the League of Nations, and could not be modified without the consent of a majority of the Council of the League.

In the second paragraph Poland agreed that any Member of the League Council should have the right to bring to the attention of the Council any infraction or any danger of infraction of Poland's obligations, and the Council could then take whatever action it considered necessary.

In the third paragraph Poland agreed further that any difference of opinion as to questions of law or fact between Poland and a League

Council member state should, if the latter so wished, be referred to the Permanent Court of International Justice (PCIJ), whose decision would be final.[28]

The League of Nations

The second step taken by the Allies, and in response to Wilson's four-teenth point, was the establishment of a League of Nations to promote international co-operation and prevent war. Acceptance of the League Covenant was an integral part of the Peace Treaties with the defeated powers. The League itself came into being on 10 January 1920 with the coming into effect of the Treaty of Versailles, signed on 28 June 1919.

The principal organs of the League were four – a General Assembly of the Member States; an executive Council of nine, consisting originally, on the one hand of the victorious Great Powers as Permanent Members (Britain, France, Italy, Japan and the United States) and on the other hand of four elected members; a Secretariat, established at the seat of the League, Geneva; and (established in 1921) the Permanent Court of International Justice (PCIJ) with its seat at The Hague. Under Article 3 (iii) of the Covenant, the Assembly, and under Article 4 (iv) the Council could deal with any matter affecting the peace of the world. Interestingly, under Article 5 (i) decisions of the Assembly or Council would require the agreement of all the Members of the League re-presented at the meeting. But under Article 4 (v) any Member of the League not represented on the Council would be invited to send a representative to sit as a member at any meeting of the Council if matters affecting that Member's interests were under consideration.

However, with the failure of the United States to ratify the Peace Treaties the United States failed to take up membership of the League. The numbers of the Permanent Members of the Council were reduced to four until Germany became a member of the League and a permanent Member of the Council in 1926.

Under Article 10 of the Covenant Members of the League undertook to respect and preserve, as against external aggression, the territorial integrity and existing political independence of all League Members. But under article 11(ii) it was also declared to be the 'friendly right' of each Member of the League to bring to the attention of the Assembly or of the Council any circumstance which might threaten to disturb international peace.

However, the intention of the creators of the League was that disputes should be settled judicially, hence the importance of the PCIJ. Under Article 12 of the League Covenant the members of the League agreed that in case of a dispute likely to lead to a rupture of relations, besides enquiry by the Council the matter would be submitted either to arbitration or judicial settlement. Under Article 13 (i) the Members of the League agreed that whenever any dispute arose which they recognised as being suitable for submission to arbitration or judicial settlement 'and which cannot be satisfactorily settled by diplomacy' they would indeed submit such a case to arbitration or judicial settlement.

Absolutely vital for defining what cases were suitable for submission to judicial proceedings was Article 13(iii):

> Disputes as to the interpretation of a Treaty, as to any question of international law, as to the existence of any fact which, if established, would constitute a breach of any international obligation, or as to the extent and nature of the reparation to be made for such breach, are declared to be among those which are generally suitable for submission to arbitration or judicial settlement.

Under Article 13(iii), any such disputes would be referred to the PCIJ, and under (iv) the Members of the League agreed to carry out in good faith any award or decision rendered. Under Article 14 the PCIJ could render not only a decision but an advisory opinion in relation to a dispute submitted to it.[29]

A major problem, however, was that the Minorities Treaties had been drafted before the League had actually come into existence. The guarantee clause – Article 12 of the Polish Treaty – had thus been imposed on the League without its prior approval. Furthermore, if the League decided to accept this imposition (and rejection was discussed in the Council) procedures to give effect to the guarantee would have to be set up.[30]

Another problem was that under the Treaties the only means of seeing that obligations were carried out was if a Council member took up the case of a plaintiff, which meant putting the host country in the dock. The Minorities treaty states argued that it should not be enough for the Council member merely to provide information that there had been a breach of obligations but that it should be prepared to go further and maintain the accusation before the League itself. Was this likely, particularly in regard to German and Hungarian minorities, seeing that the boundaries of the Minorities treaty states had been drawn to resist revanchism and all but Greece were allies of France in the so-called 'Little Entente', an alliance specifically designed to that end? As for the right of the Council to take action, was it likely to take action if under Articles 4 and 5 of the Covenant this could only take place on the basis of unanimity in decision-making yet the accused state itself had the right to vote?

To examine these problems the Council appointed its Italian representative, Tommasso Tittoni. His report was presented in October 1920. The basis of his report was that the right of calling attention to any infringement or danger of infringement of the Treaties should not be the prerogative solely of states represented on the Council, but should be extended to the minorities themselves and even states not represented on the Council. And the way for such minorities to call such attention would be by way of a petition.

The right of petition was proposed for any individual member of a minority. He or she could petition the League Council by providing information only to the effect that there had been a breach of an obligation. This petition would be forwarded to the state concerned and Council members only, but without comment. The petition could only be dealt with if one of the Council members took it up.

Since the Minority states complained that this gave free propaganda to the minority without the state being able to give its views, the procedure was amended in 1921 so that the petition, after arriving at the League's headquarters in Geneva, was first communicated to the state concerned, which was given three weeks to inform the Secretary General of the League whether or not it intended to comment. If the state did not reply in that period or said it did not wish to comment, the petition would then go to the Council as in the previous procedure. If the state said it wished to reply it was given two months in which to do so.

In order to protect against abuse of the system certain rules were laid down in 1923:

1 The Petition must have in view the Protection of Minorities in accordance with the treaties only (i.e., minorities in other countries were disqualified from the procedure).
2 The Petition had to refrain from calling for severance of political relations between the minority and the host State.
3 The Petition could not be anonymous or come from an unauthenticated source.
4 The Petition had to abstain from violent language.
5 The Petition had to contain information or refer to facts not recently the subject of a previous petition.

The origin of the petition was not considered relevant. Poland had wanted it to come only from the minority concerned, as opposed, for example, from the kin-state or a member of that state. But the problem here was the not unfounded fear that if a member of a minority petitioned, his host state might take action against him. The contents of the petition, as well as the reply of the government, were not made public until the issue had been brought before the League Council. Furthermore, the petitioner was not informed of the comments of the accused state.

In order to assist the Council in the exercise of its obligations, and also to ensure that no Council member was put into the position of having to take the initiative in accusing a government before the Council, a further proposal of Tittoni's was adopted, namely that petitions, when they arrived at Geneva, should be sent to a Committee of three Members of the Council – in exceptional cases this could be raised to four following an amendment in 1929 – so that these could decide which merited being placed on the Council agenda for discussion. This would serve to collectivise the exercise.

These three persons, all representing their states on the Council, normally consisted of the President of the Council and two others nominated by him. None of these could come from the host state, the kin-state, or a state neighbouring that of the minority. If the President should come from one of these, then the previous Council president would be the Committee's chairman.

The Committee could ask governments for additional information, oral or written. But petitioners were never permitted to make verbal statements nor were they ever asked for additional information.

The Committee had three courses of action: it could decide that the case should go the League Council; or that the case should be shelved; or third, it might find that a case, while not meriting Council attention, could not be dropped altogether (either because the information was insufficient or because it was felt that a better result could be obtained if the host government was approached and a compromise reached). In this case the Committee more or less negotiated with the host government on how best to solve the matter, and this became the general rule.

The League also created a special Minorities section within the Secretariat in Geneva, staffed by international civil servants. It was this department which handled relations with the host state, including attempting to gain additional information and advising on whether the petition was receivable.[31]

Self-determination

In the two years following the establishment of the League of Nations and the signature of the Polish Minority Treaty the Allies and the League had to tidy up the map of Europe that had been created. In some cases matters would be solved satisfactorily; in others, less so.

(a) Schleswig

The first case was that of self-determination in Schleswig. As Denmark had been neutral in the war it was for the people of Schleswig to petition the Peace Conference for the fulfilment of the promise of a plebiscite dating from the Treaty of Prague in 1866.[32] Accordingly provisions for border revision following a border poll were in corporated into the Treaty of Versailles (Articles 109–12). The area in question would be divided into two zones. In North Schleswig the population would vote as a whole while in the so-called Middle Zone polling would take place by separate municipalities. In February 1920 the voting in the former produced a 75 per cent vote to return to Denmark but in the following month 80 per cent of those in the Middle Zone voted to remain with Germany, with not one municipality producing a Danish majority. Overall there was a slight Danish majority, but the new frontier would leave 20 000 Danes in Germany and a like number of Germans in Denmark. The Danish government promised its German-speaking citizens liberal rights, and funded separate schools wherever one-fifth of the voters could present a minimum of ten German-speaking children.[33]

What was significant about the Schleswig vote was that clearly in expectation of a much closer vote, the decision on where to draw the boundary in the Middle Zone would follow as closely as possible municipal lines, rather than the area as a whole, as in North Schleswig, being awarded to the one side or the other. This method of deciding boundaries set a precedent that would soon be followed elsewhere, in Upper Silesia and Northern Ireland.

(b) Allenstein and Marienwerder

A second use of the plebiscite took place in Allenstein and Marienwerder on 11 July 1920 where some 300 000 Masurians, Lutheran Poles writing in Gothic script, lived in East Prussia. The expectation of the Allies and the Polish government was doubtless that these Poles would wish to join Poland, and provision was made in Article 94 of the Treaty of Versailles for a border poll. In the event, only just over two per cent of the 371 000 votes cast in Allenstein went to Poland.[34] In Marienwerder only 7 947 persons voted for Poland compared to 96 894 for Germany. Expectation of Polish defeat in the war that had begun with the Soviet Union may have played a part.[35]

(c) Eupen-Malmedy

A few months later the principle of self-determination failed to be used in Eupen-Malmedy. This area had become part of the Rhine province of Prussia at the 1815 Congress of Vienna. On strategic, economic, historic and linguistic grounds it was decided to transfer the area to Belgium and arrangements were made for Germany to renounce the territory in the Treaty of Versailles (Article 34). The Americans had insisted on a plebiscite but following French pressure this was not carried out. However, the opportunity was provided under the article that after six months the inhabitants would be able to record in writing whether they wanted the area to remain with Germany, and Belgium undertook to abide by the results. Two public protest lists were opened. But by July 1920 fear of reprisals or even expulsion with loss of property, as well as political indifference, meant that only 271 voters out of the some 34 000 eligible made use of this opportunity. On the basis of this 'plebiscite', organised by the military government in the area, the League of Nations recognised Belgian sovereignty over the enclave. Complete incorporation with Belgium would not, however, occur until 1925. During this five-year transition period French–German bilingualism was introduced, and the Belgian position strengthened by an inflow of teachers and administrators. But in between the wars the idea of revising the Treaty of Versailles or holding a new referendum remained alive. Conflicting views as to whether the new situation should be accepted or a new plebiscite should be sought polarised the German community.[36]

(d) Carinthia

The next use of the plebiscite occurred in the mixed German-Slovene areas along the borders of Austria's southernmost province of Carinthia with Slovenia, now part of the newly created kingdom of the Serbs, Croats and Slovenes, or Yugoslavia. In Paris the Allies were agreed – and expected – to transfer certain parts of southern Carinthia to Yugoslavia. To begin with two zones were created. In the much larger Zone A, in which, according to the 1910 census, some 70 per cent was Slovene and which was already under Yugoslav administration, a plebiscite would be held and if, as expected, there was a majority in favour of Yugoslavia, then a similar plebiscite would be held in the much smaller Zone B around the capital of Carinthia, Klagenfurt. Again expectations were dashed as on 10 October 1920 60 per cent of Zone A voted to remain with Austria. The Slovene-speaking population of Carinthia had been declining significantly over the previous half century, from 85 000 or 26.6 per cent in 1880 to 75 000 or 22.3 per cent in 1900 to 66 460 or 18.3 per cent in 1920. In 1923 it would fall to just over 37 000 or 10.1 per cent.[37]

Advanced attempts to solve minority problems

Upper Silesia

At Versailles there had been a bitter discussion between the allies as to whether the area as a whole should remain with Germany or be given to Poland or whether it should be divided and, if so, on what basis. The final decision, enshrined in Article 88 of the Versailles Treaty, was that the inhabitants should decide. However, in a six article Annex it was proposed that any dividing line should follow the voting in the municipalities. Those born in Upper Silesia but who had moved away would have the right to vote in the plebiscite and some estimates put the number of these as high as 300 000. Tension in the area was very high. Germans, bitter at the prospect of coming under Poland, rioted against attempts to create a Polish administration and celebrated Polish defeats in the war that had begun in 1920 when the Soviet Union invaded the country in order to spread communism. On the other hand, Poles tried to disband the German civil administration and security forces. The Allies were obliged to move troops into the area to restore order. However, France and Poland sought to remove the right to vote of those born in the area but had moved away, while Britain and Germany insisted on the clause in the Annex being maintained. It was not until February 1921 that Britain forced France to agree to include the non-resident votes. It was also agreed that voting should take place on one single day, 20 March, and on a municipal basis as with the Middle Zone in Schleswig for determining the Polish–German frontier.

In the plebiscite 707 488 persons voted for Germany as against 479 369 for Poland. 844 municipalities had a German-speaking majority as against 678 with a Polish majority. The number of non-resident voters amounted to nearly 200 000, almost entirely for Germany. The north and west – agricultural areas – voted overwhelmingly for Germany. The south and the east, with large untapped iron-ore deposits voted for Poland. But in the key industrial triangle in the heart of Upper Silesia the cities generally voted for Germany whereas the outlying mining communities voted for Poland. However, the overall majority in the triangle was for Germany.[38]

On 1 April Germany claimed all Upper Silesia on the grounds that the area was an indivisible economic unit. Poland called for a boundary giving it two-thirds of the population and all the industrial resources. The British, French and Italian boundary commissioners could not agree on a line. The British and Italian commissioners proposed giving only the south and east to Poland since the other areas had a German majority. In the tense situation Wojciech Korfanty, a former deputy in the Reichstag and Poland's plebiscite commissioner, staged an uprising, while French troops in the area did nothing. In response, German paramilitary units – the *Freikorps* – entered Upper Silesia to fight the Poles.[39] British and French troops forced the combatants apart and the matter was referred to the Supreme War Council of the Allies in Paris.

The British were ready to agree that the South and East should go to Poland and the French were ready to agree that the North and West should go to Germany. The problem was the industrial triangle where a few miles might mean a difference of wealth in mines and factories. Since there was no agreement it was decided in August to refer the matter to the League of Nations.

The role of the League was significant in two respects. First, in October 1921 an expert commission appointed by the League recommended a boundary line going through the triangle. Germany obtained 57 per cent of Upper Silesia as a whole, and 70 per cent of the triangle but three-quarters of the coal-mines and iron-ore reserves as well as most of the industrial undertakings went to Poland. The population of German Upper Silesia was some 900 000, of which 154 000 were Poles and 373 000 were bilingual. Polish Upper Silesia consisted of some 1.1 million of which some 250–300 000 were German.[40]

Second, a League of Nations commission recommended that Germany and Poland should negotiate an agreement on a whole series of issues, including protection of minorities, nationality and domicile, to cover a transition period of fifteen years. The result was the Germano-Polish Geneva Convention on Upper Silesia of 15 May 1922, which consisted of no less than 606 articles, including 95 on minority protection of which 37 related to education, while others related to the establishment of institutional machinery for the redress of grievances.[41]

With regard to education the Convention dealt with all levels. As with the Polish Minorities Treaty the respective minorities could establish, manage and control private schools at their own expense provided the teachers were qualified and did not abuse their position to engage in activities hostile to the state. Nor need the official language be used for instruction (Articles 98 and 99). At primary level the creation of a state minority school where instruction would be given in the language of the minority, or the establishment of minority classes in any primary school, would be obligatory if forty or more children of the minority needed it. Children were to be nationals and of an age to attend the school in question. Instruction in the language and religion of the minority was to be compulsory if at least 18 pupils came from the minority. A minority school could not be closed unless the number of pupils fell below the requisite number on three consecutive terms or, during one term, to half that number (Articles 106–108).

In secondary and higher education for their minority Germany and Poland agreed to establish the former if requests came from the parents of 200 children, the latter from 300. Parallel classes in secondary education would be established in the event of 35 children of the minority, 30 in higher education. Minority language courses would be put on if there were at least 25 minority children. Minority secondary schools could be closed if the number of pupils was 20 per cent below the norm for three successive years (Articles 115–122).

An educational Commission was established for each minority school or course of instruction to see that equipment was to hand, to obtain finance and to advise staff appointments. The staff teaching in minority schools or courses should, in principle, be recruited from that minority, and there was provision for an interchange of staff from the two areas of Upper Silesia (Articles 111–113).

Finally, of vital importance in the field of education were Articles 74 and 131 of the Convention. Article 74 stated that 'the question as to whether a person does or does not belong to a minority may not be verified or disputed with the authorities', while Article 131 stated that in order to determine the language of a child account should only be taken of a verbal or written statement by the person legally responsible for the child's education. The object of the Article was designed to cut down polemics, the fear being that a minority could be undermined if it was argued that children could not go to a school of their group on the grounds that in reality they were not members of that group.

With regard to language, that of the minority could be used in all private and business relations. As with the 1919 Minorities Treaty 'adequate facilities' would be prescribed for its use in court. However, the Convention went beyond the Treaty in providing for its oral use with the administration, that written replies by the administration to members of the minority should have an official translation, and that the language could be used in meetings of municipal councils and (for the first four years) in the German and Polish provincial assemblies (Articles 137 and 138). With regard to redress of grievances, the Convention provided for the setting up of Minority Offices in each of the territories. These offices represented the National Government. As with the Minorities Treaties the basis for action was the petition. Under Article 147 of the Convention members of the minority were allowed to appeal directly to the League of Nations Council individually or collectively, on any matter falling under the minority provisions chapter of the Convention. But this was not, like in the Minorities Treaties, for information, to be picked up or not, but a start of action. In Polish Upper Silesia the *Deutscher Volksbund* was formed to control and direct all the activities of the German minority, and this opened the door to a mass of insignificant petitions on almost every subject, so following German–Polish negotiations changes were made in 1929. All questions not considered sufficiently important to justify examination by the Council were removed from the Council agenda and arrangements were made to have them dealt with by local procedures.[42]

Articles 149–158 laid down these procedures. The petitioner had to go first to the Minorities Office, which would try to settle the matter directly between the petitioner and the government. If this was unsuccessful the petitioner could then apply to the President of the Mixed Commission. This Commission consisted of a neutral President appointed by the League and two Polish and two German appointed by their governments. The Commission's President's findings could be final, provisional or partial; but it was not a legal decision and was not binding.

His finding would then be forwarded by the Minorities Office to the administrative authorities and the Office had then to inform the President of the decision of the authorities and state the degree to which they had taken his finding into account. If the finding was unsatisfactory to the petitioner, or if the Administration did not put it into effect, then the petitioner could appeal to the League Council. The appeal had to be submitted through the Minorities Office which had two months in which to add any observations before forwarding it. If it was not forwarded within this time limit the petitioner could appeal directly to the Council as under Article 147.

Questions relating to nationality or compensation for violation of rights could be referred to an Arbitral tribunal consisting of a neutral President and one judge each from Germany and Poland. Decisions by the Tribunal were final and not subject to review. Citizens could thus invoke the jurisdiction of the court vis-à-vis their own state. This was a big break with the tradition that only states had locus standi before international courts. The whole procedure of Commission and Tribunal would provide an important precedent for the Human Rights Convention of the Council of Europe following the Second World War.

It should also be noted that Polish Upper Silesia had an autonomy statute providing for a Regional Assembly, voted by the Sejm on 15 July 1920. This was due to the influence of Polish Silesian politicians who wanted guarantees for minorities and wanted to respond to German propaganda to the effect that if Upper Silesia was given to Poland it would lose the local autonomies it enjoyed as part of Prussia. The 48 seat Assembly enjoyed a far-reaching legislative and executive competence, and the statute remained valid until abrogated on 6 May 1945 by the administration that derived its authority from the communist Lublin government at the end of the Second World War.[43] In fact polonisation in Polish Upper Silesia was very slow because the German owners of industrial undertakings only took orders from German companies and ignored orders from Polish companies.[44]

The Aland Islands and Swedes in mainland Finland

The League of Nations was also involved with resolution of a dispute between Sweden and Finland over the Aland Islands, an archipelago lying between Sweden and Finland, populated by some 20 000 people, almost entirely Swedish-speaking.

Swedes had come to the islands around 500 AD and took over almost all Finland during Crusades in the twelfth and thirteenth century. However, in September 1809 Finland and the Islands were ceded to Russia. Shortly afterwards, in view of the Islands' strategic value dominating the approaches to Stockholm, the Gulf of Bothnia and the Gulf of Finland (with access to St Petersburg), Russia fortified them. These fortifications were destroyed in 1854 during the Crimean War. Although Sweden had not been engaged in the War it claimed back the Islands during the 1856 peace negotiations in Paris. This bid was not successful but Russia was forced to demilitarise the Islands in the Peace Treaty of that year.[45]

In December 1917 following the collapse of Imperial Russia and the uncertainties of the Bolshevik revolution as well as the declaration of Lenin that all the various nationalities of Russia had the right to self-determination, the Finns declared independence. The Aland Islanders, fearing a threat to their Swedish language and culture, sought reunion with Sweden. And Sweden too wanted the Islands: a Bolshevik Russia might be even more dangerous than Tsarism.

During the Peace Conference at Versailles the Islanders formally requested annexation by Sweden. Animated by what was being proposed for Schleswig the Swedes requested a plebiscite on the future of the Islands. In the meantime the government of Finland began preparing an autonomy statute hoping to induce the Islanders to abandon the demand for reunion with Sweden. This statute was promulgated on 7 May 1920. Since it was not yet a member of the League of Nations Sweden got Britain to put the matter on the agenda of the Council. Finland maintained that the Islands belonged to it and therefore the issue was a domestic affair. The League therefore appointed a Committee of Three international jurists to examine Finland's claim. The Committee found that Finland enjoyed no natural sovereignty over the Islands and that the Council was therefore competent to decide their fate.[46]

Accordingly the Council set up a Commission of Enquiry which, in April 1921, presented its report. This confirmed Finnish sovereignty over the Islands, both on historical grounds dating back to 1643 and on political grounds that the right of self-determination which applied to national groups as a whole, could not reasonably be claimed by a fraction, the Islanders being 11 per cent of the 11 per cent Swedish population of Finland in 1920.[47] On 24 June 1921 the Council formally recognised Finnish sovereignty but added that, in the interests of world peace, Sweden and Finland should negotiate further guarantees for the cultural protection of the Islanders and the demilitarisation of the archipelago, while the League should be able to see that these guarantees were enforced. On 27 June 1921 a far-reaching agreement was reached between the two protagonists. Finland undertook to amend the 1920 Autonomy Statute in order to preserve not only the Swedish character of the islanders *but also that of the Islands.* Any petitions from the Islanders regarding the application of the Statute would be forwarded to the League Council. For its part, in what must be considered a model classic compromise, Sweden, in accepting the League decision of 24 June, withdrew its claims of sovereignty over the Islands.

The revised Autonomy Statute came into effect in 1922. Although there were revisions in 1951 and 1991 the main features of the original autonomy have remained intact. The basic principle of the autonomy was that the Islanders had the right to control their own affairs subject only to 'the maintenance of Finland as a State'. The Islands have the status of a Province of Finland. There is a unicameral legislature (30 members in 1991) from which the government is formed. The Province can legislate in regard to, *inter alia*, expropriation of property for public requirements; education (although obliged to observe national principles as regarded the ages of children undergoing compulsory schooling, standards of university entrance, and standards of teacher competence); municipal administration, taxation and electoral law (but national regulations on voting age would have to be respected); labour exchanges (but labour legislation had to follow Finnish law); housing; agriculture and fisheries, commerce and industry; planning and building regulations; health and hospital services (with respect for Finnish regulations on the qualifications of medical staff and the combating of human and animal epidemics); the postal service (Aland began issuing its own stamps in 1984); radio (and later television).

The official language of the Islands is Swedish, although a Finn can use his language before the courts. Swedish must be used in correspondence between the provincial administration and the state authorities operating in the Islands, as well as between the latter and the Finnish cabinet and all business and judicial authorities whose circuits include the Islands. No one can obtain a post in the administration who cannot prove he or she has full command of Swedish in speech and writing.

Neither the provincial government nor the municipalities are obliged to maintain any schools other than those in which the teaching language is Swedish. The language of instruction in state schools must also be Swedish. Instruction in a state school may not be given in a language other than Swedish without the consent of the municipality concerned.

Justice is administered in the Islands by the national law court system.

With regard to legislation, if the Finnish government issues administrative orders which are to apply solely to the Islands, the provincial government must be consulted. In conducting its legislative business the Islands' parliament either issues laws independently in the fields where it has competence or adopts analogous national laws for implementation in the Islands either in their original form or with appropriate amendments or additions. The laws issued by the Islands' parliament could only be vetoed by the President of the Republic. He had three months from the adoption of these laws either to approve them or to veto them, and he could only veto them on the two grounds that either the Islands' parliament has exceeded its powers or that the security of the state was threatened by the law in question.

With regard to public finance, since 1991 the Islands receive 0.45 per cent of state revenue, and may use that revenue as the Province wishes. It may also use as it wishes revenue raised from taxes – income and corporation as well as licences – the rates of which however are fixed by the national government. But the Islands' government can impose supplementary and temporary income taxes. The provincial parliament decides the Islands' budget.

In order to maintain the Swedish character of the Islands, the population enjoys the status of Aland Island citizens, the qualification for which was an unbroken period of five years residence on the Islands or by marriage when a female married an Islander.

Special regulations governed voting, the acquisition of land and the establishment of a business. Only an Island citizen could vote in local elections. In order to carry on business in the Province persons have to have either regional citizenship or to have been resident and domiciled in the Province for at least five years, and companies, partnerships etc. having their legal headquarters in the province can only operate if all their board members have regional citizenship or, if not, have been domiciled in the Province for five years. However, the Islands' government could give permission for firms or individuals to operate businesses if it felt so inclined. Special arrangements also operated to prevent land being sold to outsiders. If property is transferred by means other than inheritance or expropriation to a person who did not have Islands citizenship, or to a company whose legal headquarters had not been in the Province for five years, or which did not possess a board of directors all of whose members had Islands citizenship, then the Province, the municipality or a private individual with Islands' citizenship – in that order – had the right to redeem the property. If no agreement on the price was reached between the redeemer and the person who had acquired the property, the matter would be decided in court. However, the Islands' government could allow the acquisition of land by an outsider if it so wished.

With regard to military service the Islanders were exempt because of the 1856 demilitarisation, still in force. Instead they must serve for a comparable period in the pilotage or lighthouse service or in another section of the civil service. On the other hand, responsibility for the police lies with the national Ministry of the Interior.

Finally, according to the Statute the provisions of the autonomy cannot be amended or abolished by the Finnish state without the consent of the Islands' parliament. The effect of the Aland Islands Autonomy Statute was to create nothing less than a Swedish national park, and enabled the claim to be made, with much justification, that the Islanders were the best protected minority in Europe. As will be seen, other minorities would wish their homelands to be cultural national parks but economic and strategic considerations which did not apply to the Islands would ensure their wishes were frustrated.

But what about the status of the Swedish-speaking population on the Finnish mainland, some 11 per cent in 1920? Even though Sweden had to cede Finland to Russia in 1809 Swedish remained the dominant language and the language of administration. Indeed, it was only in 1863 that Finnish joined Swedish as an official language. After Finnish independence in 1917 Swedish continued to be an official language and thus could be used before the courts and in the administration. Significantly, the Swedes were considered not as a minority but as co-founders of the state, an attitude that would be adopted by the Quebecois in Canada and Turkish Cypriots in Cyprus in 1960.

Under the 1922 Language Act every municipality had to declare itself as either bilingual or unilingual, with the cut-off point being 10 per cent (now, since 1962, 8 per cent), or possessing at least 3 000 persons of the lesser in numbers linguistic group in the municipality in question. The municipalities are responsible for primary and secondary education, and Swedish-speaking children go to Swedish schools. Municipalities must set up primary schools for the minority whenever there are at least 18 pupils from that minority and these cannot be closed unless the number falls to 12 or less on three successive years. At tertiary level there is a Swedish-only University at Turku (Abo). There is, however, no provision for an autonomous administration in the south-western area of Finland where most Swedes in Finland live. Such an idea was floated after the First World War but got little support from either Swedes or Finns.[48]

Preparing for trouble

As the victorious Allies and the League dipped their toes into the complexity of protecting minorities, elsewhere in Europe other minorities were being created and existing or new minorities began to find out what it was like in the two decades that would see the zenith of nationalism.

Ireland

In Ireland a partial self-determination was achieved by violence. No sooner had the World War ended than it was replaced first by a war of liberation and then by civil war. In the first stage, 1919–21, Irish nationalists, triumphant at the polls in the December 1918 elections, sought to end British rule by armed rebellion. After nearly three years of guerrilla warfare the British felt ever decreasingly inclined to continue the struggle. In 1921 an Anglo-Irish treaty provided for 26 counties generally in the southern part of the island to become a 'Free State' within the British Commonwealth, but six of the nine counties of the province of Ulster,[49] which had demonstrated in the 1918 election a strong will to remain united with Britain, obtained their wish and set up a regional autonomous government in Northern Ireland, with powers devolved from Westminster. These included agriculture, education, industry, local government, and law and order. Westminster, however, controlled taxation and revenue.

Interestingly, to begin with, Protestant Unionists were not pleased with this arrangement, preferring complete integration with Britain and fearing that having a separate parliament marked them off as different from the rest of the kingdom and liable to different treatment. They were aware that during the negotiations of the 1921 Treaty the British had not been enthusiastic about a partition of Ireland, and would have preferred a 'Home Rule' united Ireland. They were also aware that although their ancestors were overwhelmingly Scottish and English they were considered 'Irish' by the rest of Britain as well as by many Irish people although, confusingly, Irish nationalists did not hesitate to refer to them as 'the Anglo-Saxon garrison'. That traditional British parties should withdraw from campaigning in Northern Ireland only fuelled the feeling of being abandoned, and would colour their attitude to the one-third Irish Catholics of the population.[50]

Much criticism has been made of Unionists that they sought a six-county situation in order to be politically secure, whereas in a nine-county Ulster the Protestant majority over Catholics would be far narrower. Leaving aside the points that the other three counties had overwhelming Catholic majorities (no less than 260 000 Catholics would have been denied their right to self-determination) and that in any case it would have been impossible to hold militarily on to such areas, the international precedents for dividing a recognised political or economic area on ethnic or religious lines rather than deciding its political destiny as a whole unit had been set already in Schleswig and Upper Silesia.[51]

In Southern Ireland the forces of nationalism split, with those who had accepted the 1921 Treaty and therefore partition accused of treason. A bitter civil war ensued in which former brothers-in-arms against the British executed their erstwhile colleagues. During this time many Southern Protestants fled to the North. The lot of those remaining was further hit by the new state's strict enforcement of the 1908 Papal decree *Ne Temere* which obliged the children of mixed marriages to be reared as Roman Catholics. The number of Protestants in the South declined from about 10 per cent in 1920 to about 3 per cent today. Finally, in 1932, Eamonn De Valera, leader of the anti-Treaty forces in the civil war came to power at the head of the Fianna Fail party on a policy of hostility to the North, triumphalist Catholicism and rampant gaelicisation. In 1937 he put forward a new constitution which, in its sensational Articles 2 and 3, formally claimed the North, the first time in which a European state claimed in its constitution the territory of another state. In doing this the Irish state repudiated the 1925 Anglo-Irish boundary Agreement, formally laying down the frontiers between North and South, an agreement officially registered with the League of Nations.[52]

In Northern Ireland the Unionists, perceiving themselves to be surrounded by an aggressive Irish nationalism and Catholicism, moved quickly to ensure that they held the reins of power. They were helped by Nationalist calls to boycott the Northern state and by intimidation of Roman Catholics thinking of serving it. One-third of places reserved for Catholics in the new police force, the RUC, remained unfilled; Nationalists elected to the Northern Ireland parliament, Stormont, abstained for ten years. Unionist and Nationalist controlled local councils were accused of discriminating in the allocation of jobs and housing. Unionist security was ensured by a draconian Special Powers Act, backed up by the recruitment of a special constabulary, the so-called 'B-Specials'. It was a particular weakness of Northern Ireland's political institutions that there were no provisions for constitutional appeal to higher institutions against acts of the Northern Ireland government for redress of grievances.[53] As 'A Catholic State for a Catholic People' faced 'A Protestant State for a Protestant People' the two parts of the island and the two communities in the North sullenly drifted further apart, with Protestants being educated in state schools and Catholics in maintained schools run by the Catholic Church and for which public funds did not cover the full costs.

South Tyrol

Since unification in 1870 the Italian ruling elite had believed in centralism as the best way to consolidate a state with a history of independent regions and to solve the economic imbalance between North and South. How would it react to the acquisition of a quarter of a million Germans living as the majority in a compact area in South Tyrol and the majority Slavs of the Istrian peninsula to add to the French of the Val d'Aosta? It was in 1920 that South Tyrol passed out of the hands of

German Austria into those of Italy. Some Italians, especially Socialists, were doubtful, fearing German irredentism and arguing, prophetically, that it would not be possible to assimilate the South Tyrolese. To avoid this some proposed holding a plebiscite. Others enquired whether Switzerland would either take over South Tyrol as a canton or swap it for the Italian-speaking Ticino, but these proposals were declined.[54]

Early on the South Tyrolese presented the Italian government with a demand for South Tyrol to become an autonomous province with control over all branches of the economy, education and the internal security forces. German would be an official language with Italian, and all civil servants should speak and write German. State employees in the province should originate, if possible, from the area. Rome should provide the finance to cover provincial requirements. South Tyrolese would be dispensed from military service in the Italian armed forces but could serve in a local militia. This programme expressed what would henceforward be the cornerstone of South Tyrolese policy: autonomy in a form wide enough to maintain as German the ethnic character of South Tyrol as well as the South Tyrolese as compensation for the loss of the right to self-determination, a right the South Tyrolese warned explicitly that they would not renounce.

Rome, however, was no Helsinki. The idea of South Tyrol being a German national park was rejected on the grounds that it would create a state within a state, and Italians resident there would be germanised. The area would not be closed to Italian economic or cultural penetration. The Italian government also denied that it had any intentions of assimilating the South Tyrolese.[55] This dialogue between the South Tyrolese and a democratic Italian government ended abruptly when the Fascists under Benito Mussolini seized power in Italy in October 1922, and the long dark night of the South Tyrolese began.

The man behind Fascist assimilation policy was Senator Ettore Tolomei who, before the war, had elaborated the thesis that the majority of the South Tyrolese were, in fact, Italians who had been germanised over the centuries and now needed to be liberated culturally as well as politically.[56] The result was one of the most far-reaching programmes of cultural genocide ever introduced.

Indeed, the only place where German culture was allowed was in the home. The only official language was Italian and therefore public notices and dealings with the administration had to be in Italian. Those without sufficient command of Italian were removed from their posts in the civil service. Schools taught only in Italian. All place and geographic names were italianised. Family names derived from Italian or Latin had to readopt their original form, and certain given names, including those that 'offended Italian sentiment', were banned. Civil and criminal cases could only be heard in Italian; decisions and documents were only in Italian; those not understanding Italian were not put on jury lists. Thus, if he could not pay for an interpreter a South Tyroler was accused in a language he did not know, had to defend himself in a language not his own, and was sentenced in a language he did not understand.[57] Professional qualifications were not recognised unless nostrificated by a year's study at an Italian institution. South Tyrolese sporting associations were taken over and italianised. Attempts were even made to change the names on tombstones. Italian Fascist contempt for the South Tyroler's German culture was expressed by the inscription on an arch set up to commemorate victory in the war. It announced that Italy had brought to the area's inhabitants speech, laws and culture. An early version proposed using the word 'barbarians'.[58] South Tyrolese property in strategic areas on the frontier was sequestered. And in order to speed up the assimilation process, but also to take advantage of the hydro-electric facilities of the Province, an industrial zone was created in 1934 on the outskirts of its capital, Bolzano (Bozen) to which firms were lured by tax and transport incentives. Italian workers were recruited from other parts of the kingdom and housing was built for them (South Tyrolese were discouraged but in any case were disinclined to work in the zone) so that by 1939 Italians formed 25 per cent of the population.

The result was that the Province became economically and socially divided. The Italians worked in the public administration and industry enjoying higher salaries and living standards; the South Tyrolese remained huddled on their poor mountain farms. A whole generation of South Tyrolese teachers and administrators and potential industrial workers was eliminated, so that the social composition of the group became unbalanced.[59]

Protests from abroad, particularly Southern Germany, were rejected. Attempts to get the League of Nations involved also failed, the Council declaring in November 1925 that it could take action only if a state was bound internationally in the way it treated its minorities, and Italy had not signed a Minorities Treaty.

Nevertheless the Fascist assimilation process failed. German language and culture was kept alive in so-called 'catacomb schools'. And time was running out. In 1933 Adolf Hitler came to power in Germany at the head of a National Socialist (Nazi) Party, with a programme of overthrowing the Versailles Settlement and uniting all Germans separated from their kin by Versailles into one Greater German Reich. The hopes of Germans in Poland, Czechoslovakia and even South Tyrol rose accordingly.

When the Chancellor of Austria, Engelbert Dollfuss was murdered by Nazis in 1934 Italian hostility to pan-germanism led Mussolini to send troops to the Brenner and threaten invasion of Austria should there be a German take-over, but Italo-German distrust did not last long. Hostility in the League of Nations led by Britain and France to Italy's invasion of Abyssinia in 1935 brought the two dictators together, and when in 1938 Hitler did take over Austria there were no Italian protests.

However, the continued anti-Italian agitation in Germany, Austria and South Tyrol itself over the Province was interfering with Hitler's plans for the future, which required good relations with Italy. The Italians were also aware that assimilation had failed. Accordingly Hitler and Mussolini came to an agreement in 1939 to liquidate the South Tyrol question. Under the so-called Options Agreement all South Tyrolese families had to decide by the end of December 1939 whether to opt for Germany and leave their 1300-year homeland or opt for Italy and accept assimilation. Under pressure from Nazi organisations and threats that those remaining might be deported to other parts of Italy or the Empire some 80 per cent of the 250 000-odd South Tyrolese voted for Germany. However, owing to the course of the Second World War which broke out in September 1939 only about 75–80 000 actually left South Tyrol, mostly urban inhabitants, to be replaced by 25 000 Italians from elsewhere in the kingdom so that the population ratio in the Province became two-thirds German : one-third Italian.[60]

Czechoslovakia

In the new and multinational Czechoslovakia the Czechs were concerned that as the dominant nation they were hardly 50 per cent of the state's population. Hence the need to include their Slavonic kin, the Slovaks, in the creation of a state identity. One of the founders of Czechoslovakia, Edouard Benes, had once declared in writing that his government intended to make the new state a kind of Switzerland, which the Sudeten Germans took to mean a multinational state in which the rights of the various people would be recognised. But the 250-strong National Committee which took control when Habsburg authority collapsed contained only Czechs, and the National Assembly which replaced it was enlarged to 270 mostly to include Slovaks. The other nationalities were not represented. In the Preamble to the

Constitution it was made clear that Czechs and Slovaks were one people and the Czechoslovak nation was the nation of the state, the rest being minorities.[61] Even worse, President Masaryk referred to the Germans as emigrants and colonists even though some areas had been German for 700 years.[62] There would thus be no 'co-founder' role for Germans, Hungarians and Ruthenians. Indeed the promises made in America to provide autonomies for the Slovaks and Ruthenians were not maintained. Czech officials even poured into Slovakia on the grounds that the latter was a backward area which needed a programme of accelerated economic and social development and there were not enough qualified Slovak personnel.[63] The fictional uniform Czechoslovak nation found its linguistic expression in an equally fictional uniform Czechoslovak language which, under Article 1 of the 1920 Language Act, became the official language of the Republic. Interestingly, Article 4 of the same Act denied its uniformity by stating that in Bohemia its equivalent form was Czech and in Slovakia Slovak.[64] The Germans complained that their minority schools were quick to be closed down when there were less than 40 pupils, whereas Czech schools with less than 40 pupils where kept open in German areas, a move seen to get Germans to send children to Czech schools and thus 'czechify' them through education. The Czechoslovak state undertook extensive land reforms, expropriating the estates of large landowners, with low levels of compensation.[65] In the Sudeten regions these large landowners were Germans and the latter complained that the land was redistributed solely to Czechs, the intention being to weaken the economic strength of the German community. The Germans further accused the Czechs of ousting Germans from jobs in the civil service and state enterprises and giving preference to Czechs for any jobs in Sudetenland. The Ministry of Defence laid down that orders would only be given to firms in Sudetenland if they employed a certain quota of Czechs, thus forcing German firms to co-operate in the czechisation of Sudetenland; there was no reciprocal decree that Czech firms should employ Sudeten Germans. The Sudeten area had been one of the most heavily industrialised in the Austro-Hungarian empire. With the onset of the economic recession of the 1930s following the 1929 Wall Street stockmarket crash, of the 500 000 unemployed in Czechoslovakia 400 000 were Sudeten Germans or one in three of the active group population.[66] It was not surprising that the arrival in power of Adolf Hitler in Germany in 1933 raised Sudeten German hopes, and provided the Führer with a chance to demolish the Paris Peace Settlement, and indeed the first Czechoslovak Republic had only five more years to live. In September 1938 at Munich Britain, France and Italy agreed that the Sudeten area should be transferred to the Reich. In November, under the first Vienna Award, the areas of southern Slovakia heavily inhabited by Hungarians were turned over to Budapest. A few months later, under pressure from Berlin Slovakia declared its independence, Hungary seized Ruthenia and in March 1939 Germany occupied the rest of Bohemia and Moravia and declared the area to be a protectorate of the Reich.

Poland

Poles had suffered greatly at the hands of Germans and Russians after being divided up in the eighteenth century. Would it renounce territorial aggrandisement beyond its ethnic boundary? How would it treat its new German and Slav minorities, to say nothing of the Jews?

In the first case the answer was negative. The collapse of Imperial Russia and the defeat of the Soviet invasion in 1920 enabled the new state under the March 1921 Treaty of Riga to push its eastern frontier 250 kilometres further eastward than originally proposed in the so-called 'Curzon line', incorporating as a result more than a million Belarusians and four million Ukrainians. And in October 1920 General Lucjan Zeligowski with a Polish irregular army pursuing the Soviets seized Vilna, the historic capital of the new Lithuania, and after the failure to hold a plebiscite the following year the League of Nations and the Allies accepted the situation[67]

To the second question the response was varied. In the east, where the Soviets had withdrawn from world affairs in order to consolidate the regime and there was a political vacuum and thus no kin state, polonisation was the order of the day. The Ruthenians and Ukrainians rejected the enforced assimilation, leading to resistance followed by severe repression and pacification. Belarusian nationalism was originally promoted for reasons of security against the Soviet threat but when it looked like getting out of hand political and cultural Belarusian was crushed.

In the West where kin states might be expected to take action the Poles were more circumspect. The situation for the Germans was well covered with the Minorities Treaty and the Upper Silesia Convention although large German landed estates were often broken up and distributed to the Polish peasantry. But in 1920 Poland had also obtained the industrial region of Teschen with large numbers of Czechs. In April 1925 Poland and Czechoslovakia signed a Convention in Warsaw. In three respects this bilateral treaty was significantly in advance of other instruments of minority protection. It was agreed that attempts to uphold minority rights should not be regarded as acts of disloyalty. Denationalisation was prohibited. In areas where there were Poles and Czechs in large enough quantities the languages should have equal status and bilingual officials should be appointed to public posts. And where minorities did not exist in numbers large enough to get public funds to set up state schools, private schools should be authorised, even subsidised, and teachers should come from the minority. Finally, as with the Upper Silesia Convention, the declaration of the individual should be the sole criterion of nationality, i.e. the authorities could not question such a declaration or punish a person for it, and a Mixed Commission and Arbitral Tribunal were established to settle differences.[68]

Romania

Romania too could not resist aggrandisement and assimilation. To the Bulgarians of the Dobrujda, acquired in the second Balkan War of 1913, Romania now added Transylvania with its Hungarians and Germans, and, like Poland, took advantage of the civil war in Russia to seize Bessarabia, a move later legitimised by the Allies at Paris, to build up the *cordon sanitaire* against the Bolsheviks. For the relatively wealthier Hungarians land reform and social legislation threatened to dispossess them.[69] For the rest, romanisation was carried out by officials sent from the traditional Romanian heartland of the Danubian principalities.

Turkey and Greece

In one area the verdict of the Paris Peace Settlement was overthrown. In Turkey national sentiment was outraged by the Treaty of Sèvres. Indeed, the Sultan only signed it after Allied forces occupied Constantinople. Armed resistance was prepared by General Mustapha Kemal (Atatürk), and when the Allies authorised the Greeks to intervene Kemal routed the Greek armies, driving them out of Smyrna, the Anatolian enclave Greece had been promised, and occupied eastern Thrace. The Italians and French also thought it wise to leave Anatalya and Cilicia respectively. Under the 1923 treaty of Lausanne Turkey regained eastern Thrace and there was a considerable – and compulsory – exchange of population. 430 000 Turks, mostly from Greek western Thrace, were resettled in Turkey, while some 1.3 million Greeks, including almost the entire Greek population in Trebizond and Sinope on the Black Sea, as well as on the Mediterranean coast, were repatriated to their motherland, leaving only a small Greek presence in Constantinople (soon to be renamed Istanbul).[70]

Arrangements for dealing with the property of the departed did not work well. Greeks were under such pressure to leave that they were unable to collect debts or take more than a fraction of moveable property. A Mixed Commission was set up to deal with immovable property – valuing it and arranging for its liquidation. In theory the emigrants would receive a declaration of the sums due to them and be recompensed with equivalent grants of land and property from the government of the immigrant state. However, the Mixed Commission's attempt to work by unanimity rather than majority and the obstructive behaviour of the national representatives ensured such unproductive disputes that in the end the two governments decided to wipe the slate clean in the Convention of Ankara, 1930.[71]

Even in countries not affected by the Paris Peace Settlement the light for cultural minorities flickered briefly before being extinguished.

Spain

In a Spain rapidly disintegrating after the First World War it was not unnatural that the rich industrial areas of the Basque country and Catalonia would seek as much freedom as possible. Many (but not all) Basques sought to regain some of the autonomy lost as a result of the Carlist wars. Catalonia, which had gained a moderate autonomy in 1913 and had been continually pressing for Home Rule, saw it destroyed by the dictator General Primo de Rivera in 1923. Galicians sought the regionalism politically recognised during the short lived First Spanish Republic of 1873.[72] But the situation changed dramatically with Primo's fall in 1930 and that of the monarchy in 1931.

Soon after the inauguration of the Second Republic, a plebiscite on Home Rule was held in Catalonia, with nearly 600 000 votes in favour as opposed to just over 3 000 against.[73] Under an original Autonomy Statute Catalonia received what was seen by Spanish nationalists as quasi-independence, with Catalan as the only official language and language of education, laws passed by Madrid being valid in Catalonia only by consent of the latter's government, and Catalan control of local finance, civil law and the transport infrastructure. However, the hostility in Madrid led to a compromise under which the Catalan and Castilian languages would have equal status and the Catalan government would not be in sole control of education.[74]

A statute similar to the Catalonian was also brought forward for the Basques but at a delegate meeting from the four provinces in June 1932 those from rural intensely Catholic Navarre rejected it. The approval of the other three delegations was ratified in a plebiscite when, of an electorate of nearly 500 000, 84 per cent voted in favour.[75] However it was adopted by Madrid in October 1936, only three months after the outbreak of the Spanish Civil War, with the implication that its adoption was linked to Basque support for the Republic against its nationalist and military opponents. Later Avala also opted out so that in the Civil War the Basques were split – Navarre and Avala for the Nationalists, Guipuzcoa and Viscaya for the Republic.

An autonomy was obtained also for Galicia, the main feature of which was that the official languages would be Castilian and Galician. The autonomy statute was massively approved in a plebiscite held on 28 June 1936, less than a month before the outbreak of war.[76]

Unfortunately for the cultural minorities it was the Nationalists under General Francisco Franco who won the Civil War in March 1939. For the next two decades Spain was a society of victors and vanquished.[77] The new regime, based on principles of national unity and uniformity, beset by the destruction of the war and for the next six years isolated as the rest of the continent experienced the upheaval of the Second World War, began its work of reconstruction on policies of economic, political and cultural self-sufficiency.[78] For the minorities there was nothing. The objective of the regime in 'red' Catalonia was the eradication of Catalan nationalism and culture.[79] It was the same in the Basque country and Galicia. The autonomies were ended (except for Navarre).[80] The languages were forbidden in schools (and pupils were punished for speaking them), public meetings, public worship, public signs, publishing and broadcasting.[81] Sometimes matters were taken to absurd lengths. In Catalonia telephone operators were meant to report speakers who spoke in Catalan. In the Basque country, following Mussolini's example in the South Tyrol, there was an attempt to remove the minority language from gravestones. And Franco followed Mussolini in promoting massive inflows of workers, teachers and civil servants from the rest of Spain to the industrial areas of the Basque country, Catalonia and Galicia in order to hasten the process of denationalisation.[82] At the end of the war the leaders of the minorities who survived fled abroad with many of their followers – the Galicians to Argentina, the Basques and Catalans to France (although a guerrilla war continued in Galicia until 1950).[83]

Yugoslavia

For many people the artificiality of the new Kingdom of the Serbs, Croats and Slovenes undermined its legitimacy, with hardly a stretch of its external frontier unchallenged by its neighbours and its internal cohesion threatened by half-a-dozen dissatisfied nationalities.[84] The beginning of the state was not auspicious with disputes as to whether it should be based on a Greater Serbia or a federation. Perhaps because of its artificiality the Serbs intended that it should be the former and just as the Czechs obscured their demographic weakness by trying to proclaim one 'Czechoslovak' people the Serbs created a Serbo-Croatian nationality which gave them 77 per cent of the state rather than 43 per cent.[85] In 1921 the so-called 'Vidovdan' Constitution was promulgated, creating more or less a unitary state with the capital in Serbian Belgrade.

From the beginning this was resisted by the Croats, the next largest group in the state. In 1928 a Separatist Croat Assembly was opened in Zagreb just after the assassination of the leader of the Croat Peasant Party, Stefan Radic, in the Belgrade parliament, had brought the country to the verge of civil war which was averted only by a royal dictatorship on the part of King Alexander and the suspension of the Constitution in 1929. It was then that a new administrative structure of the state was created, on the basis of supranationality. Nine *banovine* which deliberately ignored historic and ethnic boundaries were created and the name of the state, the Kingdom of the Serbs, Croats and Slovenes, gave way to 'Yugoslavia'.[86] Although the royal dictatorship ended in 1931 and a new constitution was adopted Croatian separatism did not abate, and in the early 1930s the *Ustasha*, a separatist pro-fascist underground group, was founded.[87] Just before the outbreak of the Second World War the Croats obtained their own *banovina*, with virtual autonomy. But another cause of concern for the Serbs was the Islamic Albanian population of the province of Kossovo. Kossovo was the traditional heartland of Serbia, with its battlefield of 1389 when the Kingdom was annihilated by the Turks, a source of national pride and sorrow. But even between the two World Wars the Albanians of Kossovo were noted for having the highest birthrate in Europe.[88]

And in Russia, following the collapse of Tsarism and the defeat of Germany, war would decide the future frontiers of the new Soviet state and therefore what countries and peoples would remain in it.

Ukraine

In the Ukraine, once the Germans had been defeated, the independence won at Brest-Litovsk in December 1917 disappeared amid a brutal and chaotic three year civil war, involving so-called 'White' Russians seeking to restore Tsardom and supported by British and French units, 'Red' communists intent on sovietising the area, and Anarchists led by

Nestor Makhno. During this period areas considered traditionally Ukrainian were lost. Eastern Galicia was seized by Poland, Bukovina and Bessarabia by Romania, while the Ruthenian kin of the Ukrainians were made part of the new Czechoslovakia.

Victory of the 'Reds' led to the re-absorption of the Ukraine into the Russian family. Kharkov, rather than Kiev, was made the capital, and a long struggle began to resist russification, centralism and subordination to Moscow.[89]

Finland

In newly independent Finland the government came under attack from left-wing Finns supported by communists from Russia. Led by General Gustav Mannerheim, 'White' Finnish forces drove the 'Reds' out of western Karelia – the Karelian isthmus – but attempts to gain eastern Karelia and thus unite the Ugro-Finnic Karelians with their Finnish kin were thwarted by a Red Russian army. At the Peace of Dorpat, October 1920, the Finnish government retained western Karelia but failed to obtain eastern Karelia.[90] This left the Karelian people divided. In Finland the government clamped down on the Orthodox Karelian church requiring the clergy to be Finnish citizens, Finnish to be the official language, to change to the Gregorian calendar and to acknowledge the Ecumenical Patriarchate of Constantinople rather than Moscow. In the new Soviet state an Autonomous Karelian Soviet Socialist Republic was established, with Finnish and Karelian as official languages and compulsory in school. Finnish-Karelian schools were only abolished in 1956.[91]

The Caucasus

Finally, in the Caucasus the newly-acquired independence of Georgia, Armenia and Azerbaijan was soon snuffed out. Whatever Lenin may have said, the region was too rich in oil to be let go by Soviet Russia. With the collapse of White Russian forces and the withdrawal of Allied contingents in the Crimea and the Kuban, the Red Army was able to turn its attention against the Republics early in 1920. Its task was made easier by the failure of the three to settle territorial disputes between themselves peacefully, let alone develop a common programme in a federation or present a united front. Armenia was involved in trying to expel Turkish troops and had even invaded Turkey in order to make good the Greater Armenia claimed at Versailles. It was also fighting Georgia for Borchalinsk and Azerbaijan for Karabakh and Zangezur. In April 1920 Azerbaijan fell to the Reds. In November, following a Soviet understanding with the Turks on the frontier, it was the turn of Armenia. Georgia would last until February 1921.[92]

Issues in the League system of minority protection

Identity

To assert that persons of one ethnic or linguistic group belong to another and treat them accordingly is a not uncommon policy which may be used in order to justify cultural assimilation as did the Fascists in South Tyrol and as Irish Nationalists have postulated in order to justify the reunification of the island.

The issue became controversial in Upper Silesia in the mid-1920s when, in Polish Upper Silesia, the authorities noted that families presumed Polish were declaring the language of their children to be German and sending them to German schools. Under Article 131 of the Upper Silesia Convention a verbal or written declaration by the person responsible for the child's education could not be questioned by the educational authorities. The article had in fact been introduced to prevent Polish national authorities from embarking on assimilation pressurising the families of the German minority to declare the language of their children as Polish. Since the Polish government thought that false declarations were being made, it decided to refer the matter to the League of Nations, asking whether the declaration should be considered objective or subjective, i.e. should the declarer give the *de facto* mother tongue of the child or should he or she give the language in which the wish was that the child should be educated. What complicated the matter was that in Upper Silesia most workers spoke a dialect and for the first seven years of their lives children did not speak anything else so that it was difficult to ascertain objectively which was a child's mother tongue.[93]

In March 1927 the League Council upheld the Polish claim that the declaration should be objective, on the grounds that Article 131 referred to a declaration of fact. But it also decided to set up a system of enquiry for doubtful cases. Following some language examinations the Polish authorities refused to let a number of children attend German schools. The German government thereupon referred the issue to the Permanent Court of International Justice. In a curious Decision the Court upheld the objective nature of the declaration but also upheld the ban on verification by the authorities. Four of the twelve judges on the panel dissented, pointing out the contradiction between the two points. In 1931, after the Court had given an Advisory Opinion by eleven votes to one (the Polish judge), that the children could not now be refused access to the schools of their parents' choice the Council ended the system of examinations and prevailed on the Polish government to let the parents have their way.[94]

Equality

To most people equality of treatment, one law for all, is synonymous with justice. But, as the South Tyrolese would question in a famous memorandum to the post Second World War Italian government, was it equal to treat equally unequal things?[95] For example, after the First World War Czechoslovakia, Poland and Romania introduced land reform, breaking up the large landed estates and distributing them to the peasantry. However, many of these estates belonged to the former land-owning class of Germans and Hungarians, and it was easy to accuse the governments of undertaking these reforms in order to reduce the economic power of what had now become a minority community. The point that the masters were now being controlled by their servants only rubbed salt in the wound. On the other hand, would not going beyond equality before the law create a situation of privilege? If the answer was in the affirmative could such 'positive discrimination' be justified?

It was the issue of minority schools in Albania that provided the League and the PCIJ with the chance to provide an answer. In 1933 the Albanian government decided to close all private schools including those of the Greek and Slav minorities on the grounds that henceforward all education would be given by the state. The Greek government took up the cudgels on behalf of the Greek minority and referred the matter to the PCIJ.

The Albanian government argued that Article 5iii of the Declaration given by Albania upon joining the League of Nations ['Albanian nationals who belong to racial, religious or linguistic minorities will enjoy the same treatment and security in law and in fact as other Albanian nationals. In particular they shall have an equal right to maintain, manage and control (their own) schools'] imposed no other obligation in educational matters than to grant minorities a right equal to that possessed by other Albanians. Once the latter had lost the right to have private schools the former could not claim to have them either.

However, in its Advisory Opinion of 6 April 1935 the PCIJ rejected the Albanian thesis on the grounds that if minorities were refused the right to manage and control their own schools it would thwart the aim of minority protection, namely, allowing the free development of a minority's consciousness and culture, 'the essence of equality'.

> For minorities to live on equal terms with the majority it would be necessary for them to have the judicial, social, economic and cultural institutions to allow them to preserve their national consciousness and to cultivate and develop their own language and culture *under the same conditions* as the majority.

> Equality in law precludes discrimination of any kind; whereas equality in fact may involve the necessity of different treatment in order to attain a result which establishes an equilibrium between different situations.

The voting in the Court was 8–3, with the British – and significantly the Polish and Romanian – judges dissenting. Their view was that minorities could not demand more than what was recognised in respect of the majority. A right which was unconditional and independent of that enjoyed by other people could not be described as 'equal'.[96] However, it is the phrase 'under the same conditions' that makes the issue clear. The Albanian government with the power structure of the state and a majority in parliament could decide freely whatever steps it considered necessary and whatever institutions were needed for the development of the Albanian culture; the Greek minority was not in such a position. The situation was therefore unequal and required 'positive discrimination' to redress the balance.

Analysis of the League system of minority protection

The question of submitting minority protection to an international organisation and introducing a judicial element into matters was something quite unprecedented.

In Article 12 of the Polish Minority Treaty, any difference of opinion as to questions of law or fact arising out of the Minority Treaty Articles could be brought before the PCIJ by any Council Member without the consent of the host state concerned being required and without any diplomatic negotiations between the parties. Under these circumstances the Court could give a decision, and it was clear that the Council would follow such a decision.

But the PCIJ could also give Advisory Opinions on points. These were not Decisions but they did decide points of law or interpretations of clauses. Under the Guarantee clause of the Treaties the Council could ask for an Advisory Opinion and this then became the basis of negotiations between the League and the host state.

Excluding Upper Silesia, some 500 petitions had been declared receivable throughout the League period. The Committee of Three put fourteen on the Council Agenda. A Council Member put a case directly on the Agenda three times, in each case Germany versus Poland, once without even receipt of a petition. On three occasions the case went to the PCIJ for a Decision, and on four occasions the PCIJ gave an Advisory Opinion.[97]

The inevitable judgement on the League system of minority protection was that it failed. And it failed for five reasons.

First, it was limited in scope. It applied to a few states only, rather than all the Members of the League. This at once caused two things: it affected adversely the willingness of the states concerned to work with the system; and it created a demand for generalising the system. In particular, the states subjected to the Treaties were incensed not only that they, as small states, had these limitations placed on their sovereignty, but that the Allied Great Powers did not have such restrictions. Yet Italy's treatment of the South Tyrolese by the Fascists from 1923 onwards was a cause of much frustrated anger in Europe, because there were no means of getting Italy to change its assimilation policies. It was also exasperating that the Great Powers on the Council – particularly Germany after joining the League in 1926 and at once obtaining a permanent seat on the Council – could put items on the Council Agenda regarding the protection of minorities without bothering about the petition procedure under the guarantee clause of the Treaties.

As a result the Baltic countries in the early 1920s sought to have the system generalised. The idea did not gain the approval hoped and the Assembly of the League merely passed a resolution expressing the hope that states not bound by the Minority Treaties would observe the same standards.[98] But no action was taken. Then in 1925 Lithuania proposed a draft general convention, to include all Members of the League, setting forth the rights and duties of Member States to minorities. The rather naive justification for rejection was that minority problems existed in specific territories only – i.e., where minorities had been transferred against their will by the Great Powers, which, as a result, felt a certain interest in their fate. A generalised system would be a dead letter in most countries and would only be partially accepted in others.[99] But another reason, powerful in times of respect for the doctrine of sovereignty, was the reluctance to interfere in the internal affairs of states more than was necessary to secure world peace.[100] The reality was that examination of what rights minorities should have might spur them to ask for them which in turn could well be perceived by states as threats to their integrity with all the consequences thereof.

Second, the League system was specifically *political* in concept, rather than legal and humanitarian. Unlike its successor, the United Nations, the League had no humanitarian aims. It was political because the aim of the Minorities Treaties was political: to preserve world peace by enabling the minorities to live amicably within their host state. As Woodrow Wilson said on 31 May 1919,[101] the chief burden for the maintenance of peace lay with the Great Powers and it was therefore not unreasonable for them to maintain that they could not agree to leave elements of disturbance unremoved which they believed might come to disturb world peace.

As a result of the two points just made the Minority Treaty states perceived the situation as having constituted a big breach in state sovereignty and state equality. In those days of the zenith of nationalism leaders of the new or enlarged states tended to think of sovereignty as an unalterable and irreducible quantity of rights and immunities which automatically accrued to any state. Either a state existed or it did not. If the existence of a state was conceded, then there was no alternative but to treat it as the possessor of a standard set of sovereign attributes, identical with that possessed by all other states. If sovereignty was a monolithic totality of rights which must be possessed in full or not at all, then it followed that every political entity possessing that totality must be considered the equal of every other such entity.[102] Yet the treaties allowed for other states to intervene in the affairs of the Treaty states by ensuring that the government of the country respected – permanently – certain rules (and in Clemenceau's letter to Paderewski of 24 June 1919 the intention of the Powers to secure permanent protection of minorities whatever changes might take place in the internal constitution of the Polish state was clearly stated)[103] and that the Treaty states could be brought before the International Court at any time whether they liked it or not.

As a result, in September 1934 Poland denounced its Minority Treaty on the grounds that it had created a position of inequality between the states subject to the system and those not, and refused to co-operate with international organisations on minority protection until the system had been generalised. In fact Poland had political reasons for its step. The Soviet Union would soon be joining the League and immediately gaining a place on the Council. Poland did not want a repeat of the German experience in regard to its large Ukrainian minority. Following Poland's action the system became increasingly ineffectual.[104]

Third, the system was inadequate.

(a) There were no arrangements for permanent supervision, so that there were no means by which the Council could determine whether an infraction had been or was about to be committed. Action could only be taken *ad hoc* following attention being drawn to the possible infraction by a Council member, or a petition.

For political reasons it was obviously going to be difficult for the League to enforce its views, even to bring about restitution or redress of grievances. All the Council could do was 'express confidence' that the measures in question would not continue to be enforced and try to exert a moral authority. Indeed violations were often overlooked in order to get host state co-operation with the League.[105]

And again for political reasons, the League could hardly prevent states from intimidating members of a minority by prosecuting them for treason, submitting petitions to Geneva containing declarations 'that they knew to be false'. Poland and Lithuania were notorious in this regard.[106]

The Council, in examining whether there should be a Permanent Supervisory Minorities Commission, rejected it on the grounds that the Treaties and League Covenant contained no provision permitting it to exercise such constant supervision. Indeed, it was feared that any change in the existing system would merely throw sand into the already precarious mechanism. All that was left therefore was to use the Committees of Three and the services of the Minorities Section.[107]

It would inevitably be asked whether a bilateral system of minority protection between host and kin state would be better than international protection. One problem was that so many minorities have or had no kin state. The Minorities Treaty aimed at impartial international supervision but, for the reasons given above, there was great resentment at what was seen as imposed direct intervention in a state's internal affairs. A bilateral agreement was at least a voluntary act, and an agreement reached between two equals rather than one imposed might well lead to better conditions for the minority or minorities. That at least was the premise of the Treaty of Warsaw.

(b) Procedures were perhaps inevitably slow. No time limits were laid down in regard to requests by the Council or the Minorities Section for supplementary or more detailed information, thus playing into the hands of a recalcitrant host state. This would often put the Council before a *fait accompli*, for example if property had been seized in alleged violation of Treaty provisions. This would be difficult to reverse and get settled equitably. But this slowness undermined confidence in the procedure, and was seized on by Germany as an excuse for shortcutting Committee procedures and having questions put directly on the agenda of the Council.[108]

(c) Because the Council had too many states intimately interested in the politics of Eastern Europe, thus raising the question of impartiality, in practice membership of the Committees of Three was often confined to representatives from America or Asia. They might be impartial but this could only be balanced by lack of expertise.[109]

Fourth, the League did not provide clear answers on two fundamental but closely related questions. Was the system intended to preserve minorities or facilitate their assimilation? And did minorities have any duties towards their host states? Minorities could well argue that their loyalty could only be expected as a result of treatment that was just and aimed at their preservation. Host states might reply that the treatment desired was contingent on their loyalty. The former question gave rise to a bitter debate in the Council in 1925. The representative of Brazil (a 'melting pot' state) Mello Franco, felt that those creating the system of minority protection had not dreamt of creating a situation under which in certain states a group of inhabitants would regard themselves as permanent strangers. It was obvious that the system provided legal protection and respect for the inviolability of the person and 'which might gradually prepare the way for conditions necessary for the establishment of a complete national unit'. This was indignantly rejected by Gustav Stresemann of Germany, who argued that the protection afforded to minorities was permanent and not merely to cover 'a transition period instituted to overcome temporary difficulties'.[110]

Fifth, the creators of the Minorities Treaty system, politicians and civil servants, were not only Westerners, but overwhelmingly from centralised states where minority linguistic cultures had been in decline over the previous century and where the emphasis was on equality of rights for all citizens without distinction as to religion or culture. Thus in the Treaties there was much on citizenship and equality of rights for individuals and toleration for religious minorities. On the other hand the treaties were weak on linguistic provisions – there was no understanding of minorities as linguistic communities whose individuals needed their group culture to survive, and that cultures needed not only to be protected but also to be able to develop and flourish. These Westerners were against areas with cultural autonomies on the grounds that they created rival authorities to the national state. Indeed, they took as their models only the minorities of which they had experience such as the Jews, who at that time in the West were considered a religious rather than a cultural minority, and the Celts, whose language, whether in the British Isles or France, was apparently dying.

What these Westerners had perhaps forgotten was the medieval concept of communities as an intermediate link between the individual and the state. But they would not have liked to remember something with not only group but beyond that, territorial implications, that might create a state within a state with separate, different arrangements – a horror for all centralists and uniformists.[111]

Nor did it help that in any case in international law it was the individual alone who was the bearer of rights, even though the individual could hardly enjoy his cultural heritage without the existence of a group to support him. But, as has been pointed out, it was difficult to try to guarantee collective linguistic rights without international legal recognition of the concept of collective existence.[112]

For all these reasons the failure of the system cannot be divorced from the international political situation at the time, namely the Paris Peace Settlement and its political aims.

Peace was alleged to be being made on the basis of certain moral principles but these principles were not applied to victors and vanquished alike. The victorious Allies had no intention of applying self-determination in their own territories and departed again from applying it in the chief states they had created or enlarged except in the most unimportant areas, economic and strategic, involving few people – Upper Silesia being the exception. Apart from the 2.2 million population of the latter, plebiscites were offered to a few hundred thousand Allensteiners and Schleswigers and some thousands in Carinthia. But there was no plebiscite for the millions of Ukrainians, German Austrians, Sudeten Germans and Slovaks, or hundreds of thousands of Ruthenians, Hungarians in Czechoslovakia, and South Tyrolese, to say nothing of the few thousand Aland Islanders and inhabitants of Eupen-Malmedy, all of these being groups compact in their territory. This failure struck a moral blow at the Peace Settlement which did as much to undermine it as any other of its shortcomings in the areas of reparations and disarmament.

3
The Second World War
– and After, 1939–47

Territorial changes and population movements

War provides the opportunity to pay off old scores. The Second World War and its immediate aftermath would see minorities massacred in or cleansed from their homelands as national majorities took revenge for the failure of these minorities to become loyal citizens and their support for if not outright collaboration with the invading armies whether from kin states or not. Added to which the first post-war European conference, held by the victorious Allies at Potsdam, would sanction the deportation of German minorities in Poland, Czechoslovakia and Hungary.[1] Altogether some 30 million Europeans (60 per cent of them Germans) would lose their homeland.[2]

In Finland the Soviet attack at the end of November 1939 (which led to the expulsion of the Soviet Union from the League of Nations) was initially well resisted but in the end sheer weight of numbers told. In March 1940 peace was signed. The entire Karelian Isthmus (Finnish western Karelia) was ceded to Russia, and 12 per cent of the population of Finland was expelled at short notice from the lost territory. In 1941 following Hitler's attack on Russia Finland joined Germany. Finnish and Russian Karelia were regained up to Leningrad and the river Svir, and the evacuated population returned home.[3] However, attempts to Lutheranise Orthodox Karelins were not successful and 'an active desire to join Finland never arose among the population of eastern Karelia'.[4] Shortly after both eastern and western Karelia were lost again as the war turned in Russia's favour.

The Baltic states ceased to exist. On 23 August 1939 Germany and the Soviet Union signed a non-aggression pact with a secret clause dividing eastern Europe up into respective spheres of influence. When war broke out between Germany and Poland the Soviet Union occupied eastern Poland and a month later, following a border agreement, Germany gave a *nihil obstat* to the Russian occupation of Lithuania. Following pressure on all three Baltic states, including military occupation and 'spontaneous' demands for annexation, by August 1940 the Soviet Union had incorporated them as Soviet republics. These incorporations were not recognised by Britain, France or the United States. Under Russian rule there were mass deportations of the Baltic peoples throughout the Soviet Union (although ethnic Germans could return to Germany). Land was nationalised and the populations terrorised. When less than a year later Germany attacked the Soviet Union in June 1941 the German forces were at first welcomed as liberators but the Germans had little time for the Baltic peoples treating them as badly as the Russians had, and making it clear that the ultimate objective was to take the countries over. When the Red Army returned in 1944 the nightmare continued as sovietisation was reimposed and the lands subjected to plunder, rape and murder.[5]

German victory in the Spring of 1940 brought Belgium and France under the control of the *Führer*. In Belgium, even before the Belgian army surrendered Eupen-Malmedy was returned to the Reich.[6] During the war, certain elements of the Flemish community flirted with the Germans in the hope of obtaining a separate state if not the widest possible autonomy. Others joined a Flemish SS unit. These forms of collaboration would bedevil Belgian relationships for many years after the war. Alsace-Lorraine was reannexed to the Reich. Initially this was not entirely unwelcome; most of the population understood German and there were hopes that the region would be granted an autonomy. Indeed the strongest supporters of Germany were Alsatian autonomists who had struggled hard since the region had become French. But the region did not receive an autonomy and as the course of the war turned against Germany and Alsatians were called up pro-German sentiment died away.[7]

In Brittany scarcely had the Third Republic fallen when a Breton National Council proclaimed regional independence. Hopes that the Germans would support this move foundered on the desire of the occupying forces not to make things difficult for the new head of the French state, with its capital in Vichy, Marshall Philippe Pétain. Thereafter the hopes of Breton nationalists focused on obtaining a wide-ranging regional autonomy, with full cultural rights including obligatory teaching of Breton. Bat Vichy did not oblige. Indeed, in 1941 Vichy even amputated from traditional Brittany one fifth of its territory, the *département* of *Loire Atlantique*, a mutilation maintained by all subsequent French governments.[8] Brittany became an area infested with the resistance and after the war the severest reprisals were taken against Breton separatists and autonomists and their paramilitary movements. Nearly 1 000 were executed. Many of the nationalist leaders fled abroad, notably to Ireland.[9] The other minorities had also hoped their languages would be officially taught, but all that was allowed were optional courses, taught outside school time, for Basque, Breton, Flemish and Occitan.[10]

It had always been part of Fascist ideology to restore Italy to its 'natural' boundaries, and that meant not only the watershed of the Maritime, Swiss and Austrian Alps (thus including Nice, Ticino and South Tyrol) and the Dalmatian and Albanian coasts but the islands as well – Malta and Corsica. As Italian relations with France deteriorated following the invasion of Abyssinia in 1935 there were calls to take over Corsica which from the thirteenth century to 1768 had belonged to Genoa. With France teetering on the brink of defeat at the hands of Germany in June 1940, Italy declared war on France, occupying Nice and, in November 1942, in response to the Allied occupation of North Africa, Corsica. Later German troops arrived on the island but the Corsicans remained devoted to France and with the collapse of Fascism in July 1943 the Italian occupation forces surrendered. However it was not until October that the island was freed from German control, the first part of French soil to be liberated.[11]

In Italy only 75 000 South Tyrolese actually left in accordance with the Options Agreement, being resettled all over the Reich but mostly in Austria. They were replaced by more than 25 000 Italians. But as the war turned against Germany few South Tyrolese left and many drifted back. With the fall of Mussolini in July 1943 the Germans took over Northern Italy. South Tyrol came under the jurisdiction of the Gauleiter of Tyrol, Franz Hofer, henceforward High Commissioner of the Military Zone *Alpenvorland*. German was declared an official language. Official communications and place names had to be bilingual. German municipalities in the Province of Trento were returned to that of Bolzano. And now it was the turn of the Italians to leave – 50 000 or just under half of the Italian population of South Tyrol in December 1943.[12] But with the defeat of Germany in May 1945 the Italians returned to the Province, labelling all South Tyrolese as Nazis and insisting that the Options Agreement be carried out in full.[13]

The end of the war saw the restoration of Czechoslovakia, but this time without Ruthenia, annexed outright by the Soviet Union. The expulsion of the Sudeten German and Hungarian minorities had been planned by the exiled Czech government in London and given expression by the so-called Kosice (Kassa) Programme of 5 April 1945.[14] During the first nine months of the peace the programme was applied to the Sudeten Germans. Mass executions and rapes were followed by confiscation of property and eventually, stripped of all their possessions, the Sudeten Germans were loaded on trains and sent to the west, brutally deported from the homeland in which they had lived for over seven centuries. Only 200 000 of the original 3 million remained. Thereafter, until the 1968 Czechoslovak Constitution, the Sudeten Germans were not recognised as an ethnic group as were the Hungarians and Poles. They did not have their own schools nor the right to form associations.

Curiously enough the victorious Allies vetoed the application of the Kosice Programme to the 650 000 Hungarians in Slovakia.[15] A Czechoslovak–Hungarian Treaty in 1946 also arranged for an exchange of populations – some 70 000 Hungarians in Slovakia moving to Hungary and a like number of Slovaks in Hungary moving the other way.[16]

For Hungary the years 1938–48 were disastrous. Throwing its support to Nazi Germany appeared to pay dividends when Hungary received Slovak territory under the First Vienna Award in November 1938 and the following year occupied Ruthenia. Then under the Second Vienna Award in August 1940 Hungary received northern Transylvania. Unsurprisingly Hungary fought on the side of the Germans during the war and paid the price afterwards. Northern Transylvania was returned to Romania and the Slovak territories to Czechoslovakia. Ruthenia was annexed outright by the Soviet Union. Some 250 000 ethnic Germans were deported to Germany by 1948, but measures against a like number still in Hungary were revoked in 1950.[17] In 1947 the theoretical Kingdom of Hungary became a communist republic.

Similarly for Romania the war years and after were disastrous. As part of Hitler's diplomacy with the Soviet Union and the Balkans, Romania was stripped by the Second Vienna Award of northern Transylvania to Hungary and the southern Dobrudja to Bulgaria. Two months previously, with German compliance[18] the Soviet Union had simply seized North Bukovina and Bessarabia. The latter annexation was followed by deportations of Romanians, especially the élites and intellectuals, to Siberia, and the creation from two-thirds of Bessarabia with the border with the Ukraine at the river Dnestr of a Moldavian Soviet Socialist Republic, the rest being annexed to the Ukraine directly.[19] Nevertheless

Romania joined the German attack on Russia in 1941 and regained the territory, but it was lost to the victorious Soviet forces in 1944. The Moldavian Soviet Socialist Republic was re-established, to which was added a strip of Ukrainian territory east of the Dnestr, and the Cyrillic script was introduced. Romania did, however, regain north Transylvania, with its substantial Hungarian minority. In 1947 Romania went the way of Hungary when the Kingdom was replaced by a communist dictatorship.

The Second World War had started with the German invasion of Poland in September 1939. After three weeks the Poles were crushed and as part of the Nazi–Soviet pact the Russians seized eastern Poland. Western Poland and Upper Silesia, the areas ceded by Germany in 1918, were reintegrated into the Reich and the rest of the country was termed the *General Gouvernement*. After the war the Soviet Union retained that part of Poland obtained in 1939 and Poland was then simply displaced 200 kilometres westwards, taking over German territory up to the Oder-Neisse line. Not only were Germans massively deported or chose to flee but 800 000 Poles were transferred from the Ukrainian part of the Soviet Union to Poland and 500 000 Ukrainians were transferred from the new Poland to the Ukraine.[20] Only some half a million Germans and less than 200 000 Ukrainians remained. What with the extermination of the Jews by the Nazis during the war Poland would begin the peace 95 per cent ethnically Polish.

Yugoslavia was fragmented. The royal Serb-dominated government had signed a treaty with Nazi Germany on 25 March 1941, but the hostile reaction led to its overthrow two days later and the conclusion of a friendship Treaty with the Soviet Union on 5 April. Hostilities began next day but Croatia, dominated by the Ustasha Movement of National Liberation refused to defend Yugoslavia, disarmed Serb forces in Croatia, declared independence and welcomed German intervention against Belgrade. By 17 April the Yugoslav army had capitulated and the federation dissolved. Croatia retained its independence but eastern Slovenia was annexed by the Reich and western Slovenia by Italy, which also received the Dalmatian coast including Montenegro. Western Macedonia was given to Bulgaria. A German military government was established in Serbia.[21] Three conflicts then occurred simultaneously. One saw the Ustasha declare a holy war of ethnic cleansing against all non-Croats, but particularly Serbs and Gypsies. The second saw the Serbs resist the Italian and German invaders and their Croatian ally. The third was a civil war between Serbs led by the Croatian Communist Jozip Broz, otherwise known as Tito, and the Cetniks, led by General Draza Mihailovic, who was supported by the royal government in exile in London, and accused by Tito of being reluctant to attack the Germans. The ferocity of these conflicts led to 1 800 000 casualties – nearly 80 per cent of all civil and military casualties in the Mediterranean.[22] The end of the war would see a communist federal Yugoslavia restored under the leadership of Tito and with the Istrian Peninsula obtained from Italy. Nevertheless the mutual antagonisms lay only too close to the surface, and they would reap their murderous harvest fifty years later.

In the Ukraine, following its attack on the Soviet Union in June 1941 the Germans were initially welcomed. As elsewhere – in the Baltic states, Belgium and Brittany – hopes for an independent state were raised. But Nazi insistence on treating Ukrainians, as all Slavs, as sub-human merely led to Ukrainian hatred of Stalinist Russia being turned on the Germans. Only towards the end of the war was Ukrainian nationalism allowed to re-emerge and an anti-Soviet Ukrainian division raised to help the Axis. This was far too late. Nevertheless, after the Germans had been driven out Ukrainian resistance to Stalin continued into the early 1950s. In return Ukrainians were deported and Russian immigrants sent in to replace them, while Moscow continued to campaign against 'Ukrainian bourgeois nationalism' and the pace of russification was stepped up.[23] Other victims in Stalin's new Ukraine were the Tatars of the Crimea and the Ruthenians. The former, numbering 265 000,[24] were deported to central Asia on the grounds that they had collaborated with the Germans. As for the latter, their homeland was incorporated into the Ukraine which in 1925 had declared all Ruthenians to be Ukrainians. The view that Ruthenians were Ukrainians was also supported after 1945 by Czechoslovakia and Poland. Only 130 000 Ruthenians remained in northern Slovakia.[25]

Finally, what of those 'unrepresented' people, the Jews and the Gypsies. It has been estimated that in eastern Europe some 68 per cent of Jews and 22 per cent of Gypsies perished. The highest death rates for Jews were found to be in areas of direct Nazi intervention – Poland (91 per cent), the Baltic States (90 per cent) and Bohemia and Moravia (89 per cent). The most unfortunate place for Gypsies was Croatia where an unbelievable 98 per cent were liquidated, followed by Poland (70 per cent), the Baltic States (64 per cent) and Bohemia and Moravia (50 per cent).[26]

From League of Nations to United Nations

Since exploitation of minorities by their kin states – and particularly exploitation of German minorities by the Nazis – was considered the main cause of the Second World War, consideration about what to do with minorities formed an inevitable part of postwar planning.

During the war itself five solutions to minority problems were examined and analysed. The first of these was that there should be an international guarantee of minority rights. Here, one thing became quickly apparent: the members of the United Nations were against merely renewing the League system on the grounds that its political aims had failed to be realised. The Poles and Czechs argued that minorities were a threat to the security of states and world peace. As one observer warned, referring to the *Führer* of the Sudeten Germans, 'Every protected minority will ultimately find its Henlein'.[27] Most of the other 'minority states' had been against the League system and did not want to undertake new commitments. Many states, particularly the United States, were dominated by the 'melting pot' approach. So what should be done? Several proposals were floated: that the Minorities System should be limited to central and Eastern Europe (proposed by the Jewish community); that the system should only be enforced on the Axis powers, i.e. Germany, Romania, Hungary, Bulgaria and Finland; that the system should be generalised; that minorities should have collective rights and be able to have access to international courts. But it was clear that international statesmen, backed up by public opinion, were more interested in curtailing minority rights and were not interested in international supervision and protection of individual minorities, whether by a renewed League of Nations or a new United Nations.[28]

The second solution was that there should be an International Bill of Human Rights. It was based on the idea that all human rights were interdependent. Thus the government which violated the basic human rights of its ordinary citizens would be unlikely to respect special rights for minorities, especially in an atmosphere of suspicion. A Bill of Human Rights would provide a general platform of rights, and any special rights, or positive discrimination, could come later. On this basis there would be no 'minorities' problem but rather that of individuals seeking to have their basic rights recognised. This idea of a Bill of Human Rights was supported by all those who did not want to see special rights for minorities. But when the question arose of how to enforce such Rights, the weakness in the idea was revealed: where was the evidence to show that enforcing Human Rights would be easier or more acceptable than enforcing Minority Rights had been in the past?[29]

The third solution was assimilation, that minorities merge culturally with the majority. The United States was inevitably an ardent supporter of assimilation. President Woodrow Wilson had said, 'America does not consist of groups. A person who thinks of himself as belonging to a particular national group in America has not yet become American'.[30]

However, even if one accepted assimilation, did that mean one could escape discrimination? For sociologists, assimilation is achieved when no separate social structures based on racial or ethnic considerations, such as schools, remain, and when there are no constraints on social mobility, i.e. in terms of employment and promotion. But was that enough? The real test was whether the minority would actually be *accepted* by the majority. The example of Jews in France and Germany was not encouraging. Alfred Dreyfus totally identified with the majority of Frenchmen; he was in an elite profession, an army officer. Jews in Germany fought cheerfully and patriotically for their country during the First World War, and became Ministers in the Weimar Republic. But their cases warned that the breaking of barriers by some individuals did not mean that they would come down for the group as a whole and that widespread prejudice need not be eliminated, and the minority would be unlikely to be accepted if it was held either to constitute a political threat (and in Germany after 1918 Jews were perceived as either finance capitalists exploiting poverty and inflation or as having links with communist revolution) or to have an inferior culture.

There were, however, two further arguments against assimilation. One was that it would complete spiritually that which persons like Hitler had tried to do physically. The other was that it violated the integrity of the individual who had a right to his or her national culture, which was a priceless heritage, and deprived of it would become a spiritual eunuch, culturally impoverished.[31]

The fourth solution, cultural pluralism, in contrast, demanded an end to the concept of the nation-state; an end to political organisation designed to express one particular culture; and demanded that majorities respect the culture of minorities and treat it as politically irrelevant, thus accepting the multinational state.[32]

The fifth proposal was the transfer of populations and/or, if need be, frontier revision. The case for transfer was simply that it ended the security threat and was therefore in the interests of the international community. The case against transfer was that it reflected pessimism about the ability of mankind to work out a means of peaceful co-existence. It would mean capitulation to a nationalist philosophy which denied the essential unity of mankind.[33]

In the meantime, in November 1943, the Allies had agreed to set up a new international organisation for the maintenance of peace and security. In June 1945 at San Francisco, delegates of fifty states drafted the United Nations Charter, and the United Nations officially came into existence on 24 October 1945. The League of Nations was wound up, officially ending its existence in April 1946.

The Allied debate about treatment of minorities was also inconclusive. On the one hand the transfer of populations solution was applied through the Potsdam Agreements of July–August 1945, but only to Germans in Poland, Czechoslovakia and Hungary back to Germany.

On the other hand, the main thrust of the Allies was that there should be Human Rights for all rather than special rights for minorities, and that if there were special positive rights to be provided it was up to the host state to provide them. Treatment of a minority should be an issue between host state and kin state only, i.e. a bilateral problem rather than an international problem. This approach was no accident. It reflected the philosophy of the Western three of the Big Four victorious powers, the United States, Britain and France, of equal rights for all citizens and thus neatly sidestepped concern about territorial community or group rights which might lead to separation or a state within a state.

The prevailing view was that the League system had been imposed on the so-called 'Minority States' in order to ward off danger to international peace arising out of the transfer of territory. The League system was thus inspired by political considerations and therefore the political consequences of mistreatment of minorities was the basis of the League system. Instead, what the United Nations hoped to do was to focus on the mistreatment itself. Whereas the League had been an organisation for dealing with political problems, the UN's view was that political problems were mostly caused by unsatisfactory economic and social conditions and non-observance of basic human rights.

The United Nations Charter therefore contained in its Preamble and several Articles references to human rights, and various bodies were established to promote them, in particular a Commission on Human Rights as part of the UN Economic and Social Council. This body began drafting an International Bill of Human Rights in 1946.

It was unsurprising therefore that these attitudes were reflected in the Peace Treaties which the former Axis powers, Italy, Bulgaria,

Finland, Hungary and Romania signed in 1947, where an Article was inserted to the effect that the country concerned 'would take all necessary measures to ensure that everyone within its jurisdiction, without distinction as to race, sex, language or religion, enjoyed fundamental human rights and liberties, including freedom of thought, press, publication, culture, opinion and meeting'.

Significantly, these Peace Treaties provided for no machinery to see that Human Rights were actually observed, and it was clear that right from the beginning the UN was against any possibility of intervention to that end, doubtless realising from the League experience how difficult it would be. The official excuse was Article 2, para.7 of the UN Charter, which stated that nothing in the UN Charter should permit interference in the domestic affairs of a state. The question avoided at that time was what would happen if a 'domestic affair' spilled over to became an international one. But there was a political dimension as well: the Soviet Union was clearly not going to tolerate any probe into the state of human rights in its Empire in eastern Europe.

The Austro-Italian Agreement on South Tyrol

In only one case did a minority receive sympathetic treatment from the Great Powers after the war – the German minority in South Tyrol. In view of their treatment by Fascism the South Tyrolese expected their land to return to Austria, and that a plebiscite on the future of South Tyrol be inserted into the Italian Peace Treaty was formally requested by the Austrian government to the Council of Foreign Ministers of the Big Four (United States, Soviet Union, Great Britain, France) in September 1945. But by June 1946 it was clear that return to Austria would not occur. Although there was much sympathy for the South Tyrolese as well as feelings of guilt for the 1919 decision, these were outweighed by two factors. First, there was the considerable body of Italo-Americans in the United States, while the Italian Communist movement, which had dominated the resistance to Fascism in the closing years of the war, could count on the support of the Soviet Union. The French, who had begun by being quite pro-Austrian, were soon bought off by the acquisition of the two small towns of Briga and Tenda and the promise of an autonomy in the Val d'Aosta for the French-speaking community. Second, there was the overall political situation, in particular the uncertainty about the future of Germany – quite apart from that of Austria, both under four-power occupation. There was considerable apprehension that a revived Germany might one day seek to reverse the verdict of 1945 as it had that of 1918. In that case, would a better watchdog be Austria, strengthened by the return of South Tyrol, or Italy, with the Brenner frontier? In reality there could only be one answer.[34]

The failure to regain South Tyrol did, however, spur direct Italo-Austrian talks about an autonomy and in keeping with the view that positive rights should be negotiated between host and kin states both sides were encouraged by the western states meeting within the framework of the Peace Conference, which had begun in Paris in April 1946. The result was the De Gasperi-Gruber Agreement on South Tyrol, named after the foreign ministers of the countries concerned and signed on 5 September 1946. And in order to provide an international guarantee of its fulfilment the Agreement was placed in an Annex of the Peace Treaty between the victorious Allies and Italy.

For the issues raised, the interpretation and application of its clauses, and the length of time over its implementation, the De Gasperi-Gruber Agreement deserves recognition as one of the most famous – or infamous – minorities treaties of all time, and the Treaty's key clauses are therefore given in full.

1 German-speaking inhabitants of the Bolzano province and of the neighbouring bilingual townships of the Trento Province will be assured a complete equality of rights with the Italian-speaking inhabitants within the framework of special provisions to safeguard the ethnical character and the cultural and economic development of the German-speaking element.

   In accordance with legislation already enacted or awaiting enactment the said German-speaking citizens will be granted in particular:
   (a) elementary and secondary teaching in the mother-tongue;
   (b) parification of the German and Italian languages in public offices and official documents, as well as in bilingual topographical naming;
   (c) the right to re-establish German family names which were italianised in recent years;
   (d) equality of rights as regards the entering upon public offices with a view to reaching a more appropriate proportion of employment between the two ethnical groups.

2 The populations of the above-mentioned zones will be granted the exercise of autonomous legislative and executive regional power. The frame within which the said provisions of autonomy will apply, will be drafted in consultation also with local representative

German-speaking elements.

3 The Italian Government, with the aim of establishing good neigh-
bourhood relations between Austria and Italy, pledges itself, in consultation with the Austrian Government, and within one year from
the signing of the present Treaty:
   (a) to revise in a spirit of equity and broadmindedness the question
        of the options for citizenship resulting from the 1939
        Hitler–Mussolini agreements;
   (b) to find an agreement for the mutual recognition of the validity
        of certain degrees and university diplomas.[35]

Article 1 of the De Gasperi–Gruber Agreement made it clear that the
objective was to safeguard the German ethnic character of the South
Tyrolese people but not to safeguard as German the ethnic character of
South Tyrol. This had already been an issue in 1920. But a new and
advanced element in minority protection was the undertaking to safeguard not only the cultural but also the economic development of the
South Tyrolese.

Further interesting questions were raised concerning the administration of the Province. Article 1(a) of the Agreement stated that the
German language was 'parified' with the Italian. Did this mean that
German was to be a local official language? Article 1(d) held out the
prospect that employment in public offices should be on the basis of
ethnic proportions – the first time this controversial issue had appeared
in an international legal instrument.

Article 2 provided for consultations between the Italian government
and representatives of the South Tyrolese about a regional legislative
and executive autonomy. What weight should be given to the word
'consultations'? And what was the definition of the word 'region'.

Finally, Article 3 provided, *inter alia*, for revisions of the 1939
Options Agreement so that optants for Germany could regain Italian
citizenship. Would this apply to all of them?

Field Marshall Smuts would refer to the Agreement as 'the highlight
of the (Peace) Conference',[36] but, as will be seen, this praise was
premature.

4
Heads (Mostly) in the Sand, 1948–72

The United Nations

In December 1948 the UN General Assembly adopted the so-called Universal Declaration of Human Rights in which Article 2 contained a blanket provision of non-discrimination on grounds of race, colour, sex, language, religion, political or other opinion, national or social origin, property, birth or other status.

There was therefore nothing special in the Declaration for Minorities. In any case, as a Declaration rather than a treaty or convention, it was not a legally enforceable document and again Article 2, para.7 of the UN Charter had its part to play. Rather, it was a standard of achievement to be attained, a moral force.

There had been attempts to get protection of minorities inserted into the Declaration but the General Assembly rejected them. It was argued that the Declaration was concerned with individual, not group rights; that the widely differing types of minorities in the world would make it difficult to adopt a uniform solution; that in some countries (like the United States) assimilation was the goal of society, and therefore preservation of a minority's characteristics could not be considered a universal aim; that political rights extending protection of minorities individually or collectively was something up to national, not international institutions; and, revealingly, that minorities might be incited to endanger the integration and integrity of states.

At the same time that it adopted the Universal Declaration of Human Rights the United Nations adopted the Genocide Convention. Genocide was defined as:

(1) Killing members of the group.
(2) Causing members of the group serious physical and mental damage.
(3) Imposing deliberately conditions of life so as to produce the physical destruction of the group in whole or in part.
(4) Imposing measures to prevent births within the group.
(5) Forced transfer of the children of the group to another group.

Interestingly, an attempt was made to have cultural genocide included in the Convention on the grounds that cultural genocide could not be divorced from physical or biological genocide since their aims were the same, namely, the destruction of a national, racial or religious group as such either by exterminating its members or by destroying its special characteristics. 'Cultural genocide represents the end whereas physical genocide represents the means.'[1]

The text adopted by the Committee on Genocide of the Economic and Social Council defined cultural genocide as:

any deliberate act committed with the intent to destroy the language, religion or culture of a national, racial or religious group on grounds of national or racial origin or religious belief such as:

(1) prohibiting the use of the language of the group in daily intercourse or in schools, or the printing and circulation of publications in the language of the group;
(2) destroying or preventing the use of libraries, museums, schools, historical monuments, places of worship or other cultural institutions and objects of the group.[2]

But the inclusion of the section was rejected in plenary on a number of grounds – cultural genocide was better protected through human rights, the definition of cultural genocide was too vague. The delegate of Belgium, none other than Georges Kaeckenbeeck, the president of the Arbitral Tribunal in Upper Silesia before the war, stated that the importance of protecting minorities had no place in the Convention. Moreover, since the acts described as cultural genocide came within the province of the domestic affairs of states, it would be difficult for the latter to recognise international jurisdiction in such cases.[3]

But the UN did not entirely wash its hands of minorities. At the same time that it adopted the Universal Declaration of Human Rights the General Assembly also adopted Resolution 217 III C to the effect that it could not remain indifferent to the fate of minorities; considered it difficult to adopt a uniform solution for this complex and delicate question; and referred the matter to a Human Rights Commission Sub-committee, the Sub-committee on the Prevention of Discrimination and the Protection of Minorities 'to make a thorough study of the problem'.

The first task of this Sub-committee was to do something not done before, but vital if norms of protection on a world-wide basis could be prepared, namely to provide a definition of Minorities. This definition appeared in 1950.

> The term 'minorities' includes only those *non-dominant* groups in a population which possess and *wish to preserve* stable ethnic, religious or linguistic traditions markedly different from those of the rest of the population.
>
> Such minorities should properly include a number of persons sufficient by themselves to *develop* such characteristics.

In addition, to qualify for protection the minority had to be 'loyal to the state of which they are nationals'.[4]

The last sentence spelled out only too eloquently that minorities were still considered political threats to states. Nevertheless, the Sub-committee did support positive action for minorities, based on the reasoning behind the decision of the Permanent Court of International Justice in the regard to the case of minority schools in Albania.[5] Drawing a distinction between Prevention of Discrimination on the one hand, and Protection of Minorities on the other, the Sub-committee ruled that Prevention of Discrimination was the 'prevention of any action which denies to individuals or groups equality of treatment which they may wish', whereas Protection of Minorities was protection of those wishing for differential treatment in order to preserve basic characteristics which they possessed. This differential treatment was justified when '*exercised in the interest of their contentment and the welfare of the community as a whole*'. Discrimination was thus any act or conduct which denied individuals equality of treatment. Protection of Minorities, on the other hand, required positive action; for example the establishment of schools in which education is given in the native tongue of the group provided concrete service to that group. Such measures were also inspired by the spirit of equality. For if a child received its education in a language not its mother tongue, this meant that a child was not being treated on an equal basis with those children who did receive their education in their mother tongue.[6] Thereafter the Human Rights Sub-Committee authorised work to go ahead on filling the gap – to draw up instruments on minorities that were binding on the signatories. In fact this would not be achieved until 1966.[7]

In the meantime one major problem still remained to be settled. The United Nations was the successor institution to the League of Nations. Were the League's Minorities Treaties still valid, and should therefore the UN assume the role of their guarantor? Or was the old system no longer in existence? These issues were examined in a document that appeared in April 1950 prepared by the UN Legal Department.

The legal validity of the undertakings concerning minorities was examined in the light of the clause *Rebus Sic Stantibus*, a clause invoked in international law when 'essential changes of circumstances from those under which a treaty was concluded' are advanced in order to justify non-compliance with that treaty's obligations.

On the one hand, there was the war and population transfers. But the UN Legal Department decided that neither in themselves was sufficient to entail the extinction of the obligations under the Minorities Treaties. Not all minorities had been transferred, only most Germans. The clauses might therefore still be valid for the remaining Germans and non-Germans, especially Hungarians in Czechoslovakia and Romania.

On the other hand, the dissolution of the League of Nations most certainly provided a change of circumstances, in that the Article in the Treaties under which the obligations of the Minority State could be reduced or terminated altogether by agreement with the League Council was no longer applicable. It was also felt that the new United Nations regime of Human Rights for all and non-discrimination had 'to a large extent supplanted' the regional regime of the League's Minorities Treaties and this had been reflected in the Peace Treaties of 1947.

Finally, the position of the states involved in the Treaties had undergone big changes since 1939 due to considerable territorial and population changes. The three Baltic states had disappeared when taken over by the Soviet Union and their obligations had gone with them. Poland had lost almost all its Germans, fled or deported, most Ukrainians and Lithuanians were now part of the Soviet Union, and only 100 000 Jews of the original three million had survived. Czechoslovakia had expelled most of the Germans, had ceded Ruthenia to the Soviet Union and had lost most of its Jews in the Holocaust.

The UN Legal Department also declared that the Peace Treaties at the end of the First World War applying to Austria, Bulgaria and Hungary should no longer be considered in force, although the Peace Treaty with Turkey (Lausanne) should still be considered valid.

With regard to Greece, obligations should still be considered in force in so far as they concerned the special regime set up between Greece and Turkey under Article 45 of the Treaty of Lausanne, according to which Greece undertook to confer on Moslems in Greece the same rights as conferred on non-Moslems in Turkey.

The conclusion of the UN Legal Department was that if the problem was regarded as a whole, then indeed 'between 1939 and 1947 circumstances had so changed that the League of Nations system should be considered as having ceased to exist'. The United Nations was therefore free to develop its own attitudes and policies.[8]

The first ten years

Back in Europe the first decade of the peace would see some countries come to terms with their minority problems. The results varied.

Italy

(a) Introduction

As the postwar democratic government viewed its country it would be affected by three issues. First, the peace arrangements looked like being kind to Italy. The only likely territorial losses were the enclaves of Briga and Tenda in the western Maritime Alps and the Istrian peninsula taken from Austria in 1918. But that still left within the Italian state the French minority in Val d'Aosta, the Germans of South Tyrol, the Rhaeto-Romansch Ladins of South Tyrol, Trento and Belluno, the Rhaeto-Romansch Friauls in north-eastern Venice, Slovenian communities along the frontier with Yugoslavia and the Sards of Sardinia. Second, a new constitution was needed, and amongst other things Italy would have to decide whether to remain a kingdom or become a republic. Third, because of the centralism with which Italy had been governed since unification, particularly under the Fascists, there was a reaction in favour of regional devolution.

This latter point was particularly apposite since, if French troops were occupying the Val d'Aosta where there was a separatist movement, the French government was not enthusiastic about annexation but thinking rather in terms of an autonomy,[9] whereas the South Tyrolese wanted separation. In order to appease the French, halt potential French support for the South Tyrolese, and appear conciliatory towards the latter in order to impress the Allies, the first measures in favour of minorities were swiftly introduced. In the Val d'Aosta, where 75 000 of the 115 000 inhabitants spoke Franco-Provençal, with pure French speakers numbering only 5 to 7per cent,[10] the Italians guaranteed to the French an autonomy for Val d'Aosta on 1 June 1945 and a regional autonomy was introduced on 7 September 1945.[11] Amongst its provisions was that the French language should be 'parified' with Italian. However, it was made clear that this autonomy was provisional, until ratified by a future Italian parliament.[12]

In October 1945 teaching in the mother tongue was allowed in elementary schools in South Tyrol. The question as to which ethnic group a pupil belonged was to be based on the declaration of the father. Provision was made for Italian to be taught in German-language schools and *vice versa*. In December 1945 South Tyrolese could use German in relations with the political, administrative and judicial authorities of the Province, and public acts and documents other than judicial ones were to be bilingual.[13]

On 2 June 1946 Italy went to the polls to elect an Assembly to prepare the constitution. On the same occasion the monarchy was defeated by 45.8 per cent of the votes to 54.2 and was replaced by a republic.[14] It would henceforth be for this Assembly to scrutinise proposals for regional devolution. The constitution of the new Italian republic was adopted by the Assembly on 1 January 1948.

Article 131 provided for the creation of nineteen regions, and Article 116 named five of them as having special statutes – Sicily, Sardinia, Val d'Aosta, Trentino-Alto Adige (Alto Adige or the Upper Adige being the Italian name for South Tyrol) and Friuli-Venezia-Giulia. Article 117 listed the nineteen fields in which the regions in general could legislate, amongst the most notable being agriculture and forestry, tourism and the hotel trade, town planning, handicrafts, public health and welfare, hospitals, professional education, local public works, fairs and markets, and local police. However, the regional legislation had to respect principles established by state laws, the national interest and that of other regions. Under Article 118 the regions carried out the administration in regard to those fields where they possessed the legislative power and could receive further administrative functions from the state.

Then on 26 February 1948 the Assembly adopted four constitutional laws providing for the special statutes for Sicily, Sardinia, Val d'Aosta and Trentino-Alto Adige. These regions had three levels of legislative power. With regard to a number of fields, variable according to region, but generally including agriculture and forestry, tourism and the hotel trade, local transport, local police, handicrafts, town planning, the regions exercised primary legislative power, meaning that legislation had to respect the constitution and the principles of the legal organisation of the state, international obligations and national interests, as well as the fundamental principles of the economic and social reforms of the republic. Under a less extensive list of fields, but including industry and public health, the regions enjoyed secondary legislative power which meant they could act not only within the aforementioned limits of primary legislative power but they also had to respect the principles established by state laws in regard to the fields in question.

Under tertiary legislative power the regions could adapt for their own requirements state laws in regard to an even smaller list of fields, particularly national insurance and social security. For those fields in which the regions exercised primary and secondary legislative power they also provided the administration. The regions also received – varying according to region – their own sources of income, usually a proportion of state taxes.

(b) Val d'Aosta

The Val d'Aosta Autonomy Statute designated the area as an autonomous Region, with 21 fields of primary legislative competence, including agriculture and forestry, tourism and the hotel trade, protection of the countryside, professional and technical education, local police, town planning (Article 2.), and 13 fields of secondary legislative competence, including industry and commerce, preparatory, primary and secondary education and health and hospital services (Article 3). The region provided the administration for those fields in which it could legislate. Article 38 confirmed the status of the French language as being 'placed on a footing of equality' with Italian but there was no mention of Franco-Provençal. Article 39 provided that in schools of all sorts and at all levels 'dependent on the region' the French language would be taught for the same number of hours weekly as Italian, but again there was no provision for Franco-Provençal. Some subjects could be taught entirely in French. Article 40 provided that the regular, i.e. state education programmes could be modified to take account of local requirements. Joint commissions should decide these modifications as well as the choice of subjects which might be taught in French. In addition to local sources of finance, the Region would receive a proportion of public funds (Article 12). Finally the Italian government and the Constituent Assembly rejected any idea of an international guarantee for the autonomy statute (i.e. by putting it in an annex to the Italian Peace Treaty).[15]

Thereafter, although most native Valdotains spoke the Franco-Provençal *patois*, it was with difficulty that the French language and culture kept its head above water. Italianisation increased as industrial workers, civil servants and policemen invaded the valley – particularly the urban centres – continuing the process of italianisation begun by the Fascists. Summer and winter tourism also contributed to the decline of French. Italian dominated professional life and French seemed to have disappeared from the capital, the city of Aosta.[16]

Things would be very different indeed in Trentino-Alto Adige.

(c) South Tyrol

The De Gasperi-Gruber Agreement had been greeted with such shock and anger in Austria and South Tyrol at the failure – for the second time in less than thirty years – to obtain self-determination for the South Tyrolese that the Austrian government had to take the line that the Agreement was the best solution possible under the circumstances and that it did not mean Austria had renounced South Tyrol. Austrians and Tyrolese – North and South – argued that self-government was not self-determination, and that the Agreement was only a temporary solution.[17]

It was true that the text of the Agreement contained no renunciation of South Tyrol by Austria and since this was essentially the one thing the Italians wanted, failure to secure it would be used by the Italian government to give a restrictive interpretation to the Agreement and apply it restrictively through the Autonomy Statute that implemented it. It did not help that the official text of the Agreement was in neither of the languages of those who had made the Agreement in the first place.[18]

Drafting the Autonomy Statute got off to a bad start when the 'consultation' with the South Tyrolese by the Italian government on the autonomy provided for was kept to a minimum. As the South Tyrolese – and other minorities – would find out, when security or state integrity was held to be at stake 'consultation' did not mean 'negotiation', let alone negotiation between relatively equal partners.[19]

The most serious blow, and one which the South Tyrolese had feared and expected, was the way the word 'region' was defined, providing for the extension of the regional autonomy contained in Article 2 of the Agreement to include not only the Province of Bolzano (South Tyrol) but the Province of Trento. This meant that since the smaller population of Bolzano was two-thirds German-speaking while the larger population of Trento was very nearly 100 per cent Italian, in the region Trentino-Alto Adige the Italians would enjoy a two-thirds majority. The significance of this development could be seen in the respective distribution of legislative and executive powers between the region and the provinces.

For it would be the region, not the provinces, that would receive primary legislative power in regard to most of the important economic and social sectors such as agriculture and forestry, the environment, tourism and health and hospital services, communications, transport and public works of regional interest. It enjoyed secondary legislative power with regard to the development of industrial production and commercial activity. In contrast the provinces enjoyed primary legislative powers with regard to, *inter alia*, place names (but Bolzano had to respect bilingualism), cultural institutions, fairs and markets, handicrafts, town planning and housing. They enjoyed secondary legislative powers in regard to pre-elementary, elementary and secondary education, art and technical schools and teacher training. The South Tyrolese complained bitterly, and with justification, that the autonomy should be for them. They were the minority. The Italians in the region did not need an autonomy since they had the state behind them. Perhaps just as shocking for the South Tyrolese was the refusal by the Italians to call the Province of Bolzano 'South Tyrol'. The Italian text of the Autonomy Statute referred to Alto Adige, the Upper Adige, Adige being the Italian name for the main river (Etsch in German) running through the province and marking the historic boundary of the German world.[20] The German text referred to *Tiroler Etschland* or Tyrolese Adige.

But merely to have the political, economic and social development of the region in their hands was not nearly good enough for the Italians who saw themselves as the watchdogs of the state against South Tyrolese separatism. Control, direct and indirect, was exercised in seven other ways.

First – and for the first time ever – the principle of institutionalised power-sharing was introduced. Thus in the Regional Assembly, composed of the members of the Bolzano and Trento Assemblies, and in the Bolzano Assembly, the *Giunta* or government had to be composed in proportion to the numerical composition of the linguistic groups represented in the respective Assemblies. Thus for the nine members (Assessors) of the regional government, two-thirds, or six members, had to be Italian and three German-speaking. Conversely, in the Province of Bolzano, of the six members of the provincial *Giunta* four had to be German-speakers and two Italian, even though in Bolzano the party that overwhelmingly represented the South Tyrolese, the *Südtiroler Volkspartei* (SVP) would, throughout the 1950s and 1960s, have the absolute majority in the provincial assembly, consistently gaining over 60 per cent of the total vote.[21] As for the decision-making process itself, regional and provincial laws were to be adopted by simple majority and implemented shortly thereafter unless challenged by the government for overstepping their competence or conflicting with the national interest or that of one of the provinces.

Certainly one important point in the development of the South Tyrol question would be the consistent support given by the South Tyrolese community to the SVP. In 1980, for example, the paid-up membership of the party amounted to 36 per cent of the German/Ladin voting population and 23 per cent of the *entire* provincial electorate![22] By contrast the Italian community in South Tyrol – and Trento – was fragmented into anything up to a dozen parties. The only similar example of party dominance of 'their' community would be the Ulster Unionists before 1968. However, the idea of institutionalised power-sharing (if a means in societies where voting was tribal rather than ideological of attempting to create an environment of partnership in which each community could feel it had a stake in society and government rather than having one community always dominating the other, and it would be the Italians who were in the minority in South Tyrol) needed two things for it to be satisfactorily fulfilled. One was territorial stability. As people in Cyprus and Northern Ireland would soon learn, power sharing was highly questionable if it was felt that the aim of one of the partners in the power-sharing agreement was to dissolve the framework within which that power was shared. Second, a compatible joint programme would have to be agreed. At first this was not a problem in capitalist, Christian-democratic, social-democratic South Tyrol. But what would happen if one community came to be dominated by either the extreme left or the extreme right?

Second, since Italy was not a federal state but a regional state with power devolved to the regions, government approval had to be given to any regional or provincial legislation before these could take effect, particularly if there was a financial implication involving the state. This approval might also require the prior issue of so-called 'executive measures', cabinet decrees having the force of law whose function was to co-ordinate the legislative and administrative powers of the regions and provinces with those of the state, including defining their respective spheres of interest. This procedure was cumbersome and usually lengthy.

Third, there was the issue of administrative powers. Under Article 14 of the Autonomy Statute, the region should 'normally' exercise its administrative powers, delegating them to the provinces, the municipalities and other local public bodies or by making use of their offices. The South Tyrolese believed that transfer of the region's administrative powers to the provinces should be the rule rather than the exception. The Italian-dominated regional government rejected this interpretation, arguing that each case should be decided on its merits. Indeed, in the debates in the Constituent Assembly the idea of automatic delegation was expressly denied. The neo-fascist *Movimento Sociale Italiano* (MSI) rejoiced at this decision, stating that 'a regular transfer of administrative functions would bring ... a decisive step towards provincial autonomy, *which the Italian minority in Bolzano could not think of accepting.'*

What was particularly nauseating for the South Tyrolese was that the transfer of executive power apparently provided for in Article 14 was not only the same as in the Val d'Aosta Statute but seemed to fit in with similar wording of Article 118 of the Italian Constitution. It had seemed to provide an important requirement for an effective autonomy. Moreover, insertion of the article had been a last minute gain for the South Tyrolese in the 'consultations' with the Italian government, part of the price being that the SVP leadership had to write a humiliating letter thanking the drafting committee of the Constituent Assembly for having granted so many of their requests and 'noting with pleasure that the De Gasperi-Gruber Agreement ... had been translated into reality in so far as the fundamental problem of autonomy is concerned'.[23]

Fourth, whereas regional and provincial laws could be contested by the Italian government before the Constitutional Court and the provinces could contest regional laws, only the region could contest state laws. Provinces could only contest state laws if the region took up the cudgels on their behalf. When the South Tyrolese sought to have direct access to the Court this was rejected.[24]

Fifth, there was the question of ethnic proportions in public employment, around which were a large number of issues. For example, what constituted 'public employment'? To what extent was the achievement of ethnic proportions compatible with equality of rights in competitions for posts? In Italy, entitled to be included in 'public employment' were not only the administration of the region and provinces but state and semi-state bodies operating in those areas such as the police and judiciary, the railways and postal service, departments of ministries, labour exchanges, health insurance offices, state housing bodies and so on. Unsurprisingly the South Tyrolese expected all public posts to be filled in ethnic proportions. The Italians were quite happy to accept the principle in regard to the provincial administration but rejected the idea for state and semi-state bodies where Italian officials comprised anything between 85 and 99 per cent of the staff.[25] In this they were supported by the Constitutional Court which ruled in regard to employment in health insurance offices that 'in the case of public bodies whose jurisdiction extended beyond the Province ... the principle of representation must be applied in a manner compatible with the structure of the body itself.'[26] As a minority of 0.75 per cent in the Italian state the South Tyrolese could well ask how would it be possible for them to win posts on merit in state and semi-state bodies, competing with Italians from all over Italy, especially as Italian was not their mother tongue?

Behind this issue lay another. In the 1950s in South Tyrol, as elsewhere in Europe, was occurring the flight from the land. Where would South Tyrolese coming off the land find jobs? Clearly the public administration was one important source, also psychologically it was important for the minority to be seen to be administering its homeland. The great danger was that if South Tyrolese could not find jobs in their homeland they would emigrate to Austria or Germany and the group would be correspondingly weakened at least politically vis-à-vis the Italians. Conversely, if ethnic proportions were applied to all public offices then it was equally clear that a large proportion of the Italian community would be likely to leave since they could hardly become farmers or business men or industrial workers overnight. With its *italianità* weakened to such an extent calls for self-determination and return to Austria would be more plausible.

Sixth, there was the issue of language. To begin with, what was the status of German? The De Gasperi-Gruber Agreement had stated in Article 1(b) that it was 'parified' with Italian. The Autonomy Statute stated that without prejudice to the principle that Italian was the official language of the region, use of German would be guaranteed in public life, i.e. in the relations between South Tyrolese and offices of the regional and provincial administrations and in the regional, provincial and municipal assemblies.

Italians denied this meant that German was therefore an official language in the province, and in this they were upheld by the Council of State (the Constitutional Court not yet having come into being) which ruled that German was only a subsidiary language, on the grounds that had those making the Agreement intended German to be a local official language they would have said so.[27]

This situation had implications for the offices of the administration. The South Tyrolese wanted the officials in them to be bilingual. The Italian view was that it was sufficient for the offices to be bilingual, i.e. that should a South Tyroler contact an office or ministry there would be someone to deal with him or her in German. For the South Tyrolese, the fact that German was not official meant that there was no incentive for Italian officials to learn German. It was not until 1959 that a Provincial law provided for bilingualism as a condition for employment in the provincial administration, followed by another law in 1961 that Italians in the public administration passing a language exam should receive a financial bonus. But the superficiality of the exam and the ease with which the bonus was acquired infuriated the South Tyrolese.[28]

As for education and the teaching of the three languages of the region, German, Italian and Ladin, the three communities all had their separate schools. The arrangements were that in German schools teaching was in German but Italian had to be taught by a native speaker and *vice versa*. In Ladin schools in South Tyrol some subjects were taught in Italian, some in German, and religion, music and Ladin itself were taught in Ladin. However, since Italian was an official language but German was not, a number of Italian schools did not teach the latter, hence the origin of linguistic problems for the Italians in the provincial administration. In the Province of Trento Ladin was taught in the places where it was spoken but the curriculum was taught in Italian. On the other hand Ladins in the neighbouring Province of Belluno had no facilities for learning their language in schools.

The seventh issue was housing, behind which lay one of the strongest sources of ill-feeling in minority relations, namely, defence of the homeland against encroachment by the majority.

According to the Autonomy Statute housing was a subject that came under the primary legislative competence of the province. But this was useless since the province did not have the financial wherewithal to plan and implement a housing policy. Yet the ability to act was vital in order to satisfy the demand for those South Tyrolese leaving the land and seeking employment in the larger towns of the province. Conversely, the South Tyrolese believed that the Italian government was secretly encouraging Italian emigration into the province in order to upset the ethnic balance. This was formally denied by Rome but in any case who could prevent Italians moving freely around Italy?

Nevertheless, housing went to the needy, and who were the most needy – South Tyrolese who had homes and relatives in the province, or incoming Italians?

The South Tyrolese felt continually snubbed. To every request for measures which might enable the minority to recover after the traumas of Fascism and the war, the Italian response was merely to ask whether they had a right to such measures. But the writing was on the wall. In September 1956 the first bombs were thrown to draw the attention of the international community to the dissatisfaction with implementation of the Autonomy Statute. Then in May 1957 the very moderate SVP leadership which had negotiated the Statute was overthrown and replaced by hard-liners.

As with Northern Ireland in 1968 it was housing that lit the fuse. First, in June 1957, the Italian government rejected an attempt by the province to take over the local administration of the semi-state housing organisation INA-Casa, mainly on the grounds that it was a state institution. Then, in October, when the Italian government announced the intention to build a new quarter in Bolzano with 5 000 housing units. The South Tyrolese saw this as a means by which to expand the industrial zone set up by Mussolini and still in being. Yet in a field in which the province held primary legislative competence, they could do nothing.

In November a massive demonstration was held outside Bolzano, led by the new hard-line SVP leadership. Calls for separation from Trento and a proper regional autonomy for South Tyrol featured prominently, although other placards called for self-determination. After that things would go downhill rapidly for the Italians.

In 1955 Four Power occupation of Austria had ended and that country regained its independence. Article 1 of the Austrian State Treaty laid down the nation's borders as those of 1 January 1938. Guaranteed by the Great Powers, this meant that henceforward there was practically no chance that Austria would regain South Tyrol, and Italian fears should correspondingly have diminished, but Italian hard-line attitudes did not change.

When the Austrians intervened in support of the South Tyrolese, questioning whether the De Gasperi-Gruber Agreement had been properly implemented, the Italians rebuffed the Austrian approach arguing that implementation was an entirely domestic affair. The result was that in 1960 Austria took the matter to the United Nations, where the General Assembly rejected the idea that the problem was solely an internal one, and called on the two sides to 'resume negotiations with a view to finding a solution for *all* differences relating to the implementation of the Paris Agreement'.[29]

The need for such discussions was hastened by the deteriorating security situation in South Tyrol. The original group of dynamitards, anxious to draw attention to the situation in the province and seeking proper implementation of the autonomy as they saw it, had been quickly arrested. Their replacements were more powerful and more ambitious, seeking not autonomy but secession. Financial support and arms were available in North Tyrol where a number of organisations dedicated to reunification and/or self-determination (and to Italians and Austrians alike they were seen as the same thing) had set up. On 11–12 June 1961 the provincial electrical pylon system was attacked plunging Bolzano into darkness and leading to suspension of work in the industrial zone, and the first death through terrorism occurred.[30] But when many of those involved in this second phase of violence were arrested the baton was taken up by pan-Germans and neo-Nazis operating from north of the border and not only seeking the re-creation of the traditional German Reich, including Alsace-Lorraine, Austria, South Tyrol and the Sudetenland, but ready to target deliberately members of the Italian police and security forces.[31]

Discussions took place intensively over the next eight years involving, crucially, not only the governments of Austria and Italy but also the SVP. The result was that in mid-summer 1969 agreement was reached between Vienna and Rome on a package deal that contained, on the one hand, a fundamental revision of the 1948 Autonomy Statute in favour of the South Tyrolese and, on the other hand, a timetable for its implementation. It was then up to the SVP to decide, in a special party congress, whether to accept or reject the so-called Package Deal. In the event, on 22 November, the Congress accepted the Package but only narrowly – by 52.9 per cent.[32]

(d) Friuli-Venezia Giulia

Backed by a state prepared to stand up for its kin, the South Tyrolese would receive an improved statute that would enable them economically, socially and culturally to flourish in the future. The Valdotains may originally have been supported by their kin state but disinterest after the granting of the autonomy would see the group struggle. Less fortunate were the Friaul and Slovene minorities in Italy's north-eastern region, Friuli-Venezia Giulia. Although the region was to be one with special statute, the statute itself did not appear until 1963. There was nothing relating to the enhancement and development of

Friaul, although there were some 600 000 Friaul speakers.[33] Apparently the Friauls at that time did not seek any special educational or cultural statute. Nor was there anything for the Slovenes in the Province of Udine. Only the Slovenes in the border province of Gorizia and Trieste enjoyed Slovene-language schools, and then only since 1961.[34]

(e) Sardinia

The Sardinian statute contained the usual array of primary and secondary legislative powers but, as with the Friauls of Friuli-Venezia Giulia, there was no mention whatever of the status of the Sard language, let alone its protection or enhancement.

Denmark

(a) Schleswig and Schleswig-Holstein

In Denmark there had been much hostility towards the 20 000 or 8 per cent German-speaking population of Schleswig on account of the collaboration with the German occupying forces during the war – 2 000 joined the German army and afterwards 3 500 were imprisoned for collaboration.[35] German schools were closed and property confiscated. In West Germany's *Land* Schleswig-Holstein however, emigration of Danes after the war at the same time as an incoming flood of one million refugees from the east was perceived as threatening the national balance. One feature of this was that because of a *Land* election law that eliminated from representation in the *Land* parliament parties obtaining less than 5 per cent of the vote as well as perceived gerrymandering, the Danish group ceased to be represented. Angered by a situation in which one German could be elected to the Danish *Folketing* with one quarter of the votes gained by Danes in Schleswig-Holstein, Denmark threatened to veto West Germany's accession to NATO, and this undoubtedly spurred the solution to both minority problems as reached in the Bonn–Copenhagen parallel but unilateral Declarations of 29 March 1955.

In Schleswig the Declarations led to the recognition of the right of the German minority to establish, in conformity with the law, institutions for general education and high schools and kindergartens; the right to maintain religious, cultural and professional relations with Germany; and the right to use the German language in law courts and public offices.

In Schleswig-Holstein not only were these rights reciprocated for the 60–70 000 Danish-speaking population, but the 5 per cent electoral rule was lifted for political parties of the Danish minority.[36] The solution of the two Declarations as opposed to a bilateral treaty was chosen because Denmark, as a democratic country, did not want to give a powerful neighbour a right of oversight, however limited, into its internal affairs.[37]

(b) The Faroe Islands

During the Middle Ages Faroese had developed into a separate Nordic language. Even if it disappeared as a written language it continued to be spoken by the people, while Danish was the language used in education, the administration, trade and the church. Only in 1938 did Denmark recognise Faroese as a language of instruction.

Faroese nationalism rose after the German occupation of Denmark in the Second World War broke communications for five years. A home-rule movement began in 1940, and it won a referendum on independence in 1946. Negotiations followed, leading to Home Rule in 1948, with Faroese as the 'principal language', the *Lawthing* (the Faroese parliament) competent in everything except foreign affairs, defence and the judiciary, and the right of the Faroese to send two representatives to the *Folketing*.[38]

Austria

The State Treaty of 15 May 1955 was significant for Austria for three reasons. First, it ended hopes of regaining South Tyrol. Second, conversely, it ended Yugoslav pretensions to southern Carinthia. Third, it provided for limited minority protection.

Article 7 of the Treaty provided for the Slovene and Croatian minorities in Carinthia, Burgenland and Styria elementary instruction in their language and a proportional number of secondary schools. Furthermore, in the administrative and judicial districts of those three Austrian *Länder* where there were Slovene, Croat or mixed populations, Slovene and Croat should be accepted as official languages in addition to German, and official signs should be bilingual.

Nevertheless, this raised a number of questions. Should classification as Slovene or Croatian depend on linguistic or other ethnic criteria, and if the former, should the yardstick be mother tongue, family language or colloquial language? How high should the proportion of Slovenes or Croatians be in a given territorial entity in order for it to be considered a mixed language area? What constituted 'administrative districts' – 'political districts' (as provided by Austria's administrative regulations) or municipal areas?[39]

In the first case almost all Slovenes were bilingual with German, but whereas some spoke traditional Slovene many others spoke the so-called Windisch dialect.[40] This meant that whereas in the 1951 census nearly 20 000 persons declared themselves Slovene, local Slovene organisations estimated the number at over 42 000.[41] In the second case the main settlement area of the Carinthian Slovenes was limited mainly to three valleys in southern Carinthia but in only a few settlements did Slovenes constitute the majority.[42]

In 1959 federal laws provided for education in Slovene in Carinthia and for Slovene to be an official language in mixed population districts of Carinthia. This situation led to considerable dissatisfaction and inter-ethnic tension. Article 7 was meant to provide educational rights for Slovenes in Styria but nothing has been done, and the accusation has been made that the ethnic group has been deliberately suppressed and assimilated.[43] In Burgenland, on the basis of a 1937 law, in most primary schools the Croatian language is taught, and in a few schools teaching is bilingual. But at secondary level it can only be studied as an option or a freely chosen obligatory subject in a few schools.[44]

In Carinthia bilingual education is given only in preparatory schools and the first three years of primary school. Thereafter pupils only receive four hours language instruction per week. At secondary level pupils could register for Slovene language instruction or for Slovene as a freely chosen obligatory subject.[45] Nevertheless, amongst the German population there has been hostility to bilingualism and also to the erection of bilingual place names in areas alleged not to be truly bilingual.[46]

The Council of Europe

The builders of the new Europe were very conscious that in totalitarian countries denial of human rights had not been accidental but deliberate. They were also very conscious that Germany and Italy did not become totalitarian in a day but had been subjected to 'salami' tactics. They therefore wanted a European system to protect society against communism as well as the creation of a society whose conscience would sound the alarm if any nation began to be menaced by the destruction of human rights. They were also aware that the United Nations Universal Declaration on Human Rights was merely a non-binding declaration.

Accordingly, in 1950 the Council adopted the European Convention on Human Rights, binding on its signatories, listing not only certain rights but providing machinery in the shape of a Commission and a

Court of Human Rights, and including a petitions system based on that of the League of Nations, to ensure that an individual's rights could be enforced against his or her government. But again the position of minorities was rather unsatisfactory. If Article 14 of the Convention forbade discrimination on any grounds such as sex, race, colour, language, religion, political or other opinion, national or social origin, association with a national minority, property, birth or other status, there was nothing in the Convention about providing minorities with the means of preserving themselves and developing their culture. In any case it was a weakness of the Convention that it was up to the contracting parties to state whether they accepted the petitions procedure or the jurisdiction of the Court. Some Member States, notably France, consistently refused to accept the former.

Accordingly in 1956 a Swedish deputy in the Council of Europe, Hermos Dickson, proposed that the Legal Committee of the Consultative Assembly of the Council of Europe set up a sub-committee in order to examine national legislation in regard to minorities, examine whether a protocol on minorities could be added to the Human Rights Convention, and present annual reports on the position of minorities in western Europe.[47]

The sub-committee duly met and published a report in October 1957 on the basis of which the Assembly adopted a Resolution which tried to balance the interests of minorities on the one hand with the realisation that minorities were still regarded as potential threats to the integrity of states on the other. The Resolution stated that whereas Article 14 of the European Convention on Human Rights already protected individuals belonging to minorities on the grounds simply of membership of a minority group, it was desirable to ensure satisfaction of the *collective* interests of the minorities 'to the fullest extent compatible with safeguarding the essential interests of the states to which they belong'.[48] But the attitude of the Committee of Ministers was negative, preferring to leave examination of minority matters to the United Nations.[49]

As a result, the Legal Committee of the Consultative Assembly had to get information via the Secretariat and individual members with a view to preparing a Report on the Laws and Regulations in force in Member States and the existing situation of minorities, as well as to state the extent to which progress could be made to ensure satisfaction of the collective interests of minorities.

The report came out in April 1959 under the name of Senator Struye of Belgium. It was disappointing, and for four reasons. First, it dealt only with minorities in Member States which benefited from an inter-national agreement. It thus did not deal with three lots of minorities, namely those in non-Member States, such as the Basques and Catalans in Spain and the Swedes in Finland; those not bound to a kin state because such did not exist, such as the Bretons, Basques, Corsicans and Flemish in France, the Welsh and the Friauls; and those with a 'kin' state but not the object of an international agreement such as the French of Italy's Val d'Aosta. All that were left were the Croatians and Slovenes in Austria, the Danes in West Germany, the Germans in Denmark, and the South Tyrolese in Italy.

Second, it rejected the proposal to set up a permanent sub-commit-tee to report to the Council of Europe on protection of minorities, on the grounds that the situation with regard to minorities in western Europe seemed much more satisfactory than between the wars, and that the idea was too much like the League system which, it was gener-ally felt, had tended to aggravate problems and in any case had not been very convincing.

Third, the Report recommended that if a dispute about treatment of minorities arose the states concerned should apply the procedure laid down in the Council's April 1957 (Strasbourg) Convention on the Peaceful Settlement of Disputes.

Fourth, despite bombs having been thrown in South Tyrol for the past three years, the Report concluded that the situation of the minorities in the report was satisfactory – at least from the legislative point of view.[50]

Unsurprisingly the Consultative Assembly was not satisfied with the Report and adopted a proposal to add a Protocol to the European Convention on Human Rights to guarantee the rights of minori-ties.[51] Accordingly the sub-committee got to work again in great depth. There were two main areas for exploration. The first related to the rights that minorities might reasonably claim, the objective being to secure those that would ensure the preservation and devel-opment of the group's culture. There were five possible fields for study: protection of culture, language, religion, education, and polit-ical rights.

The preservation of a minority's distinctive culture did not, in general, pose any difficulties. The right to publish its own newspapers, to establish cultural, social and sporting associations and to use place names and family names in the form preferred was unquestioned. Nevertheless, one issue was raised – broadcasting. In 1960 this seemed to be a matter for radio only, but a number of questions were there to be asked. Should a minority have its own station? How much air-time should, or could, a minority reasonably have? And at what time or times of day should or could a minority broadcast?

There were no problems about the use of the minority language in private life, but to what extent should it be used in public life? Should the minority language enjoy official status locally? Did the answer to these depend on the size and/or concentration of the group? If relations with the administration in the minority language was acceptable, what about the courts? Should judges and juries be bilingual? Should all codes and documents be in both languages?

Religion and freedom of worship posed no problems, but education raised the question as to if the minority had the right to maintain its own schools, should the state provide education in accordance with the wishes of the minority as regards the curriculum? And to what level? Again, would the answers depend on the size and concentration of the group?

Finally, with regard to political and administrative rights, should there be proportional or automatic representation in the local parliament or national government or the local administration?

Bearing in mind that any provisions in a Protocol to the Human Rights Convention would be of general application to all Member States of the Council of Europe, the sub-committee felt that since matters were so complex an attempt to secure political rights in the Protocol should not be made, but that it would be possible to obtain a general agreement on the other rights.

The second area for exploration was one of definition: who were the proper beneficiaries of these rights – the individual members of the minority or the group as a whole? The Human Rights Convention dealt only with the former, although groups did have procedural rights such as to present petitions.

The sub-committee felt that in a Protocol the beneficiaries of the rights to be granted should be individual persons and not the groups as such; nevertheless these rights should be granted to them in their capacity as members of the minority and not in their individual capacity because it was only in relation to other persons of a like nature that their character as a minority group could be established. The sub-committee therefore proposed the following text:

Persons belonging to a national minority shall not be denied the right, in community with the other members of their group, and as far as compatible with public order, to enjoy their own culture, to use their own language, to establish their own schools and receive teaching in the language of their choice, or to profess and practice their own religion.

This was an improvement on the United Nations definition[52] in that it covered education, omitted from the UN text. Unfortunately it was precisely the issue of education that would lead to the downfall of the draft Protocol.

In 1961 the sub-committee's draft Protocol was approved by the Legal Committee and then by the Consultative Assembly, which formally recommended to the Committee of Ministers that the Protocol be added to the Convention.[53] As it happened, the Consultative Assembly was already involved in the conclusion of a second Protocol to cover five rights not contained in the original Convention and its First Protocol, and the Committee of Ministers instructed the Experts drafting the second Protocol to add to it the text on minorities.

But just at that time a series of applications were being lodged with the European Commission of Human Rights by certain Belgian parents who alleged that the Convention and the First Protocol were being violated precisely because their children were not receiving education in the language of their choice.[54] In view of the reference to education in the Minorities Protocol the Committee of Experts felt it was unwise to start drafting a new article on the issue as long as the matter was *sub judice*, and the Council of Ministers agreed.[55] The Court rendered its verdict in 1968 but by then it was too late to add it to what would become the Convention's Fourth Protocol, and even thereafter there was no immediate progress. Indeed, in 1973 the Committee of Experts concluded that it was not legally necessary for the protection of minorities to be the subject of a special provision in an Additional Protocol to the Convention.[56]

Once again efforts to do something more positive for minorities than Article 14 of the Human Rights Convention at international level had failed. For this there were three reasons. First there was the lack of state support. It was difficult for the Council of Europe to steer between ensuring the unity of its members while promoting policies perceived as encouraging separation or inter-Member State tension. Minorities were still seen as threats to state integrity – and this was not surprising in view of the violence which had surfaced in the late 1950s and the 1960s in South Tyrol, Northern Ireland, Brittany, the Basque country and Cyprus – and the Council, like the UN, was only interested in seeking to protect and provide additional rights for minorities that were loyal.[57] Second, there were the difficulties of getting agreement on minimum standards, whether economic, social, linguistic or political because practice varied so widely from Member State to Member State. Third, the idea of group or collective rights for minorities was still not accepted.

In the absence of action by the Council of Europe the only move in favour of minorities expressed by the international community came from the United Nations where, on 16 December 1966, the General Assembly adopted the International Covenant on Civil and Political Rights. Article 1 stated that 'All peoples have the right of self-determination. By virtue of that right they freely determine their political status and freely pursue their economic, social and cultural development', without defining what was meant by 'peoples'. Article 27, on the other hand, stated that 'In those states in which ethnic, religious or linguistic minorities exist, persons belonging to such minorities shall not be denied the right, in community with other members of their group, to enjoy their own culture, to profess and practise their own religion or to use their own language', an article which begged more questions than it answered.

Collapse

Cyprus

In the 1950s Cyprus was a British Crown Colony with a population of some 577 000 of which some 473 000 or 81.9 per cent were Greek and 104 000 or 18.1 per cent were Turkish.[58] The two communities were scattered evenly throughout the island although only 18 per cent of towns and villages had mixed populations.[59]

The Greek community had never hidden its desire for *enosis*, or union with its Greek motherland. As the pace of decolonisation set in after the Second World War and accelerated after the abortive 1956 Suez crisis the pressures on the colonial administration deepened, including terrorist violence by the Greek-Cypriot organisation EOKA. The Turkish community, on the other hand, aware of the treatment of Turks in mainland Greece rejected outright the prospect of becoming part of the Turkish minority in Greece, declaring that should Britain withdraw from Cyprus the island should be partitioned (*Tacsim*) or revert to its original owner, Turkey. As Greek-Cypriot terrorism intensified, also targeting Turkish Cypriots, the latter formed their own paramilitary organisation *Vulkan* which did not hesitate either to counter-attack EOKA-dominated areas or help the British authorities. Cyprus was important to the British as a media-transmitting listening post or staging post for the armed forces in relation to the political instability of the Middle East.

Once Britain realised that it was not necessary to have the whole of the island for military purposes and was guaranteed two sovereign base areas the way was eased for a new solution. The independence of Cyprus was seen as a compromise between the rival claims of *enosis* and *tacsim*. The settlement, the so-called Zurich Agreements, closely supported by the United States, alarmed at the implications of civil war in a key area of the Cold War, consisted of a Constitution, a Treaty guaranteeing Cypriot independence signed by Britain, Turkey and Greece and giving those countries the right to intervene, even unilaterally, to restore the *status quo* should it be upset, and a Treaty of Alliance between Cyprus, Greece and Turkey.

The Constitution was a bold attempt to try and satisfy majority and minority respectively but it was an utter disaster. It was drawn up by an international constitutional commission rather than a constituent Assembly, and was signed by a representative of the British, Greek and Turkish governments and the Greek Cypriot and the Turkish Cypriot communities. The Greek Cypriots, barely consulted, felt it was an artificial solution designed to serve foreign ends or Great Power politics in the Mediterranean rather than those of the great majority of the Cypriot people. The Republic was thus founded on agreements which did not emanate from the free will of the people but were imposed on them. Archbishop Makarios, the leader of the Greek Cypriots, did not hide the fact that he was more or less forced to sign.[60]

The 1960 Cyprus Constitution is memorable for three important features. The first feature of the Constitution and of the government administration of Cyprus is that it was based on a new concept: the equality of the Greek Cypriot and Turkish Communities in setting up the new Republic. In other words, what was required for the running of the state was joint agreement. Thus there did not exist in Cyprus a majority–minority relationship. The Turkish government and the Turkish Cypriots denied that the Turks were a 'minority' in Cyprus, even though possessing only 18 per cent of the population, but rather that the Turkish Cypriots were 'partners'. And indeed the first two articles of the Constitution referred to the two 'communities' and not to any 'minority'. Second, in the 50-seat unicameral House of Representatives the Turkish community received 30 per cent of the seats – fifteen. The Turkish Cypriots also received 30 per cent of the ten-man Council of Ministers, 30 per cent of the civil service (in principle in all grades) and security forces and 40 per cent of the army. The third feature, again one arising out of the concept of partnership, related to decision-making, particularly the ability to use a veto and to require a simple double majority (i.e., a simple majority in both communities) for certain legislation.

Executive power over all except communal affairs was vested in the President who had to be a Greek Cypriot, the Vice-President who had to be a Turkish Cypriot and the Council of Ministers. Of the ten members of the Council of Ministers not only had three portfolios to go to Turkish Cypriots but one of them should obtain one of the key portfolios of Foreign Affairs, Defence or Finance. Decisions in the Council could be taken by majority vote but the President and the Vice-President could veto any decisions relating to foreign affairs, defence and security. A number of decisions within the authority of the President and the Vice President required the agreement of both, namely, the promulgation of legislation and of decisions of the Council of Ministers; the designation of Ministers, members of the Supreme Constitutional Court and of the High Court, and certain public officials and heads of the armed forces; the introduction of conscription and the decision to increase or reduce the strength of the army.

Elections to the House of Representatives took place on the basis of separate community electoral lists. Any modification of the electoral law or the adoption of any law relating to the municipalities of the five largest towns or any law imposing taxes or custom duties required simple majorities in both communities.

On the other hand, the House of Representatives could never modify the basic articles of the Constitution. These were listed in Article 182 of the Constitution and referred to whole articles or individual paragraphs of articles dealing with the rights of the Turkish community. Nearly 50 articles of the Constitution were involved. Other articles of the Constitution could be modified only following a two-thirds majority in both communities.

In addition to the parliament there were also separately elected Greek and Turkish 'communal chambers' to deal with such matters as religious affairs, education and culture, marriage and divorce and control of co-operative and credit societies. The parliament had to allocate not less than £2 million to these chambers (£1.6 million to the Greeks: £0.4 million to the Turks). The chambers had the right to levy taxes of their own (on their own communities) to supplement this grant.

The five main towns on the island were to have separate Greek and Turkish municipalities with their own elected councils. In each town there was to be a co-ordinating body of two Greeks and two Turks together with a chairman (to be agreed upon) to operate joint municipal services. There was however a provision that this situation should be examined by the President and the Vice-President to see whether the system of separate municipalities should be continued.

In the court system, in cases where Greek Cypriots were involved with Greek Cypriots then the judges had to be Greek Cypriots. In the case of Turkish Cypriots the judges had to be Turkish Cypriots. In cases involving both Greek and Turkish Cypriots there had to be both Greek and Turkish Cypriot judges. Laws and decisions held by the President or the Vice-president to discriminate against either community would be referred to the Supreme Constitutional Court, consisting of three judges, one Greek Cypriot, one Turkish Cypriot and a neutral president. In the High Court of Justice, however, there were four judges, two Greek Cypriots, one Turkish Cypriot, and a neutral president. But the president would have two votes in order to hold the balance.

The independent senior officers of state such as the Attorney General, the Governor of the Bank of Cyprus, the Auditor General and the heads of the army, police and gendarmerie could come from either community, but his deputy had to come from the other community. One of the heads of the army, police or gendarmerie had to be a Turkish Cypriot.

In addition there were provisions for the two communities to enjoy special relations with Greece and Turkey, including the right to receive subsidies for institutions of education, culture, sports and charities, and to employ, if need be, schoolteachers, professors and clergymen provided by the Greek and Turkish governments.

As an attempt to bring together the two communities the Constitution was equally disastrous. Greek Cypriots were outraged that the 18 per cent Turkish Cypriot minority should receive 30 per cent of posts in government and the administration. They alleged that there were not enough trained Turkish Cypriots to fill jobs in the higher grades of the civil service, and implementation of the false proportions was not only discrimination against the Greek Cypriot community but held back individuals from promotion to jobs for which they were qualified. They were outraged that under the double majority system of decision-making in the parliament theoretically eight Turkish Cypriots (out of 15) could veto the wishes of the other 42 members (35 Greek Cypriots and the remaining 7 Turkish Cypriots). And above all they were enraged at the veto. Furthermore the separation of justice was seen as a slur against the impartiality and integrity of judges while the provision for separate municipalities in the five biggest towns was seen as a step towards partition.

Unsurprisingly the Greek Cypriot community rejected this Constitution and the resulting outcry only deepened Turkish Cypriot mistrust. Matters came to a head when the time came to renew the laws on customs duties and taxes which were in force before the Constitution came into effect. Failure to renew the laws led to their expiry. The Government consequently had no authority to collect customs duties and income taxes, and the result was paralysis. Finally, towards the end of 1963 Archbishop Makarios proposed amending the Constitution to provide, amongst other things, for an end to the Presidential and Vice-Presidential veto, that simple majorities in parliament should replace the double majority system, that the administration of justice be unified, that ethnic proportions of 80:20 be introduced in the government, civil service and armed forces and that the big five towns should be unified municipalities.

For the Turkish Cypriots this was seen as an attempt to create a unitary sovereign state with all powers emanating from a majority that would be entitled to decide the future on a basis of a self-determination that would led directly to *enosis*. The proposals were rejected.

Both sides had been arming for months and following the Turkish Cypriot rejection of the Makarios proposals, in which they were supported by the Turkish government in Ankara, bitter and bloody communal war broke out.[61] Over a hundred Turkish Cypriot villages were destroyed, hundreds of Turkish Cypriots were killed and 25 000 became refugees, forced to flee into safe enclaves – the Turkish quarters of the big towns.[62]

With the outbreak of hostilities co-operation between the two communities came to an end. Henceforward the two communities would lead separate lives, with the Greek Cypriot 'government' responsible for the Greek community and seeing Turkish Cypriots as rebels. Turkish Cypriots set up their own administration. But there was also the considerable danger that in the ongoing inter-communal fighting advantage to one side would lead to intervention by the kin state of the other. In 1964 a United Nations force landed in Cyprus to try to keep the warring factions apart, and by 1967 an uneasy peace had settled in. The following year talks began on a more equitable constitution but although continuing off and on for a number of years they always foundered on the Greek Cypriot insistence on a unitary state and Turkish Cypriot insistence on some form of confederation.

The 1960s also saw rising dissatisfaction leading to violence among the minorities of western Europe's most centralist states – France, Spain and Britain. In all three countries minorities drew their inspiration from the decolonisation of empire, particularly in Africa.

France

In 1951 the *Loi Deixonne* proposed to promote local languages in the regions where they were in use, but the only languages referred to were Breton, Basque, Catalan and Occitan. Corsican and Alsatian were not included on the grounds that they were assimilated to 'foreign languages' – Italian and German. Indeed, it would not be until 1974 that Corsican was added. The *Loi* provided for optional classes in the language of one hour per week and for it to be an option for the *baccalauréat*.

However, the *Loi* was purely theoretical in that it only said that these languages could be taught but it did not stipulate how they should be taught. It was also 'paralysed from the beginning by the civil service and was not put into practice until nineteen years later'.[63]

(a) Brittany

In 1952 the organisation *Emgleo Breiz* (*Entente de Bretagne*) was founded, assembling under its wing most of the cultural associations engaged in the campaign for the defence and promotion of the Breton language and culture. It became a founder member of the organisation *Défense et Promotion des Langues de France*. In 1958 it was joined by *Kuzul ar Brezhoneg* (Council of the Breton Language), uniting a number of associations dealing with literature, language, education and religion and working towards obtaining recognition of Breton cultural rights.[64]

In 1957 the first Breton political party, *Mouvement pour l'Organisation de la Bretagne,* was founded, with a programme of a regional assembly, autonomous finances and for the Breton nation to be redefined within a federal European framework.[65] However, by 1966 and for the next four years, the clandestine organisation FLB – *Front de Libération de la Bretagne* – linked to the *Comité de la Bretagne Libre*, run from Ireland, began violent attacks on government buildings, electrical installations and police stations.[66] These Breton militants refused to accept that Paris should decide everything regarding Breton language, schools, culture, the media and even names.[67] They rejected the interpretation given in France to the 'non-discrimination' content in declarations on international organisations to safeguard the rights of minorities as *'tout le monde dans le même sac'* (everyone in the same bag).[68]

(b)　Corsica

In Corsica, on the other hand, matters took a different turn. Dissatisfaction with the French state originally concerned the economy; only later did cultural values come into play.

During the 1960s living standards throughout Europe, including France, had been rising, but this was not matched in Corsica. Employment opportunities on the island were few and, as indeed had been the case since the beginning of the century, emigration was extremely high. Corsicans had often taken jobs in the colonial service but those prospects were drying up; worse, with the end of the war in Algeria many French settlers (the so-called *pieds noirs*) were returning to France – and Corsica – where they received generous repatriation grants enabling them to buy land and businesses. Tourism had also been developing but Corsicans noticed that the capital and management came from the mainland – there were few jobs for Corsicans and those of only a menial character.[69] There was growing concern that because of Corsican emigration and French and *pieds noirs* immigration native Corsicans would soon be a minority in their homeland.

The response by a number of organisations concerned with the economy and culture was to argue that the island's special problems called for it to receive special and separate measures within an administrative autonomy, and therefore it needed to separate from the region Provence-Côte d'Azur with which it had been integrated in 1960.[70] On the other hand, organisations like, first, *L'Union Corse l'Avenir* and then *L'Action Régionaliste Corse* (ARC), played up the cultural line, pushing for Corsicans to benefit from the *Loi Deixonne*, and presenting the problem as one of a cultural minority oppressed by an 'obtuse centralism' that was oblivious to facts which were geographical, cultural and ethnic. The ARC's constitution aimed at promoting the economic and cultural development of Corsica within an autonomous region but within the French republic.[71]

But from 1968 onward the ARC began to engage in direct action, organising tax boycotts and protests against individual government policies. Bombs began to be thrown, and the level of violence and public disorder to increase. By 1970 the situation had begun to slip away from the authorities who had been too slow to act and would henceforward be constantly reacting to pressure by anti-government forces.[72]

Spain

By 1950 it was realised that the severe educational and cultural restrictions on Basque, Catalan and Gallego aimed at preventing new generations from learning those languages would not succeed. On the other hand the Franco regime, having survived the odium of having been seen as an ally of Fascism and Nazism in the Second World War, had recovered its confidence and felt more secure, especially when it was welcomed by the Western Powers as an ally against communism.

The result was that some small concessions to local cultures were made, but there was no official encouragement. There were no daily papers in the language. Immigration from the rest of Spain into the Basque country and Catalonia continued since these areas were the rich industrial ones in the state but the state's hope of engendering assimilation was not a secret. By the second half of the 1960s 50 per cent of the Basque working class and 38 per cent of the population had been born elsewhere, and the figures were higher for Catalonia.[73] In 1950 in the Basque country a network of special part-time schools – *Ikastolas* – was set up to propagate the Basque language and culture, but if tolerated were seen as potentially subversive with the names of all pupils, staff and financial backers being demanded by the police.[74] By 1970 a survey showed that 90 per cent of Catalonia's population understood Catalan, 77 per cent spoke it, 62 per cent read it but only 38 per cent wrote it; the comparable figures for Basque were 50 per cent, 46 per cent, 25 per cent and 11 per cent.[75]

With regard to the administration of the minority homelands, over-whelmingly officials were appointed from elsewhere. There was a heavy presence of troops and state police forces, and the latter were 'also aided by an absence of effective constraints upon their behaviour, including high incidences of arbitrary arrests, detentions and brutality towards prisoners.'[76] Political offences were handled by special courts, or military tribunals.

To the Basques their language was their badge of distinctiveness, the only thing unifying them across France and Spain, and therefore had to be maintained against the attacks of the Franco regime.[77]

In 1959 Basque youths reacted against the passivity of their parents and the PNV by forming ETA (*Euskadi ta askatasuna* or the Basque Country and Freedom), which evolved into a ferocious terrorist organisation with separatist irredentist and revolutionary socialist ends.[78] Bank robberies, attacks on the security forces and a policy of assassination led to widespread repression and declaration of a state of emergency.

No similar terrorism developed in Catalonia. A small urban guerrilla movement appeared but it was soon snuffed out. It seemed that Catalonian society was more resilient, less concerned with identity, hardly concerned with separatism. Repression was less severe than in the Basque Country but if no political concessions were made to Catalonian regionalism, gradually pressure on Catalonian culture began to ease.

Britain

On mainland Britain in the 1950s and 1960s little was heard of Scottish or Welsh nationalism. True, there were incidents to remind one that these sentiments still existed. In Scotland letter boxes with the cipher of Elizabeth II (the Queen was of course Elizabeth I of Scotland) were occasionally blown up; in Wales one saw a beginning of the phenomenon of burning the holiday or second homes of English 'incomers'. But all this was put down to the actions of a few fanatics. It was on the other side of the Irish Sea, in Northern Ireland, that things would become very serious.

(a) Northern Ireland

In 1962 a six-year campaign by the IRA had petered out, its leaders complaining of lack of support by the Irish-Catholic-Nationalist minority, although another not unimportant factor was the willingness of the Northern and Southern governments to intern potential trouble-makers without trial. Altogether some 19 persons were killed during the campaign.[79]

Matters looked as if they were about to improve as the Northern Prime Minister Terence O'Neill sought to introduce political and social reforms for Catholics, the Southern Prime Minister paid an official visit to the North, and the Nationalist party in the North agreed to abandon abstentionism and become the official opposition to the Unionist Party. But the situation flattered to deceive.

1966 was the fiftieth anniversary of the Easter Rising. This aroused a debate which contrasted the ideals of 1916 with the reality of partition and the social programme of the Rising with existing conditions in both parts of the island. The parades and demonstrations North and South signified to Unionists, however, that Irish unification was still on the agenda.[80]

But the later 1960s also saw all over Europe the sands of time running out for all those in their fifties and sixties whose mentality was marked by the experience of the Depression, the Second World War and the Cold War. In the United States the Civil Rights movement was gathering pace. In western Europe silence was being broken over the past. The authority of parents, teachers and politicians was increasingly questioned, particularly in relation to their past roles and responsibilities. This was accompanied by strident calls to change deep-set and hitherto unquestioned policies. A key year in Europe was 1968. It saw challenges by students and workers to the France of General de Gaulle, and to communism in Czechoslovakia.

It also saw a rush of organisations dedicated to changing society by force spring up or obtain a new lease of life – ideological terrorists such as the Baader-Meinhof and Red Army Faction groups in Germany and the Red Brigades in Italy and ethnic-related terrorist groups in the Basque Country, South Tyrol and Corsica. What helped make these pressures irresistible in Northern Ireland was that because of educational reforms, the Roman Catholic community was better educated than ever before, more aware, ambitious and articulate and therefore impatient for reform. Even more crucial, the way forward was seen to lie in political action rather than the negative abstentionism of the previous 45 years. Four areas where reform was seen as needed were housing, access to employment, public representation and special powers.

Housing was still controlled by local government and allocated on the basis of allegiance rather than need.

In public employment the situation was diverse. If there was little discrimination (if any) in the Northern Ireland Civil Service, Catholics were still drastically unrepresented in jobs in Unionist-controlled local councils, the judiciary and public corporations. As for the private sector, high Roman Catholic unemployment was seen as being due to Protestant owners of firms giving preference to members of their own community on the one hand, and a deliberate government policy of fostering economic development east of the river Bann whereas much of the Roman Catholic community lived in peripheral areas in the west of the province.

As for the vote, apart from the issue of gerrymandering which produced Unionist control in areas with Nationalist majorities, the issue was the ratepayers' franchise, abolished in the rest of the United Kingdom in 1948. In local government elections the vote was given to either occupiers of rateable property and their spouses to a maximum of two residents to a house – or to voters on a business property qualification. Subtenants, lodgers and servants had no vote. Thus if 941 785 persons in 1968 could vote in Stormont elections only 694 483 had local government votes. This was seen to work against the Roman Catholic population because it was economically inferior and therefore the ratepaying vote would be smaller.

The Special Powers Act, which dated from 1922, gave the Minister of Home Affairs the right to take any steps to preserve law and order, including searches without warrant, arrest on suspicion and internment without trial, and was seen as being used permanently and exclusively against anti-partitionists and not against loyalist militants.

In 1967 the Northern Ireland Civil Rights association was formed and began calling for 'One Man, One Vote'. The following year it focused on housing allocations. Protest marches began to be a feature of Northern Ireland and clashes with the police began to be seen on television screens throughout the British Isles. O'Neill proposed one man, one vote, in council elections, a points system for the allocation of housing and an Ombudsman, and an end to the Special Powers Act. But the time-scale for introducing the reforms was too long and soon the Civil Rights movement was infiltrated by the IRA, and its members were less reluctant to adopt confrontational tactics. In the blunt words of two of the founders of the Civil Rights movement 'The Republicans and Marxists took over. They spoiled everything.'

Unsurprisingly many Unionists saw these developments as attempts to get reforms by direct action rather than parliamentary means, and saw the IRA and thus Irish unification returning on the back of the movement. Civil Rights marches began therefore to be attacked by militant loyalists.

Moderates in the Unionist Party prepared to give concessions to the minority were condemned as gullible and in April 1969 O'Neill felt he could no longer carry his party and resigned. Rioting in Catholic areas of Belfast and Londonderry provoked punitive raids by loyalists, seeing a conspiracy to defy and destroy the Northern Ireland state. The RUC felt unable to hold the line so the British government sent in troops to separate the rival communities and in addition many Catholic areas barricaded themselves off as 'no-go' areas to representatives of the civil power.

From then on it was downhill all the way and the next years were among the grimmest in Northern Ireland's modern history. Behind the 'no-go' areas the IRA regrouped. Sectarian assassination exploded followed by intimidation on both sides which led to flights of more than 21 500 families from housing estates where their religious persuasion or political creed was in the minority to more congenial surroundings so that in the largest towns the trend to sectarian ghettos was reinforced. Hotels, telephone exchanges, power-stations, pubs, and post offices were bombed and buses hijacked and burned.

The British government reacted by abolishing the B-Specials and interning suspects but the loss of intelligence with the abolition of the former led to many persons on out-of-date lists being arrested and leaving unknown young activists to carry on their work. The results were a civil disobedience campaign and a massive upsurge in support for the IRA. Crucially, this time there was no corresponding internment in the South as in 1956–62.

The breakdown in law and order was paralleled by the disintegration of political groupings. After a series of splits and mergers the Unionist community would eventually be represented by two main parties, the Ulster Unionist party (UUP) and the much harder line Democratic Unionist Party (DUP) led by the Rev. Ian Paisley. The Nationalist Party collapsed and its support went to the Social Democratic and Labour party (SDLP) led by John Hume. It stood for civil rights and Irish unity by consent. Sinn Fein split. In 1970 the Party agreed to abandon non-recognition of the Dublin and Belfast parliaments. Those against this left and formed Provisional Sinn Fein (PSF) calling for immediate British withdrawal from the North and seeing violence as the only way to achieve that end. The IRA also split. Militant members, disgusted with the alleged pusillanimity of the organisation in defending nationalist areas in the North broke away to form the Provisional IRA (PIRA), dedicated to liberating the North by violence. Given their similarity in views it is no surprise that PSF acts as the political wing of the PIRA. For Unionists, however, membership is more or less coterminous.

In the South a Fianna Fail government with a number of hard-line nationalists in the cabinet was concerned that a heavily Marxist IRA might take advantage of the crisis in the North to destabilise also the South. The hard-liners therefore supported the Provisionals in the split and arranged for funds and arms to be delivered. This convinced the PIRA that the Irish government was on their side.

But perhaps the most destabilising factor of all was that in the early 1970s Conservative party policy joined that of the Labour party. Abandoning the position that Northern Ireland would forever be part of Britain, it turned to a belief in Irish unity by consent. This would lead directly to thirty years appeasement of Irish nationalism and Irish terrorism and a demoralisation of the Unionist community, made worse by its demonisation in the British press. But by placing the territorial destiny of the province in doubt the British government merely showed it had learned nothing from events in South Tyrol and Cyprus and thus ensured a deepening of the inter-community bitterness and mistrust.

In March 1972 the British government made it clear that it no longer believed the Northern Ireland government could control the situation. Stormont, with its built-in Unionist majority was suspended, and Direct Rule imposed from London. Nationalists rejoiced at this fall of a second pillar of the Unionist Ascendancy, the first being the B-Specials.[81]

5
Renaissance in the West, 1972–99

Introduction

The 1970s would see extraordinary and positive changes come for most of western Europe's regional and cultural minorities. For this there were three reasons. First, there was the process of European integration. Starting with six countries – Belgium, France, Germany, Italy, Luxembourg and the Netherlands – in 1951, the European Union today consists of 15 countries with the accessions of Britain, Denmark and Ireland in 1973, Greece in 1979, Spain and Portugal in 1986 and Austria, Finland and Sweden in 1995.

One feature of that process was the recognition of frontiers. In western Europe in 1970 only two frontiers were contested, those between Northern Ireland and the Irish Republic, and Spain and Gibraltar. Since then, with the Belfast (so-called 'Good Friday') Agreement of 10 April 1998 the first case was, in principle, solved. Removal of threats, however vague, to the integrity of host states has made it much easier for them to be generous towards their minorities. A second feature of that process was the adherence of all western European states concerned to the vast corpus of human, political, cultural and welfare rights and standards postulated by Council of Europe Conventions and European Union Regulations, Directives and Treaties. These have helped minorities to be integrated economically and socially into the lives of their host states yet enabled them to keep their cultures alive. Removal of at least direct threats to their culture has made it much easier for them to accept their place in their host states.

Second, was a significant development in the doctrine of self-determination, a change associated with the name of Professor Theodore Veiter of the University of Feldkirch. For Veiter the problem

135

was how to get round the hostility to the idea of self-determination, seen simply as a recipe for a minority to separate from its host state. The issue had become acute in the South Tyrol question. How was it possible to reconcile the statement in the Statutes of the SVP that the right to self-determination contained in the United Nations Charter remained inalienable with the continuation that the Party saw the 1946 Paris Agreement as the basis for the natural development of the *Tyrolese* minority within the Italian state?[1] He believed that a distinction should be drawn between internal and external self-determination. Thus if minorities could not have external self-determination, the right to separate, they should be compensated by internal self-determination, the right to decide upon all statutory measures necessary for the maintenance and development of their cultural characteristics, and to enjoy that degree of legislative and administrative autonomy required. External self-determination should only be sought as a last resort if the host state refused to grant such legitimate demands.[2] The great advantage of Veiter's interpretation was that it created a framework in which minorities could present legitimate demands and negotiate with the host government without separation being seen by the latter as the final goal.[3]

Third, there was the rise of regionalism. Its aim was to reverse the situation in so many countries where regions were the objects of planning by faceless bureaucrats in distant capitals and to bring about regional democracy under which regions administered themselves and took basic political decisions through regional legislatures with regional legislative, executive and financial powers. It found its greatest expression in the 1978 Bordeaux Declaration of the Conference of the Local and Regional Authorities of the Council of Europe, a document describing European regionalism in the most lyrical terms ever drafted by any international organisation:

1. ... the Region is a fundamental element of a country's wealth. It testifies to its cultural diversity. It stimulates economic development. When based on universal suffrage regional institutions guarantee the necessary decentralisation. They ensure the solidarity and the co-ordination of its local communities.
2. As heirs to the history of Europe and the richness of its culture, the regions of Europe are an irreplaceable and incomparable asset of European civilisation. They are both the symbol and the guarantors of that diversity which is the pride of the European heritage in the

eyes of humanity and to which every European both bears witness and contributes.

3. Every European's right to 'his region' is part of his right to be different. To challenge this right would be to challenge the identity of European man and ultimately of Europe itself.

4. ... Far from weakening the state autonomous regional political institutions reduce the burden upon it, and enable it to concentrate more effectively on its true responsibilities. As a result of decentralisation, the administration becomes more human and personal and lends itself better to control by the citizens and their elected representatives.

5. A state which was not able to recognise the diversity of the regions of which it is made up would be incapable of a genuinely positive approach to the diversity of the European Community.

For all these reasons the Bordeaux Conference called for the recognition and promotion of regional cultures, including minority languages, as essential for the construction of a Europe that respected cultural and linguistic diversity, and for regions to be culturally autonomous with legislative, administrative and financial powers with regard to teaching, education, leisure and sport, control of theatres and museums, and the right to conclude contracts with other European regions. Above all, there needed to be developed a regional press, radio and television, sufficiently autonomous and equipped to help the cultural promotion of the region.[4] And clustered around the Council of Europe, with consultative status, were a number of non-governmental organisations subscribing to the values of the Bordeaux Declaration, notably the Assembly of the Regions movement, based in Strasbourg, the Federal Union of European Peoples (FUEV) with its seat in Flensburg, and the International Institute for Nationality Rights and Regionalism (INTEREG) in Munich. These NGOs built up networks of regional and national representatives, civil servants, academics, holding conferences and stimulating the production of draft international instruments.

But even before the Bordeaux Declaration's call for regional co-operation some regions had seized the initiative. In 1972 the organisation *Arge-Alp (Arbeitsgemeinschaft Alp)* had been created by seven regions from four countries: Bavaria (West Germany); North Tyrol, Vorarlberg (Austria); South Tyrol, Trento, Lombardy (Italy); Grisons/Graubunden (Switzerland). And in 1978 was founded *Arge Alp Adria* consisting of seven regions from three states: Upper Austria, Styria, Carinthia

(Austria); Friuli-Venezia-Giulia (Italy); and Slovenia and Croatia (Yugoslavia).

The aim was co-operation on common problems, particularly transport and communications, the environment, agriculture and tourism in mountain areas. Significantly, those regions, provinces, and cantons came from federal/regional states and thus enjoyed legislative, administrative and financial powers enabling them to carry out decisions. Nor did they all come from countries of the European Union.

These *Arges* had no independent bureaucracy. The annual conferences of heads of their governments set policy priorities, but decisions had to be ratified by the respective legislatures.[5]

The movement seemed irresistible. In May 1980, succumbing to the argument that in many border areas not all problems could – or indeed, should – be solved by interstate foreign policy and that there was a need for a lower level decision-making capacity by local politicians and civil servants, the Council of Europe adopted the Madrid Framework Convention on Transfrontier Co-operation between territorial Communities or Authorities,[6] in which the participating states agreed to allow local and regional authorities to make agreements with their neighbouring foreign opposite numbers in those areas of competence laid down by domestic laws.

In 1983 *Arge Pyrénées* was set up between the French regions of Aquitaine, Languedoc-Roussillon, Midi-Pyrénées, the Spanish regions of Aragon, the Basque Provinces, Catalonia, Navarre, and the Principality of Andorra. In 1986 the two Hungarian districts of Gyor-Sopron and Vas acceded to *Arge Alp Adria*. By 1990 Arge Alp had expanded to eleven regions with the addition of Baden-Württemburg (West Germany), Salzburg (Austria), and St Gallen and Ticino (Switzerland), giving it a population of over forty million. And added to the list of common problems to be tackled by the *Arges* were flood prevention, cartography, waste disposal, and cross-border national parks.

The aim of the regions in the Arges in the European Union is the creation of the so-called Europe of the Regions. They seek representation of the individual regions in a second chamber of the European Parliament along the lines of the representation of the German *Länder* in the *Bundesrat* (Upper House). In the meantime they seek rectification of regional economic imbalances, cultural diversity within European unity, and for regions to be equal partners with states and the institutions of the European Union in both national and European-level regional planning.

Taking the lead in this drive for a 'Europe of the Regions' as opposed to a 'Europe of the States' were three types of region. First, there were those regions that were already regions in federations or regional type states and which already enjoyed degrees of legislative, administrative and financial power. Often they had been independent states in the past and could look to historic roots. Second, there were those regions actually or potentially economically powerful in their own right which resented having their wealth creamed off to help poorer, less competent or more spendthrift regions, or because they felt they could manage their economy or get or develop resources better on their own than from the state.

And third there were those regions with considerable indigenous or minority cultures which saw regionalism as a better means of controlling their destiny through closer popular participation in decision-making.

Since 1970 a number of these regions have made spectacular progress in their relationship with their states, bringing about enormous improvement in the fortunes of Europe's regional and cultural minorities. And some minorities would seek to go further, using the device of cross-border arrangements to try and bring about *de facto* if not *de jure* unification with their kin on the other side of the border. In a number of other regions there would be progress as well, even if not so spectacular. Again, it was Italy and South Tyrol that led the way.

Developments in states

Italy

(a) South Tyrol

The tripartite agreement on an improved Autonomy Statute for South Tyrol reached between the Austrian and Italian governments and the SVP was in three parts: 137 measures for the improved autonomy, a time-table for their implementation, and, after that implementation the requirement that Austria declare the dispute over the Paris Agreement to be over.

The principal features of the improved autonomy,[7] which came into force in 1972 through amendment of the 1948 Statute, and which provided the South Tyrolese with much, if not all, of their demands, were as follows.

First, that if the Region Trentino-Alto Adige was not abolished, as the South Tyrolese wanted, the Province of Bolzano would have transferred to its jurisdiction not only a large number of sectors hitherto controlled by the region and the Italian state, including agriculture and tourism, but the administrative powers to go with them. However the sector of industrial development remained with the region, the fear still lingering that if it fell into South Tyrolese control it would be run down and Italians would be obliged to leave the area thus imperilling its *italianatà*.

Second, the principle of ethnic proportions which had hitherto applied only to employment in offices of the provincial administration was extended to apply to all state bodies operating in the province, with the exception of the Ministry of Defence and the various police forces. Furthermore, competence in both German and Italian would henceforth be required, through examination, for entry, promotion or transfer, at every grade from chauffeur or caretaker through to director, the severity of the examination depending on the level of employment.

Third, in regard to finance, the province would receive nine-tenths of the taxes raised there as well as a proportionate share of the state health budget and state grants earmarked for the special development programme of the regions.[8] Until the mid-1980s Article 78 of the revised Statute had been interpreted to mean that the province should automatically receive 1.6 per cent of *any* state expenditure in all the important and relevant sectors of the economy and social welfare, the percentage of 1.6 being reached by adding the percentage of the provincial population to the national population (0.76) to that of the provincial territory to that of the national territory (2.46) and dividing it by two.[9]

Fourth, the Province could now contest state laws directly before the Constitutional Court without having to go through the region.

Fifth, in regard to decision-making, it was spelt out that if a provincial bill was held to violate the equality of rights of one language group, a majority of the deputies of that language group could call for a vote by language groups. If the bill was passed despite the adverse vote of two-thirds of the deputies of the language group that called for the vote, that group could contest the law before the Constitutional Court. While the appeal was in progress, however, the law adopted remained in force.

Sixth, South Tyrol was given its proper German name of *Südtirol* in place of that given originally by the Italians of *Tiroler Etschland*.

In South Tyrol the question of ethnic identity was very important. It governed the school to which a child should go, access to employment in the public administrations at all levels, the allocation of public housing and even the candidature of those standing for election.

Everyone in the province was now required to make an official declaration at the time of the national census as to his or her ethnic group, with parents making the declaration on behalf of their children and these declarations, following the precedent of Upper Silesia between the wars, could not be verified or disputed by the authorities.[10]

In fact, apart from failing to achieve the dissolution of the region the only other major concession sought by the South Tyrolese which they failed to get was to end the practice by which approval from Rome in the shape of Executive Measures had to be given to provincial legislation before it could take effect.

However it was not until 1992 that implementation of the new measures had been carried out to the satisfaction of the South Tyrolese. On 11 June of that year – nearly 46 years after the Paris Agreement – the Austrian government, having received a resolution to that effect from the SVP adopted by 82.8 per cent in a Congress Extraordinary, declared that the dispute over implementation of the De Gasperi-Gruber Agreement was over.

The high vote of approval by the SVP was in stark contrast to the slender majority that had accepted the Package Deal. The reason was that since 1969 political and economic relations in the province had been transformed, particularly to the advantage of the South Tyrolese. The South Tyrolese were enabled to begin the process of being represented throughout the administration of their homeland at all levels, crucial not only in terms of jobs and pensions but of morale. Administration expanded rapidly as the Provincial Assembly not only took over sectors and powers from the region but received considerable financial support to implement policy.

There was a tremendous economic boom. Money flowed into the province from advanced all-the-year-round tourism, sectoral government expenditure, as well as sums received from the European Community's Common Agricultural Policy, particularly from price support and farm modernisation measures applying in hill and mountain areas.

However, this situation, so agreeable for the South Tyrolese minority, brought with it unexpected problems, which raised a number of questions regarding the viability of measures such as ethnic proportions in public employment and power-sharing. The first was the decline of the Italian group in terms of numbers and morale. The economic boom had benefited the South Tyrolese-dominated countryside to a much greater extent than the Italian-dominated industrial sector, marked by unemployment, inflation, stagnation and bankruptcy following the catastrophic rises in the price of oil throughout the 1970s. Public administration was also affected. In order to reach true ethnic proportions by the year 2002, as required by the 1972 Autonomy Statute,[11] the number of Italians in state and semi-state bodies would have to be reduced over the years by 2 700.

An indication of the seriousness of this situation in regard to employment in the Italian community was that Italians began to declare themselves or their children as Germans (i.e. South Tyrolese), thus raising the spectre of South Tyrolese assimilation of Italians rather than what the Autonomy Statute had been originally designed to prevent, namely Italian assimilation of South Tyrolese.[12] But this also alarmed the South Tyrolese, who saw pedagogical problems arising for Italian-speaking children with little or no German sent to German-speaking schools.

Whether it was because of such declarations, or that the economic situation had led to Italians leaving the province, it was of considerable concern to Italian nationalists that the Italian presence in South Tyrol declined from 33.3 per cent according to the 1971 census to 27.65 according to that of 1991.[13] The result was a rise in support in South Tyrol of the Italian neo-fascist MSI (later *Destra Nazionale*) with a programme of abolition of the Autonomy Statute. But the rise of the MSI brought with it another threat. Should it become the sole or major representative of the Italian community in the Provincial Assembly, how would it be possible to continue one of the pillars of the system of political accommodation in the province, namely institutionalised power-sharing, if on the one hand there were no Italian deputies willing to share power with South Tyrolese deputies, and on the other, if there was no agreement between the communities about the framework within which power was to be shared?

A second serious problem related to those who either would not or could not give the declaration as to their ethnic group. There were those, such as children of mixed marriages, who might genuinely be unable to decide to which group they belonged. Others, alarmed at the potential loss of rights that might occur following failure to give the declaration, argued that it was unconstitutional to have to make such a declaration since Article 3 of the Italian constitution provided for equality of rights for all citizens without distinction as to sex, race, language, religion or political belief.

In the end the South Tyrolese proposal that all inhabitants of South Tyrol should be able to give a true declaration as to their linguistic membership (i.e. German, Italian, Ladin or other), but that means for the three recognised linguistic groups to maintain their claim for protective and preferential measures should continue in force, in particular that the Declaration should take two forms, one for statistical purposes and the other for maintenance of the system of ethnic proportions, was accepted.[14]

A third problem concerned the unexpected failure of sufficient numbers of South Tyrolese to apply for posts in state and semi-state bodies and get them. Such factors as the language examination, housing shortages in Bolzano, competition from the expanding provincial administration and the tourist boom played their part. The result was a crisis in some organisations, particularly the railways and the postal services. According to the Executive Measures implementing the Package, the service concerned could take on staff from elsewhere in Italy on temporary contracts but only for a twelve-month period, non-renewable. Even this had not sufficed, and Italian politicians and trade unions protested that it was absurd for job vacancies to remain unfulfilled in the province in large numbers while unemployment was high elsewhere in Italy.[15]

With the Austrian Declaration on fulfilment of the De Gaspari-Gruber Agreement the South Tyrolese minority had won a famous victory over their host state. What now? South Tyrolese ambitions about unification with their North Tyrolese kin were not long in being revealed. On 20 October 1994 there was held in Bozen/Bolzano a joint sitting of the North and South Tyrolese parliaments. The aim was to give expression to the latest SVP initiative – the creation of an Autonomous European Region Tyrol (AERT), to include North and South Tyrol, Trento and, if it so wished, Vorarlberg.

Four considerations lay behind this initiative. First there were the developments in western Europe – the creation of the *Arges*, the adoption of the Madrid Convention, and Austrian membership of the European Union. Within the framework of the Madrid Convention, Italy and Austria had already signed a cross-border agreement in January 1993 applying, in Italy to the regions, and provinces and municipalities of Trentino-South Tyrol, Venice and Friuli Venezia-Giulia, and enabling the authorities concerned to sign agreements, within the framework of the powers they enjoyed in domestic law, in regard to fourteen matters, including transport and communications, energy, environmental protection, cross-border nature parks, health, culture and sport, tourism, cross-border commuters, handicrafts and vocational training, trade promotion, agricultural improvements, economic and technological research, with the possibility of extending the list.[16] This agreement had also been ratified by the Italian parliament in October 1994.

Second, there had been startling developments in Italy itself. Disgust at the widespread corruption, involving almost all the national political parties, that linked virtually all activity, business or administration, to party connections and party deals, had led to electoral reform which in turn had caused the collapse of the old parties and their replacement by new groupings. Prominent among these was the Lombard (later Northern) League, with a programme of European federalism on the basis of the regions rather than the states, and transformation of Italy into a federal state based on three units, North, Centre and South, with the islands of Sicily and Sardinia grouped with the last.

Third was the question of population size. South Tyrol by itself with a population of 440 000 was far too small. But with North Tyrol (630 000) and Trento (450 000), the AERT would have a total population of 1.52 million. Admittedly this was still small compared to other potential Euro-regions, but a second consideration was its physical size linked to its economic functions. Using the same arguments as those advocated at Versailles in 1919, the proponents of the AERT pointed out that the region was an extensive and coherent transit area, linking two powerful economic zones, the Lombardy plains of northern Italy and the Danubian basin of southern Germany. It also provided an area of rest and recreation for those working in those zones, and indeed for Europe as a whole.

Fourth, it was essential to include Trento in the AERT. On the one hand, the existing Trentino-Südtirol region was no longer a threat; it had been emasculated by the Package Deal. Equally, in Trento, long were gone the days when the Trentini saw themselves as watchdogs over the South Tyrolese and had done much to ensure the 1948 Autonomy Statute was applied restrictively. On the other hand, Trento had a common history, unbroken at least with South Tyrol, for very many centuries and with North Tyrol for not much less. The inclusion of Trento was necessary in order to reassure Italians who might have felt abandoned as a small minority of barely 10 per cent in a purely Tyrolese region. As it was the AERT would be 61 per cent German, 37 per cent Italian and 2 per cent Ladin. And there was also the point that if the Trentini did not go in with the Tyrolese then they could be swallowed up by a large Veneto region in which they and their historical traditions and identity would be swamped. In any case the idea of the AERT was generally supported by Italian political parties and politicians in Trento with the obvious exception of the National Alliance (the successor to the MSI) and the Greens.

For the South Tyrolese all these events meant that the power structures of Versailles and Yalta had been broken. What was wanted now was a real autonomy, with full financial sovereignty on the model of the Swiss cantons, an end to the need for approval by Rome of legislation, and transfer of almost all powers to the regions, leaving Italy (and eventually all other nation-states) only with those relating to defence, foreign policy, justice and monetary policy. In the meantime in the AERT itself German and Italian would be official languages in all institutions and offices (Ladin in the Ladin-speaking valleys of Trento and South Tyrol). Ethnic proportions in public employment would continue to apply in South Tyrol and be extended to all regional offices in the other provinces, and the AERT would have its own police force.

The main hurdle, quite apart from Austrian and Italian approval for this development, was to ensure that the individual Austrian and Italian provinces possessed the same legislative and administrative powers and institutional and social organisation. At the moment the powers relating to some sectors lay with the regions or provinces in one state but with the central government in the other, while in some cases powers were divided between the state and the region.[17]

As it happened these ambitions were soon slapped down. Far-reaching proposals to have the three provinces transfer their powers to the AERT when it came into being were vetoed by both Vienna and Rome. The former argued that it would be unconstitutional for North Tyrol to cede its powers to an international authority; the latter rejected the scheme on the grounds that the perceived loss of national territory acquired by so much blood in 1918 would incite a nationalist backlash in Italy. But there were also Italian misgivings within the putative AERT itself. Some Tyrolese circles had been proposing that decisions in the AERT should be made by majority whether in one overall parliament or three. This was unacceptable to the Trentini.[18]

In the meantime in the rest of Italy the situation for cultural and linguistic minorities was improving. In November 1991 the Italian government adopted legislation enabling regions to protect the language and culture of all linguistic minorities where they composed at least 15 per cent of the regional population. According to the legislation children of the minority in question could use their language in playschools and be taught their language in primary schools; in secondary schools teaching of the language would be optional. In primary and secondary schools history, geography, art and music had to take account of local cultural traditions. The minority language could be used in meetings of designated municipal councils and school governing bodies. Place names could be bilingualised. Persons with names which had been italianised under fascism could now change them back. The language could be used in news, educational and cultural programmes on radio and television. Regions could set up institutes to protect the linguistic and cultural traditions of their minorities.

The law applied to the Albanian, Croatian and Greek communities in Apulia and Basilicata, the Ladins of Trento, the Catalan-speaking community of Sardinia, Sardes and Friauls, as well as those German and French, Franco-Provençal or Occitan-speaking communities outside Trentino-Südtirol or Val d'Aosta.[19]

(b) Friuli-Venezia Giulia

This region's special statute had not been brought into being until 31 January 1963. Article 3 of the Statute stated that in the region equality of rights was recognised for all citizens irrespective of their linguistic group, with the safeguarding of their respective ethnic and cultural characteristics. Of the population of some 1.2 million it was estimated that besides Italian some 525 000 spoke Friaul, 50 000 spoke Slovene, and 4 750 living in three small communities on the Austrian border spoke German.[20] It was not until early 1996 that the region approved a law for the protection and promotion of Friaul, involving teaching specialists the language, conservation of Friauli's patrimony, the possibility of it being taught in school and used in television broadcasts. (A private radio station in Friaul had existed for a number of years.) It was clear, however, that the region would not opt for Friaul to become a local official language.

With regard to Slovene, spread over the three provinces of Trieste, Gorizia and Udine, the minority is considered a 'national minority' and hence falling within the sphere of competence of the state. The level of linguistic protection differs according to its location: in Trieste and Gorizia the Slovene community enjoys official recognition, but not in Udine. Nor has the German linguistic community yet received any form of cultural protection.[21]

(c) Sardinia

It was not until 1997 that the regional government of Sardinia was able to adopt a law for the promotion of the Sardinian language and culture, and 'giving equal status' to Sardinian with Italian. Money would be made available for putting on courses in Sardinian in schools. There was provision for the use of Sardinian place names, and the right to use the language with the public administration where municipalities so agreed. The law had been twice rejected by the Italian Council of State on the grounds that school curricula could not be decided at regional level.[22]

Spain

General Francisco Franco died on 20 November 1975, and Spain began the transition to a democratic constitutional monarchy and membership of the European Community. One of the features of the new state was a far-reaching decentralisation even if for some, particularly in the Basque Country, it did not go far enough.

The 1978 Constitution provided for devolution of power to the regions or, as they had become known, Autonomous Communities. Within five years Spain had been divided into seventeen of these.

This Constitution laid down the areas for which the central government held exclusive responsibility, among them being foreign affairs, external trade, defence and justice. For the Autonomous Communities their exact powers would be defined later in their respective statutes, but they could be expected to include agriculture and forestry, town and country planning, housing, tourism, leisure and sport, while with regard to health and social services norms laid down by Madrid would have to be respected. Local taxes could be raised. However, there were grey areas – education and the environment were not given directly to either.[23]

(a) The Basque Country

The Basque Autonomy was set out in the 1979 Statute of Guernica. The Basque language was declared, like Spanish, to be official in Euskadi. With regard to education, pupils had three choices: to go to a school either where teaching was in Spanish but Basque was also taught; or where education was in both languages depending on the subject taught; or where the teaching was in Basque but Spanish was taught separately. In the meantime the *ikastolas* still continued. A sensitive area, however, is the level of knowledge of Basque that should be required of public service employees, especially in areas where little Basque is spoken.

The aim of the Basque government is to make Basque the language of everyday use, and the Academy of the Basque language in Bilbao has begun work on unifying the various forms of the language, particularly to make it the same in France and in Spain. A Basque-language radio and television channel was also set up.[24]

The Basque Autonomous Community was given sole jurisdiction in regard to thirty-nine areas, including, together with economic development, culture and industry, those mentioned above. However, with regard to the latter, the Basques were also responsible for implementing plans established by the state. It also had the right to establish an autonomous police force. The Basques also had to provide further legislation for and put into effect state legislation on the environment and domestic health.

With regard to finance, unusually it was the government of the Autonomous Community which collected the taxes and then handed over to the state an annual quota in respect of those areas of responsibility retained by the state. The quota is agreed for a five-year period but is subject to annual adjustment to take account of inflation. The Autonomous Community retains the rest. It can, however, also raise its own taxes.

Finally, back-tracking on original promises by Madrid, the laws of the Basque parliament were subjected to control for their constitutionality by the State Constitutional Tribunal.

Despite the overwhelming support for the Statute of Guernica, this ability to veto Basque legislation was seized upon by ETA as justification to continue its activities with more killings since 1979 than ever before, including the assassination of policemen and politicians and kidnappings for ransom. The Spanish state struck back, sending squads to eliminate ETA members living in and operating from France. France, for its part, has unhesitatingly supported the Spanish government. On occasion ETA announced cease-fires, but only after that of 1998 have the prospects of a lasting peace seemed more likely. In the meantime some 800 persons have paid with their lives for the thirty-year campaign for independence, the most important being that of Franco's chosen successor and the head of Government, Admiral Luis Carrero Blanco, in 1973.

(b) Catalonia

The Catalonian Statute of Gau was also enthusiastically endorsed by the people of Catalonia in 1982. As with the Basque country, the Catalan language is an official language in Catalonia together with Castillian. The *Generalitat* is exclusively responsible for culture in general, and for education.

The Catalan government made no secret of its intention to make the population master Catalan. According to official figures at the time the Statute was promulgated 38 per cent of the population were immigrants and 61 per cent of the Province of Barcelona, in which three-quarters of the Catalonian population lived, did not speak the language. Only 15 per cent of the population could speak, understand and write it.

Thus under the Linguistic Normalisation Law of 18 April 1983 Catalan was declared the primary language of education, with Castillian as a secondary language, used for those with no or little Catalan. All citizens could use either language before the courts and the administration. Place names, however, had to be in Catalan only unless they had a long tradition in Castilian. Public enterprises had to guarantee that employees dealing with the public could do so in Catalan. All teachers had to have both languages. Catalan had to be taught in vocational and specialised courses. All existing or prospective civil servants had to master the language. Films could be dubbed into Catalan. Some channels of the public television network broadcast only in Catalan. By 1990 some 30 per cent of children in Catalonia were being educated entirely in Catalan. According to the 1986 census 90 per cent of the population of Catalonia understood Catalan and 64 per cent spoke it.[25]

The *Generalitat* has exclusive competence in regard to 34 matters, along the lines of the Basque statute, including industry. It also had the right to establish an autonomous police force. With regard to finance, unlike in the Basque country but like elsewhere in Spain the original agreement was that the central government collected the taxes and then gave the Catalan government a sum guaranteed to cover the cost of the areas of responsibility.[26] But in 1993 the Prime Minister of Catalonia, Jordi Pujol, demanded and secured the automatic allocation of a 15 per cent share of the income tax collected in Catalonia.[27] This was increased to 30 per cent in 1996, and it is presumed that the ultimate aim is 100 per cent.

(c) Galicia

With regard to Galicia matters were very similar. According to the Statute of Santiago Galician is an official language in the autonomous community, along with Castilian. Under the Linguistic Normalisation Law of 15 June 1983 citizens could use Galician with the public authorities and in the courts, and the only official form of place names is in Galician. Galician is the official language in all levels of education, and is used on radio and television.[28] Galicia has exclusive competence in 32 matters, however its own autonomous police force is not one of them.

Belgium

Belgium was a state which, to accommodate Flemish-Walloon tension, moved, through successive gradual constitutional revisions 'by stealth'[29] from being a central to a federal state.

The first constitutional reform took place in 1970 with the establishment of the principle of three cultural communities – everyone belonged either to the Flemish or the French or the German community – and three regions – Flanders, Wallonia and Brussels. The 66 000 German community of Eupen-Malmedy was placed within the Walloon region. The reform laid down the principle of territoriality in the use of languages and regional affiliation. However, for a number of years it was difficult to take matters further and agree on, for example, financing. Brussels was also a problem. It was only 20 per cent Flemish, yet lay in the Flemish region, and was increasing in population as it developed as capital of the European Community and the headquarters of NATO.

However, in 1980 there was significant progress when the communities and regions obtained full autonomy with independent Executives outside the national government. The communities received powers relating to personal matters such as culture and health and social welfare. The regions, on the other hand, received socio-economic powers relating to energy, transport, the environment, planning, employment and agriculture.[30] Later the parliament and government of the Flemish region and those of the Flemish community were amalgamated into one Flemish parliament and government.

The second stage of reforms in 1989 saw body being given to the Brussels region, with the establishment of a regional Council and Executive. The Brussels parliament of 75 MPs, 65 French and 10 Flemish-speaking, has legislative powers but adoption of legislation requires a double majority. But 30 per cent of the region's population – nearly a million – were not Belgian, three-fifths being from the other countries of the European Community. Both Flemish and French were official languages. The existing language facilities relating to the municipalities were made permanent. In another development the cultural communities received powers relating to education. In Brussels education was supervised by both cultural communities but children can be sent to the school of their parents' choice.

The third and latest reform took place in 1993. In Article 1 of the new Constitution Belgium was explicitly declared a federal state. The federal government's powers were restricted to justice, finance, defence, foreign policy and public order.

Nevertheless, inter-community tension did not diminish. The question of what fiscal and budgetary powers the regions should have was being complicated by the growing divide in wealth between Flanders, which has successfully attracted inward investment and has high-tech industries and an unemployment rate one-third of Wallonia, and the latter, still saddled with so-called 'rust belt' industries. Catholic conservative Flanders does not wish its social security contributions to subsidise perceived free-spending socialist and atheistic Wallonia. Difficulties in the quality of the social services and education soon became apparent.[31]

Two important features of the new Belgium were the rights of Flemish and French communities to conclude treaties which can be registered with the United Nations, and even to represent the state in international decision-making. Nowhere else has the idea of the 'Europe of the Regions' been developed to a greater extent.

Indeed it was as early as September 1980 that Flanders signed a Language Union Treaty with the Netherlands with the aim of harmonising linguistic policy in regard to terminology in legal and official publications, production of dictionaries and grammars, and conditions for awarding language certificates. The contracting parties have one vote each, and thus decision-making is by unanimity. The Treaty came into effect in 1982 after ratification by the Dutch parliament and Flemish Assembly.[32] Furthermore, in concluding treaties the federal government cannot bind the Flemish and Walloon communities unless they so agree.

Under Article 146 of the Treaty of Rome as amended by the Merger Treaty of 8 April 1965, the Council of Ministers should be composed of a member of the Government of each of the Member States. That was in turn amended by article G43 of the Maastricht Treaty to provide that the Council should consist of a representative of each Member State of ministerial level, 'authorised to commit the government of that Member State.'[33] As a result regional ministers take it in turn to represent Belgium in meetings of the European Union's Council of Ministers, with the proviso that the State must concur in the decision taken.

The situation at present is that the regional government must inform the federal government of the intention to conclude a treaty, and the government has thirty days in which to issue objections. The matter is then referred to the Interministerial Conference on Foreign Policy, which has thirty days to reach a conclusion. Objections can be upheld on the basis of certain objective criteria, such as that the party with which the treaty is being signed was not recognised by Belgium, that Belgium does not have diplomatic relations with that party, or that the proposed treaty was not in accordance with Belgium's international or supranational obligations.[34]

France

(a) Introduction

In this most centralised country of Europe the situation for minorities, after a slow beginning, has improved considerably, although not nearly as much as the minorities themselves would wish.

In the latter half of the 1970s President Giscard d'Estaing sought to promote regional cultures by providing cultural charters for Brittany, the Basque Country and Corsica. The charters usually referred to the recognition of the cultural personality of the region concerned, aimed to provide some teaching of the minority language and to encourage cultural research, increase the amount of time for the languages on radio and television and provide, together with regional institutions, financial assistance for cultural activities. Consultative cultural councils were created to allocate funds.

The charters were to last for three to five years, but were seen as a disappointment: funding was small, and was not renewed, and the Ministry of Education did not intend to go beyond an optional or voluntary status for the languages.[35]

Crucial was the 1981 Presidential election campaign when the eventual winner, François Mitterrand, spoke of 'promoting regional identities'. At the end of that year Henri Giordan was commissioned by the Ministry of Culture to carry out a fact-finding report on regional languages and culture. A number of recommendations were made, but only one, on the teaching of regional languages from pre-school to university was put into effect by the Minister of Education, Alain Savary, in 1982, and even it was considered to do no more than reiterate existing conditions.[36] Nevertheless, in 1985 the French Minister of Culture, Jack Lang, was announcing the creation of the CAPES (*Certificat d'Aptitude au Professorat de l'Enseignement du Second Degré*) in regional languages, the inscription in two languages of local road signs and the creation of a National Council of France's Languages and Cultures. 1989 saw the DEUG (*Diplôme d'Etudes Universitaires Générales*) – the first stage in obtaining a secondary education teaching degree – applied to regional languages.[37]

In fact the National Council, which included a number of politicians, academics, representatives of cultural associations, civil servants, and writers in the regional languages, met rarely. Nevertheless, in 1988 a report of the Council of Europe on French cultural policy was able to comment that regional cultures had ceased to be considered elements degrading to the national identity.[38] In July 1991 Yves Dollo and members of the Socialist group in the National Assembly went so far as to submit a bill to make regional languages co-official, at least in their areas, but no progress was made.[39]

In May 1999 France signed the European Charter for Regional and Minority Languages, and the result was a heated polemic. Advocates of the regional and minority cultures argued that these were part of France's patrimony, not only a way of communication but a way of thought; it was 'their' history. Their opponents, as well as dismissing the languages as '*dépassés*' like ancient Greek or Latin, took issue with the distinction in Article 1(a) (ii) of the Charter between 'regional' and 'minority' languages. France could accept the former, used by populations well integrated into the Republic, without risk of disintegration, but for the *départements* to encourage the latter, languages like Arabic or Chinese, which could be demanded by populations 'recently implanted on French territory' risked 'balkanising' France.[40]

The President of the Republic, Jacques Chirac, referred the matter to the Constitutional Council, which ruled that certain clauses of the Charter in the Preamble and its second chapter were indeed contrary to the Constitution. The argument was that these clauses were contrary to the indivisibility of the Republic, equality before the law and the unity of the French people, in that they conferred specific rights to linguistic groups in certain territories. In other words, practice of a regional or minority language would be extended from the domain of private life to that of public life.[41] This was seen as renunciation by the state of French as the official language, as stated in Article 2 of the Constitution.[42] When the Prime Minister, Lionel Jospin, proposed a revision of the Constitution in order to protect the languages concerned and enable ratification of the Charter, the President refused.[43]

(b) Brittany

From 1967 to 1978 the FLB carried out almost 200 attacks on French public buildings, including most notably the Palace of Versailles, as well as on symbols of French domination in Brittany. The attacks were carried out in retaliation against the perceived eradication of the Breton language.[44] Breton militancy has not, however, died down.

Between 1992 and 1996 200 Bretons were arrested for sheltering ETA suspects on the run.[45]

If 'eradication' seemed over-pessimistic, the struggle to keep Breton alive has not been easy. In 1977 was founded *Diwan* (the seed), a network of elementary schools with teaching in Breton, and until recently the only form of education not subject to ministry control. Its aim was equal bilingualism, giving pupils an oral and written command of Breton and French before they entered secondary education. Two problems of *Diwan*, however, have been funding (mostly private) and its potential integration into the state education system, neither of which have yet been solved satisfactorily.[46]

In 1981 the university degree in Breton was officially created. At preschool and primary level pupils are introduced to Breton between one and three hours per week, on a voluntary basis for teachers as well as pupils. Some teachers travel between schools. But only about three per cent of the pupils in Brittany have been taking Breton. At secondary level Breton may be studied as an option, although in fifth year it can be taken as a third language. Yet in only one-third of secondary schools is Breton offered, and not at all in professional education.[47] It has been estimated that some 250 000 persons use Breton in everyday life and another 850 000 can understand or read it.[48] By 1998 only two per cent of those attending school were learning Breton. But *Bretonisants* are seeking a new autonomous regional administration with social, economic and cultural powers to put Brittany on a par with Catalonia and Flanders.[49]

(c) Corsica

Nowhere else in France has there been a region that has received such wide-ranging constitutional change yet been the scene of so much politically-motivated violence.

In 1970 Corsica was detached from the Region Provence-Côte d'Azur to become a region in its own right. And in 1982 it received a *Statut Particulier* with a 61-seat regional Assembly elected directly by proportional representation. In a 1977 draft text submitted by the Socialists when in opposition the decisions of the Assembly would have been binding on the French government but following divisions in the socialist group and the views of the *Conseil Constitutionnel* the 1982 version gave the Assembly only a consultative role with Paris having the right to veto Assembly legislative proposals.

Nevertheless the Corsican Assembly has greater powers than the regional Councils elsewhere in France. It administers the economic, social and cultural affairs of the island, principally by deciding the priorities of that portion of the national budget allotted to Corsica.[50] The Assembly's competences include planning, urban development, industry, agriculture, tourism, energy, education and culture, housing, transport, control of employment, and career prospects (*formation professionelle*), as well as responsibility for some matters previously administered by government agencies.[51]

In creating the *Statut Particulier* the French government was trying to steer a line between dogmatic centralist Jacobinism and the need to strengthen autonomists on the island instead of extremists. One feature of this attempt was the recognition, in Article 1 of the Statute, of 'the Corsican people, part of the French people.' This Article was struck down by the Constitutional Council on the grounds contained in Article 1 of the Constitution that France was an indivisible republic. The decision was severely criticised on the grounds that recognition of the existence of the Corsican people 'as part of the French people' affected neither national unity (in that a separate Corsican state had not been created), nor that ultimate sovereignty lay with the French people, nor equality of all people before the law whatever their origins. It was pointed out that in federal states with diverse peoples like Belgium and Switzerland, citizens were still equal before the law.[52]

On the cultural front the *Loi Deixonne* was applied to Corsica in 1974; the island received its cultural charter in 1979, and in 1981, as a result of years of pressure the University of Corté, founded by Pascal Paoli but closed by the French in 1770, was reopened with Corsican used and taught there.

Despite these developments violence did not diminish, whether from those wanting a much more far-reaching autonomy or outright secession, together with the refusal to recognise the Corsican people as a separate people, invasion by 'foreigners' (only 140 000 Corsicans out of 240 000 having been born of a Corsican parent) and an insensitive, heavy-handed police presence being given as further reasons.

In May 1976 was formed the most violent group of all, *Front de la Libération Nationale de la Corse* (FLNC), seeking separation of the 'Corsican nation' from France. Its bombings and shootings were not confined to Corsica but also occurred on the French mainland, including Paris. One immediate reaction was the formation of a 'unionist' paramilitary organisation FRANCIA (*Front d'Action Nouvelle Contre l'Indépendence et l'Autonomisme*). But since then there have been a large number of splits (including in the FLNC) leading to rival separatist groups which have also not hesitated to fire on each other.[53] It has been calculated that in the last 25 years well over 8 000 bombings and terrorist actions have taken place, including the assassination of the regional Prefect Claude Erignac in February 1998.

A main target of the Corsican nationalists has been the tourist trade. First, it has been estimated that of the one billion dollars a year in income generated by tourism, 80 per cent was returning to France or went to hotel and property speculators abroad. Second, its expansion was held to be destroying the eco-system of the island.[54] As a result holiday developments and private homes owned by 'foreigners', particularly French and Italians, have been blown up and the occupants taken as hostages in order to ward off 'Balearisation' of the island.[55]

Unsurprisingly a few years later it had been noted that income from the island's main source of revenue had fallen by half. This was a heavy burden on an economy where agricultural products suffered severe competition from Spain and Portugal, where 90 per cent of goods consumed were imported from France or Italy and where food prices were 8.5 per cent higher than in Paris. In July 1996 it was reported that unemployment stood at 42 per cent, and with practically no jobs available for qualified people.[56]

(d) The Basque Region

At the cultural level, as in Brittany, the attempt to keep the language alive has rested on voluntary schools. The first *ikastolas* opened in the late 1960s and at first drew the hostility of the state, the Church and the police, but since then they have gained the support of the municipal authorities and now exist in all the three French-Basque *départements* of Labourd (*Lapurdi*), Basse Navarre (*Benapara*) and Soule (*Ciberoa*).[57] In 1979 the Basque Cultural Charter was promulgated to run initially for the three years 1980–82. The movement for Basque reunification is led by *Enbata* founded in 1959, which also seeks a confederal 'Europe of the Regions'. Its alleged closeness to ETA led it to being dissolved briefly in 1974 along with other Breton and Corsican extremist groups.[58] As with many such organisations splits occurred, and in 1978 militants created *Ipartarrak*. The object of this group was to replace tourists with industry. As a result, holiday homes and villages have been attacked.[59] Since then the situation has returned to normality.

(e) Alsace

The closeness to German of the Alsatian dialect continued to cause the latter's decline. In 1985 the Head of Public Education in Alsace stated, 'There is only one correct scientific definition of the regional language in Alsace; it is the Alsatian dialect of which the written expression is German. German is therefore one of France's regional languages.' Indeed, three years previously the Regional Assembly of Alsace, together with the *Conseils Généraux* of Haut and Bas Rhin had demanded recognition of German as a regional language of France.

In 1973 German could at last be taught in primary education, for two and a half hours per week – but only if a teacher wanted to teach it. But as the teaching of German expanded, knowledge of the Alsatian dialect, which was not taught, declined. In 1945 the entire population could speak Alsatian. By 1979 it was 75 per cent. By 1997 only 30 per cent of those under 25 could speak it, and it was disappearing in the large cities. Calls for learning the dialect have been on the rise.[60]

The United Kingdom

As with Spain, the United Kingdom experienced dramatic constitutional change in the last quarter of the century. The beneficiaries were the peripheral areas of the so-called 'Celtic fringe' – Northern Ireland, Scotland and Wales, all of which would be offered devolved government.

(a) Northern Ireland

Nowhere else in western Europe was the descent into the political abyss so marked as in Northern Ireland.

The responsibility for this state of affairs lay squarely with the successive governments of Britain, Labour or Conservative. Unlike the firm attitude of Italian governments in defence of the territorial destiny of South Tyrol, where the Italian community was in the minority, British governments, with one eye on the United States, have made little secret of their preference for good relations with Dublin rather than defence of the British majority in Northern Ireland and thus signalling a desire to disengage from the province.[61] In 1973 London set up an Executive government in Belfast based on institutionalised power-sharing between moderate unionists and the constitutional Nationalist SDLP. But forgetting anything that might have been learned from South Tyrol or Cyprus, the insistence on a 'Council of Ireland' tied to the Executive while Articles 2 and 3 of the Irish constitution remained in place smacked to most Unionists as the next step to a united Ireland. A general strike by the Ulster Workers' Council brought down the power-sharing Executive, destroyed moderate Unionism and led to a further upsurge in republican and loyalist terrorism. Then in 1985 the British and Irish governments seemed to veer towards a policy of Condominium, signing an Agreement under which, if it was accepted that there would be no change in the status of the North as part of the United Kingdom without the consent of the majority there, Dublin would be consulted on most policy initiatives by London, including on appointments to significant positions, in return for co-operation against the PIRA. The British fulfilled their side of the bargain; not until much later did the Irish fulfil theirs.[62] At no time did any British government – even during the eventual peace negotiations – ever show that it had learnt anything from similar minority conflicts in Europe, particularly South Tyrol and Cyprus. The declared policy of these successive governments, that Britain would cheerfully leave Northern Ireland if that was what its population wanted merely served, on the one hand, to encourage PIRA attacks on the Unionist community in order to bring about that consent, and on the other, to demoralise Unionists. Since the British press on the whole tended to support government policy on Northern Ireland the result was a demonisation of the Unionist community, whose perceived sins were continually publicised, so that it was not surprising that in mainland Britain public opinion polls the mood supported eventual disengagement. Since the Unionists had nowhere to go their resolve not to be pushed into a united Ireland was translated into a spectacular rise in Loyalist paramilitary activity targeting prominent Roman Catholics and 'Nationalist' housing estates.

The main objective of British governments was to get institutionalised power-sharing in a Northern Ireland Assembly. This was continually rejected by Unionist political parties which refused to share power with constitutional nationalists as long as the aim of the latter was Irish unity, and certainly so long as the Irish Republic maintained its claim to the North and turned a blind eye to the PIRA's use of the territory of the Republic as a safe haven. Again, the contrast with Italy, which in 1968 vetoed Austrian talks with the European Community because terrorist attacks were being launched from Austrian soil, was marked. The refusal of the Unionists to share power merely meant direct rule of the Province from London, something which destroyed a healthy local democracy.[63]

The British government's policy of playing down the Irish claim to the North as irrelevant was rudely shattered when the Chief Justice of the Irish Supreme Court ruled in 1990 that reintegration of the national territory was a *constitutional imperative* and that the claim to the North was indeed a claim of legal right.[64]

By the end of May 1993 more than 3 000 people had been killed and 35 000 had been injured. Compensation for criminal injuries was reckoned at over £236 million and for damage to property over £692 million. The cost of policing was £1 million per day, while that of maintaining 19 000 troops in the Province was another £1 million per day.[65]

Under the impact of such violence the Catholic/Nationalist and Protestant/Unionist communities were polarised, with many housing ghettos controlled by the respective paramilitaries. Protestant-owned firms were reluctant to employ Catholics in case they were agents of the PIRA, and the fact that there was always a larger percentage of Catholics unemployed than Protestants was a major source of grievance. The police, 90 per cent Protestant, were generally perceived by the Nationalist community as the arm of Unionism although PIRA intimidation and a potential 'chill' factor undoubtedly contributed to the imbalance.

The road to peace was begun in 1993 when John Hume, leader of the constitutional Nationalist SDLP began secret talks with the President of Sinn Fein, Gerry Adams. The main aim was to convince the political wing of the PIRA that violence to bring about a united Ireland was useless: it had made not one single Unionist change his or her mind. Closer relations were also established between the British and Irish governments. In the Downing Street Declaration of December 1993 majority consent in the North for Irish unification was reaffirmed. A few months later the so-called 'Framework Documents' were produced, under which through cross-border co-operation Ireland would be more or less united economically although remaining divided politically. An Assembly would be established, but both Nationalists and Unionists would have the right to veto proposed legislation and appointments. For Sinn Fein matters did not go far enough – it wanted the British government to coerce the Unionists into agreeing to an eventual united Ireland and rejected a majority Unionist Assembly; for Unionists the cross-border and veto arrangements were constitutionally unacceptable.

1994 also saw David Trimble succeed to the leadership of the Ulster Unionist party, and the Democrat politician Bill Clinton become President of the United States. The new American administration began to play an increasing role in moves to get all-party negotiations going. These began in May 1996 but for over a year there was little movement. The Unionists refused to negotiate with Sinn Fein until the PIRA had called a cease-fire and begun to decommission its weapons as proof of conversion to pursuing its political aims by democratic peaceful means. Sinn Fein refused to accept the principles for negotiation laid down by the chairman of the Talks process, Senator George

Mitchell of the United States, which included rejection of violence by the negotiating parties (including on the part of their paramilitary wings) and acceptance of the eventual outcome.

Then in May 1997 the Labour Party, led by Tony Blair, won the British general election with a programme of constitutional reform, including devolved government for Scotland and Wales. One consequence was to cut the ground from under those Unionists who had objected to regional government for Northern Ireland because it marked the Province out as different from the rest of the United Kingdom. In the meantime in the Irish Republic the government had become a Fianna Fail-dominated coalition led by Bertie Ahern. With Blair and Clinton he shared a determination to bring about a peaceful solution to the conflict in the North. As a result of intense efforts by Blair, Clinton, Ahern, Trimble and Hume, in September Sinn Fein on the one hand agreed to accept the Mitchell Principles even though it meant almost certainly accepting continued partition and the emergence of breakaways by dissidents resolved to continue violence, while on the other hand Trimble's UUP agreed to enter the Talks even though Sinn Fein had not begun decommissioning. But when the Talks began, including parties representing the political wing of loyalist paramilitaries, two Unionist parties, including Dr Paisley's DUP, withdrew from the Talks, outraged at sitting at the same table as perceived unreconstructed terrorists of both communities who had not begun decommissioning.

The Talks, which included the British and Irish governments, three Unionist, two Nationalist, and three small non-sectarian parties, ended with far-reaching agreement on Good Friday, 10 April 1998.

At the international level, first, the Irish government agreed to amend the Articles of the Constitution that claimed the North. The new Article 3 accepted 'that a united Ireland shall be brought about only by peaceful means with the consent of a majority of the people, democratically expressed, in both jurisdictions in the island'.

Second, a North–South Ministerial Council would be established to develop co-operation on an all-Ireland and cross-border basis. Along the lines of the European Union's Council of Ministers, Northern and Southern Ministers would come together to consult and, if appropriate, agree policies for implementation separately in each jurisdiction. The twelve possible subjects for co-operation and implementation included agriculture (animal and plant health), education (teacher qualifications and exchanges), transport (strategic planning), the environment (pollution, water quality and waste management), inland waterways, social security (cross-border workers and fraud control), tourism, relevant European Union programmes, inland fisheries, aquaculture, health (accident and emergency services), urban and rural development. However, most importantly for Unionists, any decisions taken by the Council would require ratification by the respective Assemblies, i.e., the Council could not impose policies on one or both of the jurisdictions.

In Northern Ireland a 108-seat Assembly would be set up, with responsibility for the existing six Northern Ireland government departments – Agriculture, Economic Development (including Tourism), Education, the Environment (including Transport), Finance, and Health and Social Security – with the possibility of taking on responsibility for other matters.

Government would be by institutionalised power-sharing between Unionists and Nationalists. On the D'Hondt system, ministers and committee memberships would be allocated in proportion to party strengths.

Decision-making would normally be by simple majority but on key issues would be *either* by parallel consent (i.e. a majority of both Unionist and Nationalist designations present and voting) *or* a weighted majority (60 per cent) of members present and voting, including at least 40 per cent each of the Nationalist and Unionist designations present and voting. Key issues were defined as election of the Chair of the Assembly, the First Minister and Deputy First Minister, standing orders and budget allocations and removal from office. However, if a serious issue arose a significant minority of Assembly members (30/108) could bring a 'petition of concern' in which case decisions would be taken on the basis that it was a key issue.

However, unlike in Cyprus and South Tyrol where bills held to be prejudicial to one community or to the other could be referred to the Constitutional Court, there was no similar provision in the Belfast Agreement. This had already been held to be a weakness of the former Stormont régime.[66] Instead there was provision for the appointment of a Special Committee to report on whether the proposed legislation was in conformity with the European Convention on Human Rights or any Northern Ireland Bill of Rights. The Assembly would then consider the report and determine the matter in accordance with the cross-community consent procedure.

Aimed at representatives of paramilitary organisations, a condition of appointment as a minister was that those who held office should use only democratic, non-violent means, and those who did not should be removed from office. Furthermore ministers, rather than take an oath of allegiance, had to take a pledge of office which included a commitment to non-violence and exclusively peaceful and democratic means.

A number of other steps were agreed in order to promote cross-community trust and reconciliation. First, a new Northern Ireland Human Rights Commission, with membership reflecting the community balance, was established. Part of its mandate was to review the effectiveness of laws and practices, including draft legislation by the Assembly.

Second, the British government, considering signing the Council of Europe Charter for Regional or Minority Languages, agreed to promote the Irish language, including encouraging it in private and public life 'where there is appropriate demand', facilitating Irish medium education, making available Irish-language broadcasting from the South and encouraging financial support for Irish-language film and television production in the North. There was also recognition of the importance to the Unionist community of Ulster Scots (indeed it was later arranged that both languages could be used with English in the Assembly).

Third, right from the beginning of the negotiations an International Commission on Decommissioning of terrorist weapons had been set up under General John de Chastelain of Canada. The Agreement reaffirmed that 'the resolution of the decommissioning issue is an indispensable part of the process of negotiation', and the participants accordingly 'reaffirm(ed) their commitment to the total disarmament of all paramilitary organisations. They also confirm their intention to continue to work constructively and in good faith with the Independent Commission and to use any influence they may have, to achieve the decommissioning of all paramilitary arms within two years following endorsement in referendums North and South of the Agreement ...'.

Fourth, the British government undertook to scale down its military presence in the Province, reducing troops, removing security installations and ending emergency powers. Fifth, an independent Commission would be established to review policing in Northern Ireland and present proposals on recruitment, training, ethos and symbols so that a Northern Ireland police service could enjoy widespread cross-community support. Sixth, the criminal justice system would be reviewed. Seventh, there would be an accelerated programme for the release of prisoners from paramilitary organisations maintaining a cease-fire. Support for reintegrating prisoners into society, including education and training, would be provided.

Furthermore, there was provision for a British–Irish Council to be established, to include representatives of the two governments, devolved institutions in Northern Ireland, Scotland and Wales, as well as the Isle of Man and the Channel Islands. There would be consultation and possible agreement on common policies or actions with the option to participate in these or not by the individual elements. Two or more parties could develop bilateral or multilateral arrangements between them. Suitable issues for discussion were transport links, and issues in agriculture, the environment, health, culture, education and European Union policies.

Finally there was provision for a British–Irish Intergovernmental Conference which would keep under review the working of the Good Friday Agreement. 'In recognition of the Irish government's special interest in Northern Ireland' there would be regular and frequent meetings of the Conference concerned with non-devolved Northern Ireland matters, on which the Irish government could put forward views and proposals. The Conference would concern itself particularly with security, rights, justice, prisons and policing.[67]

The Good Friday Agreement was submitted to referendums in both Northern Ireland and the Irish Republic on 22 May. In the former the vote was 71.12 per cent in favour; in the latter the vote in favour was a crushing 96 per cent. The opposition in the North was almost entirely from Unionists, whose community was split down the middle. The reason for their hostility was that the Agreement contained no absolute requirement that paramilitary organisations should have decommissioned their weapons before entering the Assembly and possibly receiving ministerial office. The war was therefore not necessarily over. In the meantime terrorists would begin being released from prison.

The result was that when elections were held to the new Northern Ireland Assembly on 25 June the number of pro-Agreement Unionists was only just superior to anti-Agreement Unionists, thus posing a threat to the cross-community voting system.

Thereafter the situation deteriorated. The PIRA refused to decommission any weapons. Sinn Fein maintained that it had no authority to force the PIRA to decommission. It argued that it had a political mandate and wanted the Belfast Agreement to be implemented at once. On the other hand Unionists refused to sit in the Assembly with Sinn Fein until decommissioning had seriously been undertaken. The result was a stalemate. In the meantime dissident splinter elements of the PIRA, UDA and UVF supplied with arms by those in the groups hostile to the Agreement, have continued a campaign of bombings and assassination.

By April 1999 some 3 585 persons had been killed and over 40 000 injured in Northern Ireland and elsewhere,[68] of which the RUC share was 302 and 8 000 respectively.[69]

(b) Scotland

For most of the period under review times were unhappy for Scots. Reasons for dissatisfaction were three. First, there was the decline of the British Empire, which meant that career opportunities throughout the world decreased. Second, Scotland's major industries and sources of employment were the 'rust belt' ones of shipbuilding, coal mining, steel and textiles. By the 1970s their day had gone and in the 1980s Mrs Thatcher's Conservative government ruthlessly cut back public funding for the nationalised industries and ordered their privatisation.

Third, in the 1980s and most of the 1990s the Conservatives governed Britain as a result of a majority in the whole and massively so in England but had only a small minority of MPs in Scotland, so that it seemed as if an 'English' parliament was taking the decisions to 'destroy' the nationalised industries, cut back on funding for health and education, and experiment with a poll-tax.

In the 1960s and 1970s when Labour was mostly in power successes by the Scottish Nationalist party (SNP) in by-elections were protest votes against government economic incompetence and rising unemployment.[70] What gave the party more substance, however, was the discovery of oil in the North Sea in 1970. 'It's Scotland's oil' was the slogan launched by the SNP in 1972, and the idea that oil receipts could pay for the policies of an independent Scotland made the Party more substantive than merely one of protest.[71]

In the 1960s, 1970s and 1980s Labour was a generally centralist party, hostile to devolution for Scotland and Wales. However, following losses in by-elections the Prime Minister James Callaghan sought nationalist support by proposing devolution in both areas. However, an amendment to the devolution bills required that for the bills to be adopted and an Assembly established at least 40 per cent of registered voters had to vote in favour in a referendum. On 1 March 1979 a bare majority of registered voting Scots voted in favour of devolution (32.8 to 30.8 per cent) thus failing to reach the 40 per cent quota,[72] although the public might have been pronouncing on the government's economic policies rather than on an Assembly.[73] Two months later the Labour government fell and the Conservatives under Mrs Thatcher were swept to power. The SNP was decimated: the 11 MPs and 30 per cent of the vote in Scotland in 1974 were reduced to 2 seats and 17 per cent.

Mrs Thatcher's victory in May 1979 had a profound effect on Scottish politics. It would be quite untrue to suggest that all Labour and Conservative supporters in Scotland were ardent centralists; many were sympathetic to devolution. But the way the Conservative 'English' majority in Westminster was perceived to ride roughshod over the Labour majority in Scotland shocked Labour into becoming devolutionists.[74]

The beginning of the 1980s saw the SNP in ideological disarray but by the end of the decade support for independence was hovering around 30 per cent.[75] The party also changed its stance on Europe. From hostility on the grounds that it was a 'capitalist club', 'independence in Europe' was seen as a means of escaping English domination.[76]

By the mid-1990s Labour and the Liberal Democrats, some Conservatives, and the SNP who saw devolution as a stepping stone to independence provided an overwhelming consensus for devolution. In the May 1997 general election Tony Blair's Labour manifesto proposed devolution. The Conservatives clung to official centralism and were utterly destroyed: in the 1955 general election the party had actually gained a majority of the vote in Scotland; in that of 1997 no Scottish Conservatives were elected to Westminster.

On 11 September 1997 the Scottish people voted in a referendum in favour of the Labour government's devolution proposals. On a 60 per cent turn out, 74.3 per cent voted in favour with 25.7 per cent against.

According to the Government of Scotland Act the first Scottish Parliament since 1707 would begin work in January 2000. The new 129-member parliament would be responsible for, *inter alia*, agriculture, the arts, economic development, education, the environment, fisheries, forestry, health, housing, law, local government, social work and sport. Unlike in Northern Ireland, cases of dispute with the central government would be referred to the Judicial Committee of the Privy Council. There would be a Scottish Office representative in Brussels, but the Scottish government would have to implement European legislation in its areas of competence. The parliament would control a block grant of £14 billion.

Unusually, the parliament would have the right to increase or decrease the basic rate of income tax set by Westminster by a maximum of 3 pence in the pound. Raising that maximum was seen as providing an extra £450 million *per annum*, and it was stated that should that index-linked figure be eroded, the Assembly would be guaranteed the shortfall.[77] The question of tax-raising powers was the subject of a second question in the referendum, with 63.5 per cent voting in favour and 36.5 per cent against.

With regard to language, the SNP had already called in 1994 for Scots Gaelic to be recognised and promoted as the national language.[78] Alarm was expressed that the language was dying. In 1991 only 1.37 per cent of the population – 66 000 – spoke it, most of them in the Western Isles. Less than 0.75 per cent of those aged 5–9 spoke it, and this fell to 0.57 per cent for those aged 3–4. Contrasts were drawn with the healthy state of the language in Wales.[79] Scholars called for funding for updating grammars and dictionaries and pre-school training.[80] In the meantime there is provision for Scots Gaelic to be used in the Assembly, and the expectation is that the government would include it if and when it adhered to the Council of Europe's Charter on Regional and Minority Languages.

(c) Wales

In contrast to Scotland, the language in Wales has made great progress whereas interest in devolution, let alone independence, has been lukewarm at best. This was precisely because language was the key to national unity – Wales did not enjoy the comprehensive range of national institutions, legal and educational, available to the Scots.[81]

In 1962 the Welsh dramatist, poet and political essayist Saunders Lewis made his famous broadcast *The Fate of the Language* on the BBC. He felt that the trend of decline in the Welsh-speaking population would lead to the death of the language by the 21st century. Wales without the Welsh language would not be Wales. He therefore called for Welsh to be put on a footing of equality with English in the administration and advocated using organised and prolonged civil disobedience. As for self-government he stated that in his opinion if any self-government for Wales was obtained before Welsh was acknowledged and used as an official language in local authority and state administration, then the language would never achieve official status at all, and its demise would be quicker than under English rule.[82]

His fears seemed justified. According to the 1971 census under 21 per cent of the 2.7 million population claimed to be Welsh-speaking, and most were to be found in rural north and west Wales.[83] In education the problem was that there were three lots of pupils, those for whom Welsh was a foreign language, those from a bilingual area but without much Welsh in their personal background, and those for whom Welsh was the natural language of their community.[84]

Nevertheless, the situation was not hopeless. In the 1940s and 1950s an increasing number of Welsh-medium primary and secondary schools had opened, and protests and demonstrations by the Welsh Language Society calling for equal status of Welsh and English had led to the Welsh Language Act of 1967. This act was designed to embody in law 'the accepted principle of equal validity of Welsh and English' in the Welsh courts and provide for bilingualism in the public services.[85] But, rather like the 'parification' of German and Italian in South Tyrol, 'equal validity' was not the unambiguous official status demanded by Welsh nationalists. Civil disobedience demonstrations began, including demands for increased broadcasting in Welsh, to which the Welsh Office responded by allowing bilingual road signs and road licence disks, while Independent Television established Harlech Television in 1968 which would lead to an exclusively Welsh channel in 1976. There were also calls for restricting English incomers to rural Wales, held to pose a threat to the language and force up house prices.[86]

But the rise of nationalism in the 1960s and 1970s was, like in Scotland, bound up with the performance of the central government. As in Scotland, economic decline had set in, unemployment rose, and the Welsh Nationalist Party *(Plaid Cymru – PC)* gained protest votes.

Debates on governmental reform inevitably involved the Welsh factor. Some sections of the Labour Party, which dominated Wales, wanted an elected Welsh Council, but other Welsh Labour members, if not most, as well as Labour throughout the country, were centralists, hostile to anything like devolution which was perceived as endangering the unity of the working class.[87] But with the loss of seats at Westminster at by-elections the 1974–79 Labour government needed minority parties to stay in power, with the Liberals as pro-devolution as the SNP and PC.

The result was the introduction by the Labour government of the 1978 Wales Bill, which promised a Welsh Assembly, but without legislative or taxation powers, only administrative ones, exercising functions given hitherto to ministers. As with Scotland, the bill would require approval by 40 per cent of the registered electorate in a referendum before implementation.

The outcome was a crushing defeat for those in favour of devolution. The view that devolution would bring democracy closer to the Welsh was swept away by arguments that it endangered the unity of the United Kingdom by setting Wales on the road to separation and that the Assembly was a useless – and costly – extra tier of government. For

PC supporters the Assembly's powers did not nearly go far enough, while Labour supporters and the English-speaking-only population feared the Assembly would be filled with a Welsh language élite obliging everyone to be fluent in Welsh before they could get a job. There was also the point that the Welsh economy was felt to be so tied in with that of England that control might as well be left as it was. On a 58.3 per cent turnout only 11.8 per cent (243 048 or 6.7 per cent of the electorate) voted in favour of the bill while 46.5 per cent (956 330) voted against.[88]

Despite this defeat neither the issue of the language nor that of devolution went away. In 1992 Welsh was to become compulsory in all schools, but parents in anglicised areas were angered at having their children being forced to learn Welsh instead of a major European language. Some schools obtained an exemption.[89] And a County Council, where two-thirds of the population spoke Welsh, was held to be guilty of race discrimination when it refused to employ two women who did not speak Welsh.[90]

In 1992 the Conservative government introduced a new Welsh Language Bill, stating that English and Welsh would have 'equal standing' in public services and justice in Wales. Every public service would have to provide facilities in Welsh. But this did not apply to the privatised industries such as water, electricity and gas, so as not to place them at a disadvantage with rival firms elsewhere, nor did it apply to Crown bodies.[91] The Bill was criticised for not making Welsh official as well as for omitting the privatised industries. Also demanded was that a Welsh speaker could be tried by a Welsh-speaking jury, and that every child in Wales should have the right to Welsh-medium education.

Following Labour's victory in the May 1997 general election, Wales, too, was promised devolution. However, the desire for a separate political entity remained far less than in Scotland, and this was the argument for giving a Welsh Assembly far fewer powers. As in 1978 the Assembly would have no legislative or taxation powers. Its 60 members would merely administer education, health, agriculture, roads and planning, on an annual budget of £37 million.[92] The fact that there were such few powers, so that even QUANGOs could not be abolished, enabled the proposals to be attacked as a costly extra layer of bureaucracy, a failure to address the democratic deficit. In the event the referendum held on 18 September 1997 voted very narrowly to accept the proposals by 50.3 per cent (559 419) to 49.7 per cent (553 698).

(d) Cornwall

As in so many other parts of Europe economic decline and central government neglect provoked demands for recognition of cultural identity.

In the 1980s a determined effort began to revive Cornish. Later this took two forms. One was to have the Cornish recognised as a national minority in their own designated territory under the terms of the Council of Europe's 1994 Framework Convention for the Protection of National Minorities, on the basis that potentially some 250 000 persons – about 50 per cent of the population of Cornwall – belong to the Cornish ethnic group. The second was to try and have Cornish registered under the Council's 1992 Charter for Regional or Minority Languages. Support has been received from Brussels, with the European Commission designating Cornish as an officially recognised living language and Cornwall being designated as an Objective I region for support under the European Union's Structural Funds. A Cornish dictionary has been launched, and the language is taught in a number of schools. It has been estimated that up to 2 000 persons speak Cornish with varying degrees of fluency. On the other hand, successive British governments have been reluctant to recognise both the Cornish language under the terms of the Charter (recently abolishing it as a GCSE subject on the grounds of lack of demand) and the Cornish as a national minority under the Convention, most recently in its 1999 Compliancy Report to the Council. The intention is to appeal the issue to the Council's Committee of Ministers via its monitoring Advisory Committee.

Switzerland

For most people Switzerland, with its three national but four recognised languages and two religions, Catholic and Protestant, has been a model for harmonious and stable linguistic relations. In 16 cantons and 6 half cantons the German language dominates, while French is the dominant language in 6 cantons and Italian in one. The Swiss population in1977 was some 7.0 million but of these no less than 1.37 million, 19.4 per cent, were foreigners. Of the 5.7 million Swiss citizens some 73 per cent were German speakers, 20 per cent were French speakers, 5 per cent were Italian speakers and 1 per cent was Rhaeto-Romansch. Four cantons were officially bilingual: Bern, Fribourg, Grisons and Valais.

The case of Fribourg is instructive. The Franco-German linguistic border in Switzerland, the river Sarine, runs through the canton which is two-thirds French and one-third German-speaking. Under the canton's constitution the French and German languages are used on a basis of territoriality: all but two of the cantons' 256 municipalities are majority-French or majority-German, but one can go from nursery school to university in either language. It is possible to live in one language municipality and work in another language municipality, or even another language canton. Thus many firms based in German-speaking Zürich would like to expand to Fribourg. However, two principles of the Confederation are liberty of language and territoriality, and the cantons have the right to intervene to protect the language in its traditional locality.

But in one spectacular case these kinds of arrangements failed, and a new canton was born in 1979 out of the inability to heal linguistic and religious divisions.

(a) The Jura

The area known as the Jura formed seven districts in the north-west of Canton Bern – Courtelary, Delemont, Franches-Montagne, Laufen, Moutier, La Neuveville and Porrentruy. All but Laufen were predominantly French-speaking. The area had come to Bern (and Switzerland) in 1815 as a result of decisions taken at the Congress of Vienna. Bern was almost entirely German-speaking and Protestant. In the Middle Ages the French-speaking Jura had belonged to the Bishopric of Basle, an autonomous political entity, but in 1528, following the Reformation, the Bishop was forced to move to Porrentruy. Significantly the four northern districts of Delemont, Franches-Montagne, Laufen and Porrentruy remained Roman Catholic but the southern three of Courtelary, La Neuveville and Moutier converted to Protestantism. In 1792 France took over the Jura; French continued to be the official language, and the values of the French Revolution were introduced.

The decision of 1815 meant that suddenly an area with a long history of autonomy was subsumed by a body six times greater and with a different language.[93] This prepared the way for instability. It has been pointed out that in mixed language cantons, such as Fribourg and Valais, the fact that the populations were of the same religion seemed to reduce tension. Similarly in mixed religion cantons, such as Aargau, a common language served the same purpose.[94] There would be no such common loyalties when single language, single religion Bern acquired the Jura. And indeed, in the period up to the end of the First World War there would be no less than five separatist movements. These were provoked at various times by Bernese conservative authori-

tarianism, anti-Catholic legislation and discrimination,[95] and germanisation. This germanisation occurred as the southern Jura became
industrialised (particularly with watch-making). French-speaking
Jurassians left the agricultural sector to work in the factories and their
places were taken by German-speakers escaping the overcrowded agricultural sector in Bern.[96] The aims of the separatists varied between a
regional autonomy, a new canton (based on the historic unity of the
Jura) and even unity with France.[97]

Rarely has a short sentence produced such long-lasting effects as the
words of the German-speaking Bernese deputy Hans Tschumi who, in
September 1947, called on the parliament to refuse the post of the
canton's Director of Public Works and Railways to M. Georges Moeckli,
on the grounds that 'the Department is too important to be confided to a
French-speaking State Councillor'. This slur on Moeckli who had even
been president of the canton a few years earlier, launched the sixth and
most successful separatist movement,[98] involving such un-Swiss activities
as bombing, damaging memorials, burning hayricks (and even farm-
houses), as well as street battles in which riot police used tear gas.[99]

The Bern government opposed the creation of a new canton, proposing instead constitutional reform, including official recognition of
the Jurassian people and the French language, and two seats for the
Jura in the canton's government. These reforms were accepted in
October 1950.[100] However the separatists, under the banner of the
Rassemblement Jurassien (RJ) intensified their activities, playing on the
theme of domination by Bern, and in July 1959 organised a
referendum that, if accepted, would have prepared the way for a later
referendum on the question of separation. In the event the initiative
was massively rejected by the canton as a whole, but in the Jura itself,
on an 85 per cent turnout, the difference between the Yeas and the
Nays was thin – 15 159 to 16 355.[101]

This result led the RJ to change tactics. Realising the large Yes francophone vote, it changed from stressing the unity and centuries-old
autonomy of the seven-district Jura to stressing that of Jura's French
ethnicity, by leaving the German-speaking district of Laufen to decide
its destiny for itself.[102]

In March 1970 the Bern parliament adopted a constitutional amend-
ment allowing for self-determination of the Jurassian people. However,
Germanophones in the area would be allowed to vote whereas ex-
patriates, held to number more than 60 000, would not. Then in
December 1973 the Bern government decided to hold a referendum in
June 1974 in the Jura on the question of creating a new canton.

On a turnout of 90 per cent, 36 802 voted Yes (52 per cent) and 34 067 voted No (48 per cent). The creation of the new canton was approved in the northern French-speaking districts of Delemont, Porrentruy and Franches-Montagnes, but rejected by the three southern districts of Courtelary, Moutier and La Neuveville as well as German-speaking Laufen.

The result was that the anti-separatists called for another referendum to ensure that the districts that voted No, apart from Laufen, could remain with Bern. This referendum was held in March 1975. Again the turnout was over 90 per cent, but two-thirds of the voters repeated their hostility to being part of the new canton, remaining faithful to Bern. However, municipalities bordering the new canton had the right to decide whether to join the new canton or remain with Bern. In the autumn of 1975 three further referendums were held, in which eight municipalities in Moutier voted to join the Jura but two in Delemont chose to remain with Bern.[103]

The Canton of the Jura officially came into being on 1 January 1979, following ratification of its creation, as constitutionally required, by a nation-wide referendum involving the people of Switzerland and the cantons. The voting, on a 41.5 per cent turnout, was 1 309 722 (82.3 per cent) and all 22 cantons in favour, and 281 917 (17.7 per cent) against. The greatest hostility was in Bern, with 30.4 per cent against.[104]

It may come, therefore, as rather a surprise that following such a comprehensive settlement the RJ has again taken up the cudgels, this time in order to get the southern French-speaking districts to rejoin their northern cousins, arguing that the three districts now constituted only 6 per cent of the population of Bern, and that their Francophone characteristics were being endangered, particularly by germanophones taking second homes in the area.[105]

(b) The Rhaeto-Romansch

According to the 1990 census some 66 000 persons speak Rhaeto-Romansch, almost all in the canton of Graubunden/Grisons, calculated on the basis of both 'Best Command' and 'Most Spoken' languages. In 1990 they formed 23.6 of the population of the canton and 1.0 per cent of the Confederation. Taken on the basis of 'Best Command' alone, they form 17 per cent of the canton and 0.6 per cent of the Confederation. On the latter basis the rest of the canton is composed of 65.3 per cent German-speakers, 11.0 per cent Italian-speakers, and 6.6 per cent miscellaneous.[106]

Rhaeto-Romansch belongs to the same linguistic family as the Ladins and the Friauls, but the unity of all these languages is very relative.[107] The status of the Romansch language is curious. In 1938 it was declared one of Switzerland's four national languages but not an official language. However, in 1996 an amendment to the Swiss Constitution provided for Romansch to be an official language for the purpose of dealings with persons of Romansch tongue. By the same amendment the government of the Federation was required to promote Romansch.

In the Canton of the Grisons, since in Switzerland language sovereignty is vested in the cantons, it is up to the individual municipalities to decide their official and school languages. For the last twenty years there has been concern for Romansch. First, spoken in remote rural Alpine villages, there are three variants of the language – Sursilvan, Sutsilvan and Ladin, and it is slipping behind the times in regard to the general evolution of technology and civilisation. It has, for example, been difficult to provide publication of a Romansch cantonal newspaper.

Second, the historic territory of Rhaeto-Romansch is not guaranteed by the cantonal constitution. Because of the economic dependence on the German-speaking part of Switzerland and the influence of the German language press and the electronic media, together with the principle of municipal autonomy it has been impossible to resist the germanisation of ever more municipalities, which has also served to separate the different varieties of the language from each other. Attempts to establish constitutionally a Romansch homeland based on its traditional territory – with all the linguistic and administrative advantages thereto – have not yet succeeded.

Nevertheless, matters have improved. Romansch can be used in the cantonal parliament and the courts. It is compulsory as a subject in the canton's primary and lower secondary schools. On the radio it can be heard for up to 14 hours per week, and if Romansch does not have its own channel it is allotted time on nation-wide channels. Much, however, remains to be done, particularly unifying and up-dating the language.[108]

The Netherlands

(a) The Frisians

Friesland is a province of the Netherlands. Frisian, a language lying between German and English, was the official language in the government and the courts in the Middle Ages, but after the 1648 union with the Netherlands the language declined, being used only in the home and in rural areas. Like elsewhere, nineteenth-century romanticism saw a revival but the area was still subject to Dutch incomers while many Frisians left to seek work elsewhere.

Matters improved after the Second World War. In 1980 primary schools in the province were obliged to teach Frisian as a subject and it was allowed as a teaching language. But efforts to make it compulsory at secondary level failed. It could be taught as a subject, but only if twenty students per school year demanded it. Since 1956 Frisian could be used as a spoken but not a written language before the courts. However, in the administration documents and communication can be in Frisian. The language is now spoken by some 400 000 people.[109]

The Sami of Scandinavia

Just over 50 000 Sami live in the northernmost regions of Norway (30 000), Sweden (15 000) and Finland (6 500 – 7 000), with a nomadic lifestyle concentrated on reindeer herding. During the nineteenth century there was much hostility to their way of life, particularly in Norway which, on the basis of racial theories and social Darwinism, felt that they should be either extinguished or raised to a higher level. Policy was to get them to settle down, be educated and conform to Norwegian dress, way of life and language. Settlers were sent into traditional Sami areas.

The first changes came in the 1950s with acceptance of the Sami way of life and an end to assimilation policies. Co-operation on policies towards the Sami was begun by the three states and in 1956 a Nordic Sami Council was created.

In 1988 an amendment to the Norwegian Constitution required the State to create conditions in which Sami culture could flourish. The following year a Sami parliament was established and the language was made official in some municipalities. In Sweden in 1992 a Sami Assembly was set up but it only has advisory powers. However, teaching in the Sami mother tongue is given in some primary schools. In 1996 it was Finland's turn to create a Sami Assembly. It can decide on disbursement of monetary allocations, and the Finnish government must negotiate with it on Sami language and cultural issues.[110]

International organisations

The progress being made within national states as regards the institutionalisation of their minorities made it easier to have that institutionalisation extended to the international level.

The European Community

In 1981 the European Parliament led by Gaetano Arfé, and supported by John Hume (Socialist, SDLP) and Joachim Dalsass (Christian Democrat, SVP) adopted a Resolution which made in its Preamble the point that linguistic and cultural heritages could not be safeguarded unless their economic development was also assured. The main thrust of the Resolution was that the teaching of regional languages and cultures should be obligatorily included in official curricula right through from nursery school to university. Opponents of the Resolution, especially French members, accepted the voluntary nature of such language teaching, but not that it should be obligatorily included in curricula.[111] Other resolutions in favour of recognising regional languages and providing full educational facilities for them followed.[112] Against the background of the 1981 Arfé Resolution it was decided to support financially an institution to promote these languages and accordingly in 1982 the European Bureau for Lesser-used Languages was set up, with offices in Dublin and Brussels.

Then in response to the spirit of regionalism and particularly to the pressure from Belgian, German and Spanish regional leaders, powerful in their own countries and angered that they had no seat in Brussels, as well as from the Assembly of the Regions movement, the Maastricht Treaty on European Unity (TEU) of 7 February 1992 provided for a Committee of the Regions.

This advisory Committee, composed of 222 elected local or regional representatives, had to be consulted by the Council of Ministers or Commission in regard to five topics – economic and social cohesion (i.e. the structural funds), transport and communications, public health, education and youth, and culture – and could submit formal opinions on other matters where it believed specific regional interests were involved.

This was the first time that an EU Treaty had recognised the existence of local and regional government, so making a slight breach in the consideration of Europe in terms only of its Member States. Regions had thus obtained a part in the construction of Europe.

Nevertheless, full participation in the process of European integration as sought by 'regionalist' movements, remains some way off. Belgium might be one example of regional ministers representing the country in meetings of the Council of Ministers, but regions are not represented on the European Court of Justice nor indeed can they be brought before the Court. Rectification of this situation has become a main aim of the Assembly of the Regions movement.

Even so, before a Europe of the Regions can begin to take off it would be necessary to reach agreement on what basic powers Regions should have, and in regard to which sectors. And as with the question of minority rights, might there not also be a need for a definition of a region?

The Council of Europe

The failure of the Legal Committee in the early 1970s to arrange for a text on Minorities to be a Protocol to the ECHR led to one of the organisations with consultative status with the Council, the Federal Union of European Nations (FUEN), trying to fill the gap.

In the 1990s the FUEN produced a number of draft texts[113] which reflected the German school of thought on minority protection, stressing group rights, and territoriality. This was hardly surprising since these efforts were supported by the South Tyrolese provincial government and the experts involved came mostly from Central and Eastern Europe. Three presidents of the FUEN from the 1970s to the 1990s were prominent South Tyrolese.[114] And perhaps because of the South Tyrolese experience, the texts were admitted to be maximalistic in their demands.[115]

That of 1992, for example, on the Fundamental Rights of Ethnic Groups in Europe, began by providing a definition of such groups as an ethnic community compactly or dispersedly settled on the territory of a state party, which was smaller in number than the rest of the population of a state, whose members, who were nationals of that state, had ethical, linguistic or cultural features different from those of the rest of the population, and were guided by the will to safeguard these features. It was affirmed that to belong to an ethnic group was a matter of individual choice and no disadvantage should arise from the exercise of such a choice. Members of the group should have the right to their own names in their own language. Groups should have the right to exist, i.e., to enjoy the respect and development of their identity and be free of attempts at assimilation, including the right to their homeland as an inseparable part of their ethnic identity and development and rejection of measures aimed at modifying the demographic composition of such areas. They should have the right to dispose freely of the natural wealth and resources of their homeland. They should be able to use their language before all public institutions in their homeland. They should be taught in their mother tongue at all levels of education, which would be financed by the state, and they should be instructed in their own history and culture. They should have unimpeded transfrontier contacts with their cultural kin; have not only access to the state's mass-media but the right to their own. In public employment the aim should be proportional representation, with compulsory multilingualism. And finally, where they were in a majority groups should have the right to autonomous legislative and executive power to conduct their own affairs, wherever possible in the form of a territorial autonomy. Acceding states would have to report on the way these rights were being implemented.[116]

This was strong stuff, so it was not surprising that the text eventually adopted by the parliamentary Assembly was much weaker in comparison. Recommendation 1201 (1993) recommended to the Committee of Ministers that it adopt an Additional Protocol to the ECHR. The text itself began with the definition of a minority as a group of persons in a state who:

(a) resided on the territory of that state and were citizens thereof;
(b) maintained longstanding, firm and lasting ties with that state;
(c) displayed distinctive ethnic, cultural, religious or linguistic characteristics;
(d) were sufficiently representative, although smaller in number than the rest of the population of that state or of a region of that state;
(e) were motivated by a concern to preserve together that which constitutes their common identity, including their culture, their traditions, their religion or their language.[117]

In regard to the principles listed in the Recommendation a number of those relating to individual rights could be seen in the FUEN text, but there was no provision for proportionality in employment or institutional bilingualism in the minority's area of settlement, and that if members of the minority had the right to learn their mother tongue and be educated in it, the level or levels of that education were not specified. There was no mention of a minority's right to the natural resources of its homeland but, interestingly, a clause was included to the effect that in regions where minorities were in a majority, they should be allowed to enjoy a local autonomy.

The Recommendation was rejected by the Committee of Ministers on the grounds that its obligations were too far reaching.[118] If this decision more or less brought to an end the fight for an Additional Protocol on Minorities to the Human Rights Convention, and it has been said that as a mere Assembly document it had no legally binding force, nevertheless it was important since the Assembly considers itself bound by it. For example, Order 484 (1993) of the Assembly instructed the Committee on Legal Affairs and Human Rights to 'make scrupulously sure' when examining requests for accession to the Council of Europe, that the rights included in the Protocol were respected by the applicant countries.[119] It was significant that some eastern European countries referred to the Recommendation in the Treaties between them.[120]

The 1990s may have seen the failure to obtain an Additional Protocol, but relative success was achieved with two other instruments. The approach of the European Charter for Regional or Minority Languages, adopted by the Committee of Ministers in 1992, eschewed central and eastern European thinking on ethnicity and linguistic communities, and reflected instead the western European emphasis on the rights of the individual as a user of his or her language in relation to identity. These languages were defined as being ones, different from the official language(s), traditionally used within a given territory of a state by nationals of that state who formed a group numerically smaller than the rest of the state's population. Excluded were dialects of the official language(s) of the state or the languages of migrants.

The principle of the Charter was that signatory states should specify, at the time of ratification, each regional or minority language to which it intended to apply measures of promotion or protection. As a minimum, each signatory state undertook to apply thirty-five paragraphs or sub-paragraphs chosen from Part III of the Charter, which related to the use of the languages concerned in education, the judiciary, the media, cultural activities, economic and social life, and transfrontier exchanges. At least three paragraphs or sub-paragraphs had to be chosen from the articles on education and cultural activities, and one from the rest. In determining policy with regard to the languages concerned states were enjoined 'to take into consideration' the needs and wishes of those using the languages.

Under the system of monitoring implementation of the Charter, not only would Member States' reports be examined by a Committee of Experts, but legal non-governmental bodies could draw the attention of the Committee to matters, and submit statements, thus widening the scope for relevant information.[121] By 31 December 1999 the Charter had been signed by 20 states and ratified by eight,[122] coming into force in March 1998 for the languages concerned.

Then in November 1994 the Council adopted the Framework Convention on the Protection of National Minorities. The Convention provided for the usual features on equality and non-discrimination normal in such international instruments. Some features of Recommendation 1201 were also present, including the right of choice to belong to a minority with no disadvantage thereto; the right to official recognition of surnames and first names; prohibition of measures to alter the demographic composition of a minority's area of settlement; and no interference with cross-border contacts with cultural kin. More importantly, measures to promote equality between members of the minority and the national minority in all areas of economic, social, political and cultural life should not be considered acts of discrimination. On the other hand, compared to Resolution 1201 clauses on the use of the minority language in public and on education were considerably watered down. If members of the minority could use their language in private and in public, in the minority area of settlement 'if those persons so request and where such a request corresponds to a real need, the Parties shall endeavour to ensure, as far as possible, the conditions which would make it possible to use the minority language in relations between those persons and the administrative authorities'. If members of a minority had the right to learn their language in areas of their at traditional settlement, the Parties 'shall endeavour to ensure, as far as possible, and within the framework of their education systems, that persons belonging to those minorities have adequate opportunities for being taught the minority language or for receiving instruction in this language'. As for education, the Parties agreed 'where appropriate' to take measures to 'foster knowledge' of the culture, history, language and religion of their national minorities and of the majority. Private schools could be established – but within the framework of national systems, and without any financial obligations by the Parties. And there was certainly nothing about territorial autonomies. Nor, to start with, was the monitoring procedure as good as that under the European Charter. Member States' reports would be evaluated by a Committee of Experts but there was no provision for other bodies to participate in the information process.[123] This would not be rectified until 1997 when Resolution 10 (97) of the Committee of Ministers authorised the Committee of Experts not only to receive but also to invite information from other sources. By the end of 1999 the Convention had been signed by 37 states and ratified by 27.[124]

6
Eastern Europe

Introduction

During the period of Soviet domination of Eastern Europe the problem of minorities lay dormant, even if it had not gone away. Generally control by the Communist Party of states and the media meant that minorities got as much or as little attention as the authorities allowed.[1] The communists could try assassination or elimination of minorities, as Bulgaria did with regard to its Moslem population. For example, in the 1970s and 1980s using arguments similar to those used by Mussolini with regard to the South Tyrolese, claiming that Roma and ethnic Turks were really ethnic Bulgarians who had been forcibly converted into Turks under Ottoman rule, these were obliged to change their names. Villages also had to take new names. Eventually in 1989, after Turkey had agreed to accept them, 370 000 Turkish Bulgarians were expelled.[2] For its part, Poland ignored its some half-million Germans.[3] In Romania treatment of minorities varied according to the regime and the minority. Immediately after the war a Hungarian Autonomous Province was created, although its organisation was no different from Romania's other provinces and it was autonomous in name only and was eventually abolished in 1968. It was also possible for Hungarians, who formed 40 per cent of Transylvania, to receive education in their own language from nursery school through to the Hungarian-language Bolyai University in Cluj. But after the 1956 revolt against communism in Hungary this was dismantled through 'downgrading'. This was achieved, on the one hand, by merging Hungarian and Romanian educational establishments but keeping Hungarian language sections, and on the other by stipulating a minimum number of pupils for classes given in Hungarian and educating them in Romanian if that number was not reached. Between 1976 and 1986 the number of Hungarian children being educated in primary and secondary school had fallen from 63 to 23 per cent. An area of particular concern to the Hungarians was the clear intention of the Romanian authorities to keep Hungarian-language technical and vocational education to a minimum in order to limit the minority in key jobs at a time of rapid Romanian industrialisation. In addition, links with their Hungarian kin were severely restricted, Hungarian cultural institutions were deprived of materials and increasingly had Romanian officials put in charge or were run by front collaborators. Cultural patrimony was removed or destroyed, while history textbooks in whatever language played down to the point of exclusion the Hungarian presence and contribution to the area. In the last decade of Romanian communism Hungarian language broadcasting was reduced to thirty minutes a day. Many Hungarian newspapers became mere translations of their Romanian counterparts, and their print runs were reduced. Hungarian language publications had to give place names in Romanian. Hungarian personal names without Romanian equivalents were also banned. Hungarians were increasingly excluded from senior positions in government, the civil service and the armed forces. In so far as Hungarians were concerned the deliberate aim was to break the process of upward mobility.[4]

But in its history Transylvania has been a multicultural area, with, in 1930, some 745 000 Germans. In the years after the war some 100 000 returned to Germany. Romania did not expel its German population but permitted emigration. However, from the 1950s onwards the numbers emigrating continued to increase until they reached 7 000 a year in the 1970s. In 1978 Germany and Romania agreed a quota of 12 000 per year, for which the German government paid, allegedly, 10 000DM per person, with 6 000DM for a pensioner and 4 000DM for a child. In 1990, the year after the overthrow of the Ceaucescu government, some 111 150 Germans emigrated. According to the 1992 census only 119 436 were left.

The Jewish population of Romania was also sharply reduced. There were 728 000 according to the 1930 census, but the events of the war and emigration to Israel thereafter left only a small minority of 25–30 000. The Ceaucescu government was also believed to have an arrangement for payment for emigrants with the state of Israel. According to the 1993 census the Jewish community numbered less than 10 000.[5]

For their part Czechoslovakia and Yugoslavia provided for federalism on a territorial basis for their dominant nationalities and educational facilities for their non-dominant minorities.

The CSCE/OSCE

At international level in the 1970s and 1980s Europe was still dominated by the politics of the Cold War. The Soviet Union wanted formal recognition of the postwar territorial *status quo* (the West had never recognised the 1940 annexation of the Baltic states and West Germany made no secret of the desire for German unity) while the West, if not interested in recognising territory, sought progress in the fields of security and human rights.[6]

As a framework within which political matters could be discussed both sides set up in 1972 the Conference on Security and Co-operation in Europe (CSCE), with a Council of Foreign Ministers as the governing body and a Committee of Senior Officers (CSO) to implement decisions.

In August 1975, 35 European states signed the Helsinki Agreement. According to Principle VII of the Declaration on Principles Guiding Relations between the participating States,

> The participating states on whose territories national minorities exist will respect the right of persons belonging to such minorities to equality before the law, will afford them the full opportunity of the actual enjoyment of Human Rights and Fundamental Freedoms and will, in this manner, protect their legitimate interests in this sphere.

But the Helsinki Agreement contained another interesting principle. The text of Principle III on the Inviolability of Frontiers seems explicit:

> The participating States regard as inviolable all one another's frontiers as well as the frontiers of all the states in Europe and therefore they will refrain now and in the future from assaulting these frontiers. Accordingly they will also refrain from any demand for, or act of seizure and usurpation of part or all of the territory of any particular state.[7]

The Soviet Union could seem well satisfied with such a text, but questions as to its interpretation would be raised not in Eastern Europe but in the West, where Ulster Unionists would later believe that the Constitution of the Irish Republic, a signatory to the Agreement, contravened Principle III because of the claim to the North in Articles 2 and 3. However, the British government has argued that the Declaration on Principles Guiding Relations between participating states in the Helsinki Final Act contains ten such principles and the wording makes clear that all these have equal importance and must be interpreted taking account of the others. Principles III and IV covering Inviolability of Frontiers and Territorial Integrity of States were applications of the general principle of international law regarding the non-use of force, and their interpretation had to take account of that part of Principle I which stated that 'Frontiers can be changed, in accordance with international law, by peaceful means and by agreement'. *The maintenance of a territorial claim by one signatory state against another is thus not incompatible with the Helsinki Final Act provided it is pursued by exclusively peaceful means.* And in this regard the Irish government, referring to Article 29 of the Constitution, according to which Ireland pursued the settlement of international disputes by peaceful means, has always maintained that it is for it to decide how the claim should be pursued, that it has always used negotiation, and has condemned the violence of the PIRA as having no mandate. However, as the Fine Gael leader John Bruton devastatingly pointed out, reference to Article 29 was irrelevant since under the 1937 Constitution matters concerning Northern Ireland were not international but national.[8]

But behind any interpretation of the Agreement lay the more fundamental issue as to whether the Agreement – or any documents of the CSCE (later OSCE) for that matter – were legally binding on states as opposed to being merely a guiding statement of principles similar to the 1948 UN Declaration of Human Rights. It has been stated that OSCE commitments are generally not considered to form part of international law legally enforceable between participating states.[9] But even if such instruments are considered legally non-binding entailing 'merely' political or moral obligations, the question remains as to what this means. For the eminent United Nations jurist Oscar Schachter, 'stating that the Agreement does not engage the legal responsibility of the state is quite different from stating that the Agreement need not be observed or that the Parties are free to act as if there were no such agreement'.[10] In any case, even if the OCSE instruments are politically rather than legally binding, 'a commitment does not have to be legally binding in order to have binding force ... violation of politically but not legally binding agreements is as inadmissible as any violation of international law'.[11]

Whatever the status of CSCE commitments – and a number of future inter-state treaties would specifically declare that the parties accepted as legal obligations the relevant CSCE instruments – its efforts in the field of what became known as the Human Dimension became particularly relevant in the dying years of the Soviet Empire.

Thus, in Part IV of the Document of the Copenhagen meeting of the CSCE in 1990, the Conference on the Human Dimension laid down the basic premises for the development of any viable minority regime.[12] These included recognition of the importance of a democratic political framework based on the rule of law, with an independent judiciary to resolve questions relating to minorities; reaffirmation that the rights of persons belonging to minorities formed a part of universally recognised Human Rights; that it was a person's individual choice to belong to a minority; and that persons belonging to minorities had the right freely to express, preserve and develop their ethnic, cultural, linguistic or religious identity and to develop their culture in all its aspects free from any attempts at assimilation against their will.

The Conference recognised that for persons belonging to minorities to enjoy full equality, to protect and create conditions for the promotion of the cultural identity of minorities as groups, and to protect against forced assimilation required special measures. In particular protection of the collective identity of minorities was 'fundamental to any system for minority protection'. Specific provisions included measures in education, the use of language before the public authorities, and a local or autonomous administration to promote and protect the identity of the minority group.[13]

But as well as laying down guidelines the CSCE established the relevant machinery. In Vienna in January 1989 the Concluding Document on the Human Dimension Mechanism created the possibility for participating states to institute exchanges of information, representations and bilateral meetings in order to examine problems 'with a view to resolving them'.[14]

At Copenhagen the following year the Mechanism was developed further. Written requests for information had to be answered within ten days; if the state concerned agreed, an expert mission could be sent to address a specific issue. If the expert mission failed to solve the problem a mission of three Rapporteurs could be set up to get the facts, report on them and give advice.[15]

In April 1991 it was agreed that the CSCE should have a Parliamentary Assembly. At Moscow in 1991 a qualitative change in the mechanism was introduced. If the states felt that a situation was threatening to the Human Dimension a mission could be sent with or without the consent of the state concerned. However, any action on the basis of the mission's reports had to be decided by the Senior Council (which had replaced the CSO in 1992). However, since decisions had to be taken by consensus it was not unreasonable to suppose that decisions might not be taken.[16]

At the Helsinki summit in July 1992, as a direct result of the violent dissolution of Yugoslavia,[17] it was decided to establish the post of a High Commissioner on National Minorities (HCNM), and in December the Netherlands Minister of State Max van der Stoel was appointed. His main duty was the prevention of conflict by providing early warning of potentially critical situations. It would be up to him to collect information, meet and discuss with the parties to a dispute, promote dialogue and co-operation between them, and make recommendations to them. He could request the assistance of experts. On the other hand, the HCNM does not investigate individual minority rights violations – he is no receiver of petitions nor is he a Minorities Ombudsman. Furthermore, he is specifically excluded from considering national minority issues in situations involving organised acts of terrorism, thus conveniently removing him from the possibility of being called in to consider the problems of the Basque Country, Corsica or Northern Ireland.[18]

In Stockholm in December 1992 a Directed Conciliation Mechanism was established under which the Senior Council could 'direct' a state to seek conciliation in order to help resolve a dispute. This 'direction' could be taken without the consent of the parties to the dispute, but could not be used in cases involving issues of territorial integrity, national defence, or title to sovereignty over territory.[19]

Conciliation was mandatory under the CSCE's Convention on Conciliation and Arbitration if one party so requested, but the parties had to decide whether they would accept the proposed solution of the Conciliation Commission. On the other hand, if arbitration was optional the award was binding.[20]

At the Budapest Summit in December 1994 the CSCE became the OSCE in order to underline the organisation's permanent status. In 1996 the CSCE went on to draw up the Hague Recommendations on the Educational Rights of National Minorities, including that in primary schools the curriculum should ideally be taught in the minority language and the minority language should be taught on a regular basis; that at secondary level a 'substantial part' of the curriculum should be taught in the minority language; and that there should be the required number of teachers available to do this. With regard to vocational and tertiary education, this should be provided in the minority language if a need is demonstrated for it and numbers justify it.[21]

In 1998 at Oslo the OSCE adopted a series of Linguistic Rights of National Minorities, including the right to one's names in the minority language, to apply also to private businesses; that in areas inhabited by significant numbers of the minority and where there was sufficient demand place names should also be in the minority language; persons belonging to national minorities should have the right to establish and maintain their own minority language media, with independent programming safeguarded; that where members of a minority were in sufficient numbers they should have the right to acquire official documents in their language, use their language with the administration, the courts, in prison and in local and regional government, with the authorities providing public services in the language and adopting appropriate recruitment and training policies.[22]

The need for developing standards and monitoring machinery became evident following the collapse of communism and the dissolution of the Soviet empire, including the Soviet Union itself. Within a few years fifteen new states came into being or were reborn – Armenia, Azerbaijan, Belarus, Bosnia, Croatia, Estonia, Georgia, Latvia, Lithuania, Macedonia, Moldova (formerly Moldavia), Slovenia, the Ukraine, and, following the so-called 'velvet divorce' of 31 December 1992, the Czech Republic and Slovakia. Almost immediately Armenia and Azerbaijan went to war over the latter's province of Ngorno-Karabakh, where the 75 per cent Armenian population attempted to secede. In predominantly Romanian-speaking Moldova it soon became clear that the minority Slavic population of the Trans-Dnestr region would be most unwilling to accept the new state. And in Georgia the population of the Abkhazia region, supported by Russia, declared independence and fighting broke out, while South Ossetia declared independence and sought union with North Ossetia, part of the Russian Federation.

Six existing states were under new management, sometimes in name only – Albania, Bulgaria, Hungary, Poland, Romania, and what was left of the once model Yugoslav Federation in the shape of Serbia and Montenegro.

In the new and reborn states those in charge reverted to the mentality of those in charge of the states that had newly emerged or been enlarged after 1919 – emphasising the nineteenth or early twentieth century Germanic school notions of 'the nation'.[23] This meant focusing on issues of territorial integrity; citizenship (and particularly the position of citizens of the former imperial power); the use of the national language to enhance identity and the national culture; and concern for kin in neighbouring states.

In the existing states, however, the minorities expected their rights to be improved, but fear of separatist ethnic nationalism remained no less rife. In two countries, Albania and Bulgaria, an attempt was made even to ban political parties based on ethnic criteria.

But why did minority issues become so important after the fall of communism? Liebich argues that the explanation that with the collapse of iron communist control nationalism was able to rear its head again was unsatisfactory, as was the theory that nationalism stepped into the ideological void left by the disappearance of Marxism, and that a more cogent explanation was that ethnicity had become one, sometimes the principal, criterion for the distribution of scarce resources.[24]

A simpler explanation is that one looked for security within one's own community in a world that was disintegrating. On the one hand, there was the spectre of economic dissolution and collapse of living standards in the slower than expected transition to western European capitalism; on the other hand, there was the spectre of political dissolution – three federations, Czechoslovakia, Russia and Yugoslavia had collapsed, leaving everywhere the fear of granting autonomies that could be the first step to secession. There was the threat of aggrandisement by a number of states that had considerable exploitable diasporas abroad, notably Albania, Hungary, Russia and Serbia.

Unsurprisingly, therefore, apart from the Caucasian states and Belarus, all the others wanted to become part of the western world as soon as possible. They wanted to be members of the European Union in order to receive funds for economic reconstruction and to receive advice on changing from a command to a free market economy. They wanted to belong to NATO in order to ensure defence against the return of a crusading communism in Russia or against Russian attempts to regain the territory that had once been part of the Soviet Union, and in many states of which Russian troops were still stationed. And they wanted to join the Council of Europe, in order to ensure high standards of human rights. Membership of all three, it was hoped, would bring about and ensure democracy, political stability, a thriving economy, and defence against external aggression.

In three countries minority problems were minimal. In the Czech Republic and Poland the main issue was not a minority within the state but one that was not.

Individual minority problems

The Czech Republic

Almost immediately after the fall of communism the new government of Czechoslovakia faced demands from Germany that the Sudeten Germans be compensated for the loss of their property and possessions. A 'Good Neighbour' treaty signed on 27 February 1992 was criticised in Germany for its lack of provisions on the property rights of those expelled. In fact legislation adopted in May 1991 providing for the restitution of private property seized under communist rule specifically ruled out restitution to the Sudeten Germans. In January 1997 a Joint Czech–German Declaration was signed, in which the German government apologised yet again for Nazi policies towards the Czechs while the Czech government apologised for the first time for the expulsion of the Sudeten Germans. Nevertheless the Agreement explicitly acknowledged that the legality of the expulsions was not in question, and therefore there were no grounds upon which individual compensation claims could be pursued.[25]

Poland

Similarly in Poland German families expelled in 1945 demanded back their property. But there was no law, in contrast to the Czech Republic, providing for compensation for citizens deprived of their property even by the communist regime precisely because of the fear that it would open the door to German claims. Refugee organisations demanded that Polish entry into the European Union be vetoed unless the properties – and the right to return to them – were restored.[26]

However, that still left some 500 000 persons speaking the Silesian dialect which children acquire first and use in everyday life. Silesian was encouraged after the war as German was discouraged but was nevertheless heavily germanised. In the group German is used in everyday speech and is 'code switched', i.e. German words are inserted into sentences to convey emphasis in the sentence.[27] Since the 5 per cent hurdle for political parties needed to obtain a seat in the Polish parliament under the proportional representation system does not apply to parties of ethnic minorities the group is able to send an MP to parliament.

As for the 300 000 Ukrainian minority, a kindergarten and some primary and secondary schools exist where instruction is given in Ukrainian. Some Polish primary schools teach Ukrainian. There is no shortage of books and press in Ukrainian and links with the Ukraine via the Church and other socio-cultural bodies are strong.[28]

Karelia

In Finland the disintegration of the Soviet Union raised the question of regaining at least western Karelia. Repossession was seen as matters of history and justice. Proposals included its unconditional return, purchase or leasing of the area, or remaining with Russia but with an autonomy enabling expelled Finns to return.[29] However, redrawing the border has been rejected by both Russia and Finland. President Koivisto of Finland declared that Finland had lost Karelia in two wars and three peace treaties, and cross-border co-operation was more important than the border. To pursue the matter would be economically unjustified, politically unwise, and, if successful, Finland would acquire a Russian minority. His views seemed to find general support amongst the Finnish population. In eastern Karelia, however, where some 80 000 Karelians numbering 11 per cent of the population declared themselves Karelian but only half of these named Karelian as their mother tongue, the demand was for the language to be official again, with teaching in the language for those who wanted it and increased cross-border co-operation.[30] In 1992 a Russo-Finnish treaty of Good Neighbourliness and Mutual Co-operation was signed, with agreement to base relations on OSCE accords and respect for the inviolability of their joint frontier.[31]

The Baltic states

In the Baltic states the issues were citizenship and language. Half a century of enforced incorporation into the Soviet Union had seen Russians take up senior and managerial posts in the economy and many had entered while serving in the armed forces. A substantial number had preferred to stay in the perhaps more agreeable society in those states, so that Russians formed one-third of the population of Estonia and Latvia and 10 per cent of Lithuania, but when other language groups such as Ukrainian and Belarusian were added then barely 61 per cent of Estonia was Estonian and 52 per cent of Latvia was Latvian. By contrast in Lithuania, even when a Polish minority of 7 per cent was added to the Russians, Ukrainians and Belarusians, the Lithuanian percentage of the population was still 80 per cent.[32] Another aspect of the situation was that most of the Russians lived in the big towns. Narva, on the Estonian border with Russia, was practically an entirely Russian city. The great fear in Latvia was that if citizenship was granted to non-Latvians any change in the composition of the population might lead to Latvia being voted back to Russia. The example of Belarus more or less returning to the Russian fold in 1999 was not encouraging.

The last decade of the century therefore saw the adoption of harsh Estonian and Latvian laws on citizenship, possession of which was essential for voting and property rights, gradually amended under pressure from international organisations. The initial laws were based on an attempt to emphasise the legal continuity of the two Republics over the Soviet occupation. What complicated matters was that in both republics citizenship laws were based on *jus sanguinis* yet many of those coming to the republics under communism now had children born there.

In the Estonian Constitution of July 1992 only those who were citizens before 1940 and their descendants could vote in elections. Earlier, laws provided that applicants for citizenship would have to pass stringent language examinations. In June the following year the Estonian parliament adopted a law defining 500 000 ex-Soviet citizens as foreigners, who would be required to apply for a residence permit or face expulsion. Residence rights would be refused to Russians who had been members of the Soviet armed forces or security services. In the meantime the remaining Russians would receive a residence permit for two years, after which they would be expected to apply formally for the citizenship of their choice. But in May of 1993 Estonia had become a member of the Council of Europe, and the Council criticised the law, following which the law was revised. Later, minorities numbering at least 3 000 were given the right to establish cultural, educational and religious institutions for which funds would be provided by the state. In 1995 a new citizenship law extended the minimum period of residence required for naturalisation from two to five years with citizenship, if approved, being granted a further year after application. Then, from 15 May 1997, former Soviet passports were declared no longer valid in Estonia, and the holders were therefore obliged to apply for non-citizen passports or become citizens of another country. In 1998 the citizenship law was amended to provide that stateless children born after 26 February 1992 would be eligible for Estonian citizenship if their parents were stateless and had lived in Estonia for at least five years. 6 500 children would benefit and the amendment was welcomed by Russia and the OSCE.

Efforts to establish the Estonian language in public, however, ran into difficulties. In November 1997 Parliament amended the language laws requiring MPs and local government officials to prove a suitable knowledge of Estonian if they had not been educated in an Estonian-language primary school. The government was also given powers to regulate the use of Estonian in the services sector. The six Russian deputies voted against, arguing that the laws were unconstitutional and in February 1998 the Supreme Court upheld them. But in December Parliament returned to the attack, approving legislation that required all elected officials to know Estonian well enough to take a proper part in the workings of local and national elected bodies and to understand the contents of legislative texts. The OSCE's HCNM urged the President not to approve the law on the grounds that it contravened Article 25 of the 1966 UN Covenant on Civil and Political Rights.[33] Nevertheless the law was promulgated by the President, and the question now is whether it will be challenged before the European Court of Human Rights.

In Latvia the Supreme Court adopted citizenship laws on 17 October 1991. It would be granted automatically to anyone who held Latvian citizenship before 1940 and their descendants, even if not currently resident in Latvia. Anyone else seeking Latvian citizenship had to have lived in Latvia for sixteen years, be fluent in Latvian and conversant with the Constitution, renounce Soviet citizenship and swear allegiance to the Latvian Republic.

In 1992 language laws guaranteed education only in Latvian. All employees in both the public and the private sector were required to take language exams. Then in June 1994 the parliament adopted a language bill which stipulated that in order to obtain Latvian citizenship one needed to pass a language exam, but former members of the military, 'chauvinists', 'nationalists' and 'fascists' could not apply. This was expected to exclude up to half a million of the 700 000 non-citizens inhabiting the state. Furthermore, from the year 2000 there would be an annual quota of 0.1 per cent of the total Latvian population who actually would be able to obtain citizenship. Following protests from the Council of Europe and the OSCE's HCNM a revised bill was adopted. The quota provision was deleted; applications had to be processed within a year, but the applicants still had to pass a language exam and former Soviet armed forces personnel remained excluded.

In February 1995 Latvia became a member of the Council of Europe. Its application had been held up because of its treatment of minorities.

Following further consultations with the HCNM the citizenship law was revised again in April 1998 to provide that all persons born in Latvia would be entitled to apply for citizenship at the age of sixteen; those born outside would have to wait until 2001. Nevertheless applicants would still have to pass exams in Latvian language and history. However, all children born in Latvia after 21 August 1991 would be granted citizenship provided the parents had been legally resident in

Latvia for at least five years. These moves, coupled with measures simplifying the language exam for the over-65s were welcomed by the OSCE.

Because Lithuanians were a comfortable majority in their own land their treatment of minorities was very different. Using *jus solis* rather then *jus sanguinis*, an early citizenship law of 3 November 1989 allowed all current foreign residents of Lithuania, irrespective of their ethnic origin, to apply for Lithuanian citizenship. The law was revised in 1995 to allow persons who had been forced to leave the country against their will before or after the proclamation of independence (11 March 1990) to be included. In May 1993 Lithuania became a member of the Council of Europe, and in August the last Russian troops left the country. However, it was not until January 1995 that Lithuanian was declared the official state language. Nevertheless there had been some tension when Lithuania banned all school textbooks printed abroad – Poland protested as Polish-language schools used history books printed in Poland.

If language and citizenship were the issues in the Baltic states it was language and autonomy in those areas where the Crown of Saint Stephen cast its shadow.

Hungarian minorities

Article 6, para.3 of the 1989 Hungarian Constitution affirms that 'The Republic of Hungary *feels responsible* for the fate of Hungarians living beyond its borders and promotes the cultivation of contacts with Hungarians'.[34] On 19 August 1992 the Prime Minister, Josef Antall, addressing the World Federation of Hungarians, stated that Hungary had no territorial claims on neighbouring countries but nevertheless the Hungarian government had a duty enshrined in the Constitution to protect the interests of Hungarians living beyond the borders.

In Slovakia, according to the 1991 census, 556 000 persons, 10.8 per cent of the population, were Hungarian. In Romania it was 1.62 million and 7.1 per cent. In the Serbian province of the Voivodina in 1981 it was 425 000 and just under 19 per cent (present day estimates are 15 per cent).

In Slovakia Hungarian culture was perceived to be in decline. Hungarian-only primary schools with small enrolments in rural areas were being closed from the 1970s onwards and the pupils and teachers sent to larger establishments, but in those areas there was an irreparable loss of local culture. Some 25 per cent of Hungarian pupils attend Slovak schools. A lower percentage of Hungarians attended secondary schools, and it was noted in 1980 that Hungarian standards of education were markedly lower than the rest of the population, with a knock-on effect on university applications. More Hungarians were going to Slovak grammar schools, and this was proving necessary for higher and technical education. Most Hungarians generally believed that the existing number of Hungarian-language schools was inadequate; most Slovaks thought the number was sufficient. Another cause for low admission to university was poor knowledge of Slovak, in which the entrance examinations were held.[35]

Slovakia became independent on 1 January 1993. Following complaints from Hungary about the treatment of the Hungarian minority in Slovakia, and from Slovakia regarding the treatment of the Slovak minority in Hungary, the HCMN sent in a Team of Experts to analyse the situation in both countries. The initial duration of the Team's mandate was two years. It was then extended by one more year, after which Slovakia stated that it had fulfilled its task and there would be no agreement on a further extension.[36] In two areas progress was made. Where the minority represented 20 per cent bilingual road signs were agreed, and Hungarians were allowed to register their names in the Hungarian version. Previously they had had to register Slovak given names and women had to add 'ova' to their family names.

On 19 March 1995 Slovakia and Hungary signed a Friendship Treaty described as unprecedented in contemporary international law in terms of the breadth of obligations undertaken in relation to minority rights.[37] First, the parties confirmed that they respected each other's territorial integrity, had no territorial claims on each other, and would not raise any such claims in the future (Article 3).

Second, the parties recognised that the protection of national minorities was an integral part of the international protection of human rights and was therefore not an exclusively domestic affair of the states concerned. In protecting minorities the parties would be guided by the following principles: membership of a national minority was to be a matter of free personal choice and no disadvantage should result from such a choice; members of a minority were equal before the law; they should have the right freely to express, maintain and develop their cultural identity; the parties would refrain from policies aimed at assimilating members of the minority against their will; members of the minority could use their language in contacts with the public administration and in judicial proceedings, have the right to bilingual topography in areas where they lived, to register their first and family names in their language, and, without prejudice to the learning of the official language or the teaching in that language, to have adequate opportunities in the framework of the state educational system for being taught their mother tongue or for receiving instruction in it; and the right of access to public mass media and the right to their own media (Article 15, paras.1–2).

Third, the parties agreed to respect accepted principles and norms of international law, applying the Council of Europe Framework Convention for the Protection of National Minorities adopted and signed by both parties on 1 February 1995 'as from the date of the ratification of the present Treaty and the Framework Convention' by both parties. They also agreed to accept as legal obligations both the CSCE's Copenhagen Document of 29 June 1990 on the Human Dimension and Recommendation 1201 (1993) of the Parliamentary Assembly of the Council of Europe (Article 15, para.4).

Almost immediately differences of opinion arose on the Treaty's interpretation. The main issue was the reference to Recommendation 1201. According to one eminent authority it seemed legitimate to con-clude that the Recommendation conferred group rights, on the basis that Article 11 of the Recommendation provided that in regions where they were in a majority, persons belonging to a national minority should have the right to 'appropriate local or autonomous authorities'. When the Treaty was ratified in March 1996 the Slovak parliament entered a *caveat* to the effect that the Slovak Republic had 'never accepted ... in the Treaty formulations ... a recognition of the principle of collective rights for minorities and those ... rights, which would allow establishment of any autonomous structures or special statute based on ethnicity'.[38]

Matters did not improve when in November 1995 Slovakia adopted a new language law which stated that Slovak was the only official lan-guage, and there were restrictions on the use of other languages in public life. Hungarians denounced it as violating the Friendship Treaty, and concern was expressed by the European Parliament and the Council of Europe. The government promised to submit a bill on the use of minority languages but one was not forthcoming until July 1999. In the meantime, first in March 1996 the Slovak parliament approved a law which included penalties of up to two years' imprison-ment for those 'disseminating false information abroad damaging to the interests of the Republic', or organising demonstrations 'deemed harmful to the constitutional system, territorial integrity or defence capabilities'. Then in September 1997 the Slovak Prime Minister, Vladimir Meciar, proposed a voluntary mutual repatriation pro-gramme. The Hungarians refused to discuss the matter.

When the Use of National Minority Languages Act was adopted on 10 July 1999, it was immediately denounced by the Hungarian political parties. *Inter alia*, nowhere could a minority language be official; individual members of a minority could only use their language in official communications with their municipality where they constituted at least 20 per cent of the inhabitants (the Hungarians wanted 10 per cent); official documents were not allowed to be issued in a minority language; officials of the public administration were not obliged to know a minority language (and thus knowledge of a minority language could not be a condition for recruitment of staff); since, according to the State Language Law all public authorities had to use the national language, Hungarian mayors exchanging official letters would be breaking the law (a repetition of the situation in South Tyrol before 1972).[39] However, the law was considered by the HCNM as in conformity with the Slovak Constitution, applicable international standards and recommendations from international institutions.[40]

Much the same situation existed in Romania where, since the fall of communism at the end of 1989 the Hungarian minority had been trying to obtain adequate linguistic and cultural rights. In particular the calls have been for an all-Hungarian language university in Cluj, and for areas with a compact Hungarian population to be designated as special zones where the Hungarian language would have the same official status as Romanian. There were also calls in 1993 for regional self-administration.

The results have not been encouraging. In 1993 Romania joined the Council of Europe, and bilingual signs were allowed in areas where minorities formed 30 per cent of the population. But the following year the government introduced penalties of up to three years' imprisonment for flying foreign flags or for playing the anthems of foreign states. Calls for cultural autonomy were dismissed as unacceptable.

In 1995 a language law prescribed Romanian as the language of tuition and examinations in all universities and colleges, including the entrance examination to these.

These measures aroused the concern of the HCMN who, on visits to Bucharest, focused on issues such as the freedom of parents to choose a school for their children, the fact that the law did not allow the existence of private religious schools and the possibility that these should receive state funding, and the revision of Romanian history textbooks to contain the contribution of minorities.[41]

On 16 September 1996, with the support of the HCMN, Hungary and Romania signed a Treaty of Understanding, Co-operation and

Good Neighbourliness which in its key aspects of respect for territorial integrity, minority rights, and the status of certain international instruments was practically identical with that signed between Hungary and Slovakia the previous year. Interestingly, mindful of the controversy relating to the latter Treaty, it was explicitly stated in an Annex that the Contracting Parties agreed 'that Recommendation 1201 does not refer to collective rights, nor does it impose on them the obligation to grant to the concerned persons any right to a special status of territorial autonomy based on ethnic criteria'. Nationalists on both sides condemned the Treaty. And on two subsequent occasions, December 1997 and June 1998, the Romanians showed themselves hostile to the idea of a separate Hungarian-language university, insisting on a multicultural approach to education.

In addition to the Slovak and Romanian Treaties Budapest signed other Treaties and Conventions disclaiming any threat to their territorial integrity and providing for mutual protection of minorities with the Ukraine (31 May 1991), Slovenia (6 November 1992), the Russian Federation (11 November 1992) and Croatia (5 April 1995).

By contrast, in Hungary itself minority rights for the nation's some 200 000 Germans, 100 000 Slovaks, 50 000 Croatians, 10 000 Slovenes and anything from 500 000 – 700 000 Roma and Sinti are extensive and ungrudging.

Legislation[42] adopted in July 1993 defined national and ethnic minorities – and hence able to qualify for protection – as all groups living in Hungary for more than a century and having their own linguistic and cultural traditions. Choice of identity was voluntary. Minorities were guaranteed their names and education in their mother tongue. Unusually, it is nowhere stated that Hungarian is the national official language, but that any one could use his mother tongue anywhere and at any time in the Republic. In the introduction to the Act it was expressly stated that minority rights could not be fully guaranteed within the bounds of individual civil rights so that group rights were also necessary. A chapter in the Act headed 'Collective Rights' provided for the right to establish social organisations and self-government at both national and local level, including educational, training, cultural and scientific institutions, the right to develop direct international relations with their kin in other states, with the implication of funding from central resources. Another chapter dealt with the machinery for the election of local self-government bodies by members of the minority group, whose representatives then elect national self-government. Minorities also have the right to be represented in the national parliament.[43]

Moldova

In 1990 of the some 4.3 million population of Moldavia 64.5 per cent were ethnic Romanians, 14.2 per cent were Ukrainians, 12.8 per cent were Russians, and 3.5 per cent Gagauz (Orthodox-Christian Turks). Under Soviet rule the Romanians were denied the status of Romanian nationality.[44]

With the Soviet empire disintegrating, the Russian-Ukrainian population, the majority east of the Dnestr, sought to create the Dnestr Republic. A separate state was called for by the Gagauz group of Christian Turks. Both claims were rejected by the Romanian majority which had already in 1989 rejected the Cyrillic script imposed by Stalin. In May 1991 the name of the state was changed to Moldova and in August independence was declared. There was also a strong movement west of the Dnestr for the area to return to Romania. Fighting broke out as the Slavs of the Trans-Dnestr sought independence, and matters were complicated by the presence in the territory of the Russian Fourteenth Army.

In 1995 Moldova became a member state of the Council of Europe but differences continued. Schools in Trans-Dnestr were ordered to teach only in the Cyrillic script, rejecting the Latin script as 'creeping Romanianisation', while those wanting union with Romania wanted the Constitution to designate the country's official language as Romanian rather than Moldavian. On the other hand, the Moldovan parliament had granted a cultural and economic autonomy to the southern part of the state where the Gagauz were concentrated.

The situation remained confused during 1996–98 as both parts of the state held presidential elections, and talks involving also the HCNM were held to find a solution. The Moldovan government was ready to accept a special status for the Trans-Dnestr, but the government of the self-declared Dnestr-Moldovan Republic saw negotiations as between two equal states.

The Ukraine

The disastrous experience of Yugoslavia is recounted in the next chapter. But in one other area, the Ukraine, the OSCE took the lead in brokering an autonomy for one of its regions, the Crimea.

In 1989 the Ukrainian population numbered some 51.4 million, 22.1 per cent of which were Russian. To the west of the Dnepr there was a high degree of Ukrainian national consciousness, a greater liberality in politics and a desire to look toward central Europe. To the east where the heavy industry of the Soviet era was situated was also located most of the Russian population heavily imbued with Soviet authoritarianism. Russians also formed 70 per cent[45] of the 2.5 million population of the Crimea, mainly as a result of tourist-led immigration and the stationing of the strategically important Black Sea Fleet at Sevastopol.

Under Soviet rule the Crimea had been first an autonomous region and then an *oblast* (province) of the Russian Soviet Federated Socialist Republic (RSFSR) but in 1954 Nikita Kruschev allowed it to become part of the Ukrainian SSR, but remaining an *oblast*. After the Ukraine declared 'state sovereignty' in July 1990 the vast majority of Crimea voters voted in a separate referendum in January 1991 for restoration of autonomous region status within the RSFSR, and in 1992 the Crimean parliament adopted a Constitution of the Republic of the Crimea that, if acknowledging that the Crimea was part of the Ukraine, bore all the hallmarks of an independent state.

Matters were complicated by the return in 1989 of some 300 000 of the Crimean Tatars deported in 1944. These wanted to reclaim property, including land rights and rights to natural resources, to re-establish cultural traditions including re-introduction of place names, to be guaranteed more than proportionate representation in Ukrainian and Crimean decision-making bodies and, to distinguish themselves from other minorities, to claim special status and rights as an 'indigenous people'.

The OSCE had originally been called in to ease tensions between Russia and the Ukraine over holdings of nuclear weapons and control of the Black Sea Fleet, but the organisation was soon involved in the tension between the Ukraine and the Crimea.

Negotiations between the two brokered by the OSCE began in July 1993. In November 1995 a new Crimea Constitution was adopted but it was opposed by the Tatars since it failed to give them a guaranteed representation. On the other hand, most of the provisions of this Constitution were acceptable to Kiev, the exceptions being some 20 articles on symbols of statehood, an internal citizenship, and the status of Sevastopol.

In April 1996 the Ukraine adopted a Law on the Autonomous Republic of Crimea (ARC) approving all but the disputed articles, and providing for agreement on them to be reached within a month. This did not, in fact, occur. Nevertheless, in June 1996 the new Ukrainian Constitution provided for an Autonomous Republic of the Crimea.[46]

On the other hand, criticisms have been made of the apparent lack of law-making power by the ARC in that under the Ukrainian Constitution the ARC is not expressly granted the power to make laws but can adopt 'normative legal acts' and exercise 'authority' in a large number of fields, but any such acts and decisions by the Crimea government must conform to the Constitution, laws and decrees of the Ukraine. The expectation is that the working of the relationship between the Ukraine and the Crimea will depend heavily on the Ukraine's Constitutional Court, and that relaxation of the watchdog nature of the autonomy by Kiev is likely only to occur within the framework of improved wider relations between Kiev and Moscow.[47]

In the meantime the position of the returning Tatars had not improved – there had been long delays in granting them Ukrainian citizenship, with the result that many were unable to vote.

As for the Ruthenians taken over by the Ukraine in 1945, since Kiev does not believe that the Ruthenian language is different from Ukrainian, there is no mention of them in the new Constitution, although there is a reference to 'indigenous peoples'.

The Caucasus

Throughout the 1990s the situation in the Caucasus continued to be dominated by the ongoing dispute between Armenia and Azerbaijan over Ngorno-Karabakh. The OSCE brokered a number of peace plans – in 1992, 1993, 1995 and 1997. At one time Ngorno-Karabakh actually declared itself an independent republic, which even the President of Armenia denounced as unrealistic. The Minsk group of the OSCE proposed an autonomous status for the province and the right to its own constitution. This was accepted by Azerbaijan but rejected by Ngorno-Karabakh. New proposals by the Minsk group were consequently rejected on the grounds that they threatened Azerbaijan's territorial integrity.[48]

7
No Lessons Learned

Western Europe: freedom of movement versus defence of the homeland

As the third millennium dawns what are the prospects for regional cultural minorities? The omens are less favourable than one might suppose.

In western Europe the minorities have seen the process of western European integration as a liberating factor as the Member States of the Union, the traditional oppressors, decline, and they hand ever more power over to Brussels. But these minorities would do well to heed the old saying 'Better the devil you know than the devil you don't'. The last three decades of the millennium showed that most states were increasingly willing to be generous to their minorities in their homelands, whether as a result of armed conflict or not; that dialogue between minorities and their host states, or between host states, were more likely to bring about improved conditions for minorities than regimes imposed by international organisations. Indeed it can be argued that it was the relative success of arrangements at state level that paved the way for instruments adopted at international level.

The European Union, however, is quite another creature. The fanatic drive for a level playing field in economic and social matters, and the rigid centralism which is the mainstay of that drive does not augur well for the decentralised tolerance of local arrangements necessary for the maintenance and development of minorities on their unique habitat, their homeland. It is also far less accountable to its people than any member state. The supreme decision-making body, the Council of Ministers, cannot be removed as a body; the individual ministers can only be removed by the electorate of their own countries. The European Parliament has no government-making powers and can only dismiss as a whole the collegiate body of the European Civil Service, the European Commission, responsible for drafting legislation; it cannot dismiss individual Commissioners. And there is no appeal against decisions of the European Court of Justice in regard to the implementation of Union legislation.

A main pillar of the process of European integration is the principle of freedom of movement: that any citizen of any member state may move to another member state to live and work. The threat of an invasion of minority homelands is therefore unambiguous. Freedom of movement is governed by Article 48 of the 1957 Treaty of Rome. It entails the abolition of any discrimination based on nationality between workers of the Member States as regards employment, remuneration and other conditions of work. Acceptance of offers and the ability to move freely for this purpose could only be limited on grounds of public policy, public security or public health. However, according to paragraph 4 of Article 48 its provisions did not apply to employment in the public service. The European Commission was aware that what constituted the public service varied considerably in the Member States, and was concerned that if Member States were at liberty not only to decide what constituted the public service but also to impose a nationality requirement for employment in the public service the policy of freedom of movement could be substantially thwarted.

In the view of the Commission, employment in the public service was itself a Community concept.[1] Action to eliminate the nationality requirement from conditions for access to certain posts in the public service was therefore essential.[2]

This need for a restrictive interpretation of derogations to Article 48 was supported in a landmark ruling of the European Court of Justice. In its judgement of 17 December 1980 relating to the case brought by the European Commission against Belgium, the Court stated that it was 'necessary to ensure that the effectiveness and scope of the provisions of the treaty on freedom of movement of workers and equality of treatment of nationals of all Member States shall not be restricted by interpretations of the concept of public service which are based on domestic law alone and which would obstruct the application of Community rules.'[3]

In the view of the Commission, Member States could only restrict the entry of aliens to public posts if these posts put the holders thereof in the position of directly participating in the exercise of official authority or of making use of prerogatives in the nature of powers conferred in law in regard to members of the public.[4]

But how were these posts to be defined? In a case brought by the European Commission against France in 1984, relating to a nationality requirement for the employment of nurses in public hospitals, Advocate General Mancini delivered the opinion that

> ... for him who exercised the sovereignty of the state, it implies ... privileges of official power and powers of coercion over citizens ... the duties must involve acts of will which affect private individuals by requiring their obedience or, in the event of disobedience, by compelling them to comply. To make a list ... is practically impossible, but certainly the first examples which come to mind are posts which involve the exercise of powers relating to policing, defence of the state, the administration of justice and assessments to tax.[5]

The Court upheld the Advocate General's view, stating that in view of the nature of the functions and responsibilities which they involved, posts of nurses in public hospitals did not constitute employment in the public service within the meaning of Article 48 (iv) of the Treaty of Rome.

In the view of the Commission, derogations were seen as covering posts in state ministries, regional governmental authorities, local authorities and other similar bodies, central banks and other public bodies where the duties of the post involved the exercise of state authority, such as preparation of legal acts, monitoring their application, and supervision of subordinate bodies. Considered 'sufficiently remote' from the Court's definition of the public service were such activities as public transport, electricity and gas supply, posts and telecommunications, public health care services and teaching in state educational establishments.[6]

But the issue was not only one of the employing institution but also the career structures within them. Exclusion on grounds of nationality would only apply to the most senior posts. Thus, of the some 29 000 posts in what was considered the public service in South Tyrol falling under the requirement of ethnic proportions under the revised Autonomy Statute, and involving some 17 per cent of the active population, as few as 2 000 could be described as being held by 'persons participating directly in the exercise of official authority.'[7]

To the threat of being swamped by incomers taking up all but the most senior and decision-making posts in their homelands lies the possibility of requiring language competence in the language or languages spoken in the area concerned. But even here European Union regulations pose a number of problems. Community regulation 1612/68 lays down in Article 3(i) that although national provisions or administrative practices of a Member State were not to apply where, though applicable irrespective of nationality, their exclusive or principal aim or effect is to keep nationals of other Member States away from the employment offered, that provision did not apply to conditions relating to linguistic knowledge required by reason of the nature of the post to be filled.

However, in 1989 the European Court of Justice ruled that if the Treaty of Rome did not prohibit the adoption of a policy for the protection and promotion of a language of a Member State which was both the national language and the first official language, 'the implementation of such a policy must not encroach upon a fundamental freedom such as that of the free movement of workers. Therefore, the requirements deriving from measures intended to implement such a policy must not in any circumstance be disproportionate in relation to the aim pursued, and the manner in which they are applied must not bring about discrimination against nationals of other Member States.'[8]

But this ruling did not say anything about the need to know languages that were *not* official. Practice in the European Union varied. In Finland the minority language, Swedish, is official throughout the state. Basque, Catalan and Gallego are official in their Spanish homelands. But French is only 'parified' with Italian in Val d'Aosta. German is only 'parified' with Italian in South Tyrol, according to the 1946 Paris Agreement, a word that was interpreted as specifically denying official status,[9] and the same word was used in Article 99 of the revised Autonomy Statute. At the moment, for obvious political reasons and common-sense, German is considered official in South Tyrol, but it is nevertheless a case of 'letting sleeping dogs lie'. Testing the word before the Constitutional Court rather than the Council of State, or simply declaring German official, might lead to complications; failure to do so, yet requiring a prospective employee to know what the European Court might consider a non-official language in addition to the official language in order to gain employment might be considered an encroachment upon a fundamental freedom such as the free movement of workers. And even if German (or any other minority language elsewhere) was made official, would the requirement to know a second official language be considered an encroachment? Indeed, what should be done about Ladin? Under Article 17 of Decree 752 it was laid down that wherever possible Ladin-speakers should be placed in public offices in Ladin areas. These areas were to be found not only in the

Province of Bolzano but also in the provinces of Trento and Belluno. But if it was decided that, for purposes of protection, fluency in Ladin should be made obligatory for public employment in Ladin areas, either through Ladin being 'parified' with Italian or being made an official language, would not the requirement to know *three* languages for public employment in the Ladin areas of the Province of Bolzano be considered an encroachment? And is it likely that the Italian government would take the necessary steps?

As Advocate General Darmon put it, a minority language cannot be preserved without the adoption of voluntary and obligatory measures. The preservation of language was one of those questions of principle which could not be dismissed without striking at the very heart of cultural identity. Was it for the Community to decide whether a particular language should survive? Was it for the Community to set Europe's linguistic heritage in its present state for all time? Was it to fossilise it? It seemed to him that it was up to the individual state to try and ensure the diversity of its cultural heritage and, consequently, to establish the means to carry out such a policy. Such means concerned primarily public education. Likewise every state had the right to determine the importance it wished to attribute to its cultural heritage.[10]

There are, therefore, a number of significant grey areas in the field of minority protection which need clarification. For the moment the preservation of a minority's culture is likely to continue to remain with nation states rather than as the minorities wish, namely, with the minorities themselves. But if the criterion – at least for the Community – for the preservation of a minority's language now seems to be that it obtains official status, then it will be up to the individual member state to make it so, or at least make it so in specific parts of the national territory. States may indeed have the right to determine the importance they wish to attribute to their cultural heritage, and in the Europe of today states may not be unwilling to let their minority languages have official status locally, at least in cases where the minority is numerically large or when a major European culture is involved. The fate of Europe's lesser used languages, such as Basque (in France), Breton, Ladin, Friaul or Welsh still remains in the balance. Here ratification of the European Charter of Regional and Minority Languages will be crucial.

However, the last word is likely to lie with the course taken on European integration. Should protection of all minority cultures become part of that 'public policy' referred to in paragraph 3 of Article 48 of the Treaty of Rome as justifying limitations on that Article?

In Article 4 of the 1948 South Tyrol Autonomy Statute, outlining the powers of the region, the latter's primary legislative powers had to respect not only the Constitution, the legal principles of the state, and the fundamental rules governing the social and economic reforms of the Republic, but also 'national interests'. In the negotiations on the Package Agreement the SVP had pointed out that the phrase could be used to restrict protection of minorities. Accordingly, Article 2 of the Constitutional Law setting out the new powers of the region, which would become Article 4 of the improved Autonomy Statute, was drafted specifically to make it clear that protection of local linguistic minorities was included in the term 'national interests'.[11]

Article 3(p) of the Maastricht Treaty on European Union states that the activities of the Community include 'a contribution to education and training of quality *and to the flowering of the cultures of the Member States*'. Even this phrase is highly dubious since it could be interpreted restrictively to apply only to the official cultures of the Member States. By contrast, the 1991 draft Treaty's draft Article 3(p) referred to '*the flowering of the cultures of Europe in all their forms*'.[12]

Upon the extent to which Article 3(p) of the Maastricht Treaty can be reconciled with the objectives of Article 3(c) 'an internal market characterised by the abolition as between member States, of obstacles to freedom of movement of goods, persons, services and capital', the fate of Europe's many regional cultural minorities may come to depend.[13]

Interestingly, in the Aland Islands, the only part of Europe which could be said to be a 'national park' for a minority, the Swedish-speaking inhabitants of the Islands and the Finnish government had to consider, when Finland applied to join the European Union, whether the provisions of the Autonomy Statute were compatible with EU membership. If they were not, should the Islands be outside the EU, enjoying the same type of status as the Isle of Man or the Channel Islands?

It was agreed in the negotiating between Brussels and Helsinki that the provisions of the Accession Treaty would not apply to the Islands unless the Islanders so indicated their wish in a referendum.

Accordingly a Protocol was inserted into the Accession Treaty which provided for the continuation of the existing restrictions on the right to purchase property, exercise a profession and offer services on the Islands for those not having Aland regional citizenship. The restrictions, however, would be non-discriminatory, i.e., applying to all citizens of the Union.

The referendum was held in November 1994 and the Islanders voted by 74:26 per cent to accept membership of the Union under the terms of the Protocol Accession Treaty. Above all, this meant that the provisions of the Protocol, as part of the EU's primary legislation, could not be altered by EU regulations. Thereafter, if the Islanders have not been guaranteed a place on the Finnish representation in the European Parliament, they are represented in the Committee of the Regions, have their own special adviser in the Finnish delegation in Brussels, and are represented in the Finnish parliament's committee for consideration of EU matters.[14]

In areas that do not enjoy the status of the Aland Islands other defences against territorial encroachment have been tried. Belgium has refused to implement an EU law allowing nationals of Member States of which there are some 560 000, to vote in local elections. Hostility to the law has been expressed by the Flemish community, especially in the Brussels region, on the grounds that the persons concerned, some 140 000 or 15 per cent of the population, working for the European institutions, NGOs, and business and professional organisations, would be more likely to vote for French-speaking candidates because they themselves speak French rather than Dutch. The Flemish fear they would be practically eliminated politically from the capital, 85 per cent of which is French-speaking. There is also the fear that the EU law would open the way to voting rights for the many non-EU immigrant workers from Turkey and North Africa.[15]

Another technique pursued by some Flemish communes is aimed to bar residency to anyone without ties to the Flemish community. For example, the commune of Overijse in the Brussels region obliges persons wishing to sell land for residential purposes to sign a contract with the council requiring potential buyers to appear before a committee, one of whose tasks was to vet their cultural and linguistic credentials. One fear is that international incomes drive up the price of houses so that local people can no longer live there. Another is resentment that the incomers make no effort to speak Flemish, do not mix locally, and do not send their children to the local Flemish school – and might well vote for Francophone councillors and tip the balance.[16]

Control of property to prevent encroachment has also occurred in Northern Ireland. In order to stop Protestant farms mainly in border but also in other areas from falling into Catholic hands, often following murder operations by the PIRA, the Orange Order was reported as setting up a fund to buy properties or provide loans to prospective Protestant tenants.[17]

Minorities often live in scenically beautiful areas, and thus attract members of the majority to buy second or holiday homes, or even to retire there. In Wales Welsh nationalists have expressed their hostility to incomers by intermittently burning such homes, or even attacking estate agents' offices selling such homes in England.

There is also growing resentment in Scotland at the purchase of property by English persons able to pay high prices for property in Scotland, above what Scots can afford, because of the sale of their more highly priced property south of the border.

Of course, no method of control of territory can compare in terms of horrific brutality with ethnic cleansing. In Europe, apart from PIRA attempts ethnically to cleanse Protestants from border areas in Northern Ireland, two areas where this crime against humanity occurred were Cyprus and Yugoslavia.

Southern and Eastern Europe: ethnic cleansing

Cyprus

In 1974 the military government in Athens, hoping to gather domestic support, supported a move to overthrow President Makarios of Cyprus, whose views on *enosis* had changed considerably in view of comparative poverty and an end to democracy in Greece. Following a *coup d'état* on 15 July, a government was set up in Nicosia by a former EOKA terrorist, Nicos Sampson. When Britain, as a guarantor of Cyprus, refused to act, on 20 July Ankara ordered Turkish troops to invade. Greek Cypriot forces were swept aside and the Turks occupied the northern and eastern part of the island, amounting to 37 per cent of the whole, effectively partitioning it, as Turkish Cypriots had really always wanted, and establishing an 'independent' Turkish Republic of Northern Cyprus (TRNC) that has not, however, been recognised by any other country.

During the course of the invasion, according to the European Commission on Human Rights, the Turkish army massacred unarmed civilians and forced 180 000 Greek Cypriots to leave their homes in the face of physical expulsion and a campaign of terror. Thereafter they were prevented from returning. Only some 900 Greek Cypriots now live in the territory of the TRNC. The fate of some 1 619 Greek Cypriots is still unknown. The property of those who had fled was distributed to Turkish Cypriots and to the some 50 000 Turks brought in as settlers from the Turkish mainland. Some 35 000 Turkish troops had also settled in as a permanent garrison. There was systematic destruction, or looting, or dispersal abroad of northern Cyprus's Christian and Hellenic archaeological and antique treasures.[18]

On the other hand, in the territory controlled by Greek Cypriots, whose government is now recognised by the international community as the legitimate government of Cyprus, Turkish Cypriots, living in the ghettos into which they had been forced before 1974, were likewise forced to flee so that only a few hundred remained.

Twenty-five years of intermittent discussions between the Greek and Turkish Cypriot authorities brokered by various international organisations, and innumerable Security Council resolutions have failed. Whereas Greek Cypriots and the international community support the idea of a single state in the form of a bizonal confederation, the Turkish Cypriots insist that the TRNC be recognised, and that the two parts of Cyprus negotiate, as equals, a two-state confederation. This has been considered unacceptable since it is contrary to UN Resolutions.[19]

The issue of reunification has been complicated by the application of Cyprus to join the EU, as well as the desire of Turkey to join that organisation. Greece has made it clear that it will veto Ankara's application unless the Cypriot issue is solved. In the meantime negotiations have begun between Cyprus and the EU but the Turkish Cypriots have refused to participate in the island's negotiating delegation.

The problem for Turkey and Turkish Cypriots is that when a Greek Cypriot, Titina Loizidou, formerly resident in Kyrenia now in the TRNC, petitioned the European Court of Human Rights against Turkey for compensation for deprivation of land and property and the right to return to it, the Court first rejected Ankara's argument that the TRNC was a sovereign state for which it had no responsibility, and then ordered Turkey, as the occupying power, to pay her £CYP 300 000 (£432 000) compensation. Since the case opened the way for a like decision regarding compensation claims pending by all other Greek Cypriots deprived of their property, membership of the Union, which requires adherence to Human Rights standards and Court judgements, holds out the prospect of Turkey, if it becomes a Member State, having to pay massive sums in compensation.[20]

Yugoslavia

But even the events in Cyprus, grievous as they were, paled in comparison with those following the collapse of Yugoslavia with the breakaway of Slovenia, Croatia and Macedonia in 1991 and Bosnia-Herzegovina in 1992, leaving only Serbia and Montenegro in a rump

Federation. The scale of the genocide, crimes against humanity in an area where there was no love lost between Croat and Serb and between Christian and Moslem, had not been seen in Europe since the days of the Third Reich.

Hoping to profit from the collapse of the Federation were those who dreamt of a Greater Serbia. In 1991 the composition of the Federation of 23.5 million was Serb 36.2 per cent, Croat 19.9, (Bosnian) Moslem 10.0, Albanian 9.3, Slovene 7.5, Macedonian 5.8, Montenegrin 2.3, Hungarian 1.6, Gypsy 0.9, Turkish 0.5, with 3 per cent also declaring themselves 'Yugoslav', and 3.1 per cent 'other/unknown'. All the constituent republics had mixed populations but there were wide differences as to the dominant group. In Slovenia Slovenes formed 87.6 per cent of the population with Serbs only 2.4 per cent, of the 1.7 million population. Croatians formed 78.1 per cent of Croatia, with Serbs 12.2 per cent, of the 4.4 million population. Macedonians formed 66.4 per cent of the population of 2 million but Albanians formed a strong minority of 23.1 per cent. Of Serbia's population of 9.7 million 65.7 per cent were Serbs. As in Macedonia, Albanians (in Kossovo Province) were the strongest minority with 1.68 million, or 17.2 per cent, followed by the Hungarians of the Voivodina with 345 000 or 3.5 per cent. On the other hand, of Bosnia's 4.3 million, Moslems formed only 43.7 per cent, with Serbs 31.4 per cent and Croats 17.3 per cent.[21]

Two days after the declaration of Slovene independence, on 27 June 1991, the new state was attacked by the Serbian-dominated federal army, invading Croatia in the process, ostensibly to hold the Federation together. The Yugoslav civil war had begun. Since Slovenia was overwhelmingly consolidated ethnically the Serbs withdrew after a few weeks leaving pursuit of a policy of accession to the EU by the new state. Very different was the situation in Croatia where the Serbs, supported by the Serbian army and paramilitary Cetniks occupied a third of the country, including eastern and western Slavonia, and proclaiming a Serbian Republic of Krajina. An EU-brokered peace conference at The Hague in September 1991 engineered a series of cease-fires, all of which were broken. 300 000 Croatians were expelled or fled from the Serb-occupied areas, but many thousands were also murdered by militant Serbs. In November the EU ordered sanctions against Yugoslavia and on 17 December formally recognised Slovenia and Croatia.

Worse was to follow. In a referendum on 1 March 1992, boycotted by the Serbs, the Bosnian population voted overwhelmingly for independence. This independence was recognised by the EU on 7 April, and immediately the civil war escalated and spread, with Serbia seizing

70 per cent of the country, setting up a Serbian republic of Bosnia-Herzegovina (SRBH) and embarking – again – on a deliberate policy of ethnic cleansing. Many civilians were massacred, and 670 000 persons fled the country. In May the United Nations followed the EU in ordering sanctions against Yugoslavia. In July the Croatian element of the population set up their own mini-republic of Herzeg-Bosna in 10 per cent of the territory, leaving the Bosnians with 20 per cent and the capital, Sarajevo, under siege, in desperate plight, and in some areas under attack also from Croats. Indeed, Croatian officers would later be indicted for war crimes against Bosnians. UN forces sent in to separate the combatants and see that cease-fires were observed were largely ineffectual.

Subsequently, in August 1995 Croatian forces drove the Serbs out of eastern and western Slavonia and Krajina. Now it was the turn of 150 000 Serbs, many of whom had come – or been sent – to those areas after earlier Serb victories, who were forced to flee, while many of those remaining became victims of atrocities.

By the Dayton Accords of 21 November 1995, brokered by the United States, it was agreed that Bosnia should be maintained as a bi-zonal state with 51 per cent going to a Moslem-Croat Herzeg-Bosna and 49 per cent going to the SRBH.[22]

By 1996 an uneasy peace had come to the war zone but inter-ethnic hatred and distrust did not diminish. Croatians were reluctant to accept Serbs originally resident but who had been forced to flee, although the OSCE argued that return was a right. There was practically none but Serbs in the SRBH, while Moslems and Croats kept to their own areas in Herzeg-Bosna. Supporters of the Greater Serbia idea had made some gains, but at a fearful cost to the lives and reputation of their community, with several members of the military being indicted for genocide and war crimes. Their next attempt would be even more disastrous, unbottling the genie of a Greater Albania, the vision of which had existed since the beginning of the century.

Of all the peoples of Europe it is Albanians that in this century have had the highest birthrate. In Albania itself they increased from an estimated one million after the war to 3.25 million in 1990. But up to a third of Albanians make up a diaspora. In the former Yugoslavia they were concentrated in Macedonia and the Serbian province of Kossovo, numbering over 500 000 in 1931, or 3.6 per cent of the population, rising to 1.3 million or 6.4 per cent in 1971, and 2.1 million or 9.3 per cent in 1991. In Macedonia in 1994 after the collapse of Yugoslavia they numbered 479 000, or 23.1 per cent of the population, an increase of nearly 200 000 and 6.1 per cent since 1971. In Serbia the number of Albanians had increased from 985 000 or 11.7 per cent in 1971 to 1 687 000 or 17.2 per cent in 1991.[23] The problem was that they were almost entirely concentrated in the historic heartland of the Serbian people, the province of Kossovo, where, according to the 1981 census, Serbs only constituted 13.2 per cent compared to the Albanian 85 per cent.[24]

Even in the 1960s Kossovo Albanians were demanding the status of a full republic rather than that of a province, but for Serbs this was officially seen as the first step towards a Greater Albania, to be achieved first by unification of Albanian areas in Serbia and Macedonia and then with Albania itself as, indeed, Albanian nationalists were demanding.[25] Throughout the 1970s and 1980s the situation in Kossovo deteriorated, with massive demonstrations by Albanian nationalists being met, on the one hand, by massive arrests, and on the other by a rise in Serb nationalism.

In May 1989 the Serb communist Slobodan Milosevic came to power in Yugoslavia, and immediately began to exploit Serbian nationalism. The provincial autonomy of Kossovo was reduced. Serbs took over direct control of policing and drafted in more policemen. By the end of May 1990 all Kossovar (ethnic Albanian) members of the government had resigned. When, in July, the Kossovar members of the Kossovo Assembly called for self-determination the Serbian authorities dissolved it and the government was taken over by the Serbian Assembly. Kossovar civil servants were dismissed.[26] Thereafter Albanian language schools began to be closed and the Serb police used violence against demonstrating students – drawing protests from the OSCE.

As long as the attention of Serb forces was focused on Croatia and Bosnia a sullen confrontation continued in Kossovo. But in 1997 a clandestine Kossovo Liberation Army (KLA) began operating, targeting Serb police forces and even gaining control of some towns and villages. In March 1998 Serbs began a crackdown against the KLA, systematically destroying areas under the latter's control and murdering civilians and children, causing many others to flee. For their part, in March 1998 Kossovars declared a republic and elected a legislature.

But the state of anarchy and the ethnic cleansing which had caused so many Kossovars to flee to Macedonia and Albania prompted European fears of destabilisation and wider conflict throughout the Balkans. In August 1998 the Contact Group of six countries (USA, Britain, France, Italy, Germany and Russia) proposed that Kossovo be given a wide-ranging autonomy within Serbia, with legislative and executive powers and control of the judiciary, police and taxation, and with the rights to fly its own flag and engage in foreign policy. This was rejected by the Kossovars for not advocating independence, and they also refused to negotiate with the Serbs.[27] But ominously for the Serbs, as evidence of atrocities by Serb Special Forces increasingly came to light, NATO began holding manoeuvres in Albania 'underlying the West's determination to discourage any move by Serb forces to drive ethnic Albanians from the Province'.[28]

In March 1999 the Serbs refused to sign a peace deal with the Kossovars after three months of negotiations in Paris, in which the latter had been promised an eventual independence referendum. Instead they launched a scorched earth policy designed to remove all Kossovars from the province. 500 000 Kossovars had left their homes during the past year and 800 000 were still displaced there. On 24 March NATO air forces intervened, attacking Serb military and strategic targets, and as Serb forces retreated ever more sites of atrocities were uncovered.[29] In May President Milosevic himself was indicted for war crimes – the first Head of State in office to be so charged.

But the wheel of fortune was now turning with a vengeance. As Serb forces retreated Serb civilians were left to face the incoming KLA and a Kossovar programme of ethnic cleansing of Serbs. By September nine-tenths of Kossovo's Serbs had fled the province to escape revenge attacks.

However, it is now NATO and the EU that are on the spot. The aim of intervention was to ensure political stability and human rights for all in a Kossovo with a large autonomy that would still be part of Serbia. But few Albanians believe that after all the atrocities it could ever be part of Yugoslavia again. The fervent hope is that an independent Kossovo would one day merge with Albania to bring about the dream of the Greater Albania.

All this then turned the spotlight on Macedonia. Officially Albanians formed 23 per cent of the population and, after the declaration of independence by Skopje, they sought nation-status within Macedonia and threatened to set up an Albanian Autonomous Republic of Illyria in their settlement area in the north-west of the country. But this – and the attempt to argue that Macedonia was a two-people state – was rejected as a first step to secession and a Greater Albania. Albanians also believe that they number some 40 per cent of the population in that many Albanians are still waiting for citizenship: under Macedonian law fifteen years residence is required in order for it to be acquired. However, since *jus solis* exists in Macedonia, Albanian children born there can become citizens, and Macedonians fear that because of the high Albanian birth-rate they would one day become a minority in their own state.

In December 1994 the Macedonian parliament rejected a proposal that Albanian be an official language, and a few months later rejected the use of Albanian in Macedonian passports and identity cards.

In order to diminish the rising tension the HCMN became active in trying to get the government to improve secondary education facilities for Albanians, higher education in their mother tongue within the framework of national legislation, as well as recommending that citizenship be granted in five years and that ethnic Albanian representation in the public administration, police and army be increased.[30] But tension returned when, as the Serbs began the ethnic cleansing of Kossovo, Kossovars fled to Macedonia, overwhelming Macedonian reception resources and its economy.

At the time of writing it is too soon to say how the situation of the Albanian minority in Macedonia will develop.

Conclusions

The nineteenth and twentieth centuries have seen a struggle between two approaches to the problem of minorities and their protection, and the outcome of that struggle will have its effect on the future development of Europe.

One approach focused on the individual. Its supporters today argue that in the fast changing contemporary world where freedom of movement, globalisation in terms of financial movements, of the electronic information of the Internet, and the ever-increasing numbers of mixed marriages, the ground is being cut from under cultural communities who have occupied their land for centuries if not millennia, and this makes it unrealistic to think in tribal terms of ethnic purity or the need to maintain community solidarity in order to preserve identity. For them three things are enough when considering majority–minority relations. First, that individual members of a minority should enjoy rights equal to members of the majority. Second, individual members of a minority should be able to enjoy a basic cultural autonomy, i.e., the right to have their own language taught in schools, and to have books and newspapers in that language, and (usually) to use it in relations with the public authorities. Third, that rights granted to members of the minority should be on an individual rather than a group basis. The vision is one of a fluid, bold, open, progressive, unsegregated, interactive, optimistic society, welcoming change. It is not surprising that they are usually to be found amongst western Europeans or North Americans who have never been conquered or subdued, whose cultures dominate the world and which can survive the 'melting pot' which their approach inevitably invites.

The other approach, based on the *volkisch* ideas of Herder, focuses on the group. Its supporters argue that maintenance of group solidarity is essential for survival. The individual flourishes better, is better able to preserve his culture and identity within the framework of a group. And in any case the preservation of culture is a collective enterprise. Their vision is one of a closed, inward-looking, pessimistic society, on the defensive against a formidable army of destructive forces. And these destructive forces truly are formidable: either the hostility, or the contempt, or the benign neglect of the host state, as well as precisely those features of the contemporary world so attractive to the advocates of the first approach, freedom of movement, mixed marriages, dominant languages brought even into the home by electronic means. It was therefore essential to be continually on guard against degenerating into a mish-mash, 'half spaghetti, half knödel' as the SVP leader Silvius Magnago contemptuously put it.[1]

They also see uncertainty in the outside world: the decline of traditional values in the terms of the family and the church and their replacements by 'rights' to this or that which nevertheless may have great difficulty in being accepted nationally or, if accepted, being swiftly applied, leaving the individual a spiritual eunuch in a rootless, alien world. Ethnicity is therefore an anchor in that sea of economic and social change. Above all, minorities come from the defeated and conquered. History has not dealt kindly with them. There is no cause for optimism. That is why if the European Union slogan of 'Unity in Diversity' is to have any meaning there must be a territorial defence aimed at ensuring that the maintenance and development of their culture rests largely in their own hands: government of their homeland (or at least power-sharing), their own administrators, priority in employment, official status of the language, education in the language. As another SVP leader, Alfons Benedikter, put it, 'It is said we are pawns. But we must work to ensure we remain pawns.'[2] The responses of the countries of Europe to the problems of their regional, linguistic and cultural minorities have inevitably varied considerably, depending on the ethos of the states and the size and demands of the minorities.

Clearly there must be some place for territoriality, with governmental and employment rights for the minority in its homeland if at least the weakest minorities in the terms of numbers are to survive. What is perhaps surprising is that in the western Europe of the Union, the Union of Human Rights and Freedom of Movement, there are so many examples of territoriality. Nevertheless, there are still great differences between, at one level, the cultural protection afforded for the Aland Islanders, the Flemish and Walloons, and South Tyrolese, and to which Catalonia aspires, where knowledge of the languages concerned is a formal requirement by all local inhabitants; at a second level, where the state supports the minority's linguistic and educational rights, and the minority can use its language with the public administration, which is the usual situation, for example, in Austria, Denmark, Germany, the Netherlands, Spain, Wales in the United Kingdom, and Val d'Aosta in Italy; while at a third level learning of minority languages is more or less a voluntary effort, with a few educational establishments teaching them, and the public administration under no compulsion to know them, as in France and other parts of Italy and the United Kingdom.

Consideration of the ever increasing number of international instruments does reveal a move towards a general consensus as to what rights minorities should have, and after the lead given by western European countries one must hope that they will eventually be introduced in eastern Europe so that an integrated continent will one day enjoy that cultural diversity postulated by its leaders.

However, one thing is sure: history has shown that uncertainty as to the territorial destiny of a minority's homeland is, even more than contempt for the minority's culture, the greatest obstacle to satisfactory majority–minority relations. With regard to South Tyrol after the war, the refusal to renounce self-determination led to a restrictive Autonomy Statute restrictively applied and the threat that if the South Tyrolese actually did call publicly and officially for self-determination the Autonomy Statute would be revoked. In Cyprus the imposition of a solution not supported by the 80 per cent Greek Cypriot population ensured the collapse of the Republic within three years. In Northern Ireland British government tolerance of the Irish Republic's claim to the North and disinterest in the Province destroyed trust between the Ulster-Irish and the Ulster-British communities. In Yugoslavia, after the recognition of Croatia and Slovenia against the advice of Britain and France no one knew what would be the boundaries of states as Greater Serbia and Greater Croatia grubbed in the ruins of Bosnia.

From which it follows that it is better for agreement to be reached between the minority and the host state if the interests of both are to be maintained, and therefore it will be difficult to disagree with the thrust of three conclusions by the OSCE arising out of its experience in eastern and central Europe but which are equally valid in western Europe. First, the lack of developed structures for dialogue in many states negatively affects the quality of communications, leading to prejudices continuing and hampering negotiations. Second, respect for human rights can contribute significantly, if not conclusively, to the settlement of most situations involving minorities. Third, decentralis-ation and enhancement of self-government, local, provincial or regional, contributes substantially to giving people greater power over their own destinies, something absolutely vital for ensuring effective participation of persons belonging to national minorities in public affairs,[3] which gives them a stake in the future.

Appendix 1: Linguistic and Religious Minorities in Europe[1]

Country	Total population	Minority	Minority population	Percentage
Albania	3 255 000	Greeks	58 750	1.80
Armenia	3 580 000	Azeris	107 400	3.00
Austria	7 860 800	Croatians	22 000	0.28
		Slovenes	16 000	0.20[2]
		Hungarians	12 000	0.15
Azerbaijan	7 145 000	Armenians	428 700	6.00
		Russians	430 000	6.00
Belarus	10 259 000	Russians	1 354 200	13.2
Belgium	9 978 681	Flemish	5 747 720	57.60
		Walloon (Fr)	3 243 070	32.50
		Germans	66 445	0.66
Bosnia	4 479 000	Bosnians (Muslim)	1 957 300	43.70
		Serbs (Russian Orth.)	1 402 000	31.30
		Croatians (Roman Cath.)	775 000	17.30
Bulgaria	8 600 000	Turks	860 000	10.00
Croatia	4 601 469	Italians	19 041	0.004
		Serbs	580 000	12.2[3]

Cont'd

Country	Total population	Minority	Minority population	Percentage
Cyprus	701 000			
		Greeks	556 400	80.00
		Turks	129 600	18.00
		Maronites	9 000	2.00
Czech Republic	10 362 000			
		Slovak	425 000	4.1
		Poles	70 000	0.7
		Germans	49 000	0.5
Denmark	5 147 000			
		Germans (N.Schleswig)	20 000	0.38
		Faroese	38 700	0.75
		Greenlandic	50 000	1.00
Estonia	1 583 000			
		Russians	488 000	30.30
Finland	4 998 478			
		Swedes	300 000	6.00
		Sami	1 730	0.0003
Former Yugoslav Rep. Of Macedonia	2 075 000			
		Albanians	479 033	23.10
		Turks	82 000	3.90
		Serbs	40 000	1.90
		Sinti/Roma	47 000	2.30
Former Rep. Of Yugoslavia	10 411 000			
		Serbs	6 350 000	60.00
		Albanians	1 890 000	18.00
		Montenegrins	573 000	5.50
		Hungarians	420 000	4.00
France	57 206 000			
		Alsatians	1 160 000	2.03
		Basques	80 000	0.14
		Bretons	2 600 000	4.54
		Catalans	200 000	0.35
		Corsicans	162 500	0.28
		Flemish	100 000	0.17
		Occitans	1 500 000	2.60

Cont'd

Country	Total population	Minority	Minority population	Percentage
Georgia	5 456 000			
		Armenians	491 000	9.00
		Russians	403 750	7.40
		Azeris	278 250	5.10
		Ossetians	174 600	3.20
		Abkasians	92 750	1.70
Germany	79 951 000			
		Sorbs	60 000	0.075
		Danes	30 000	0.037
Greece	10 269 000			
		Turks	110 000	1.07
		Albanians	95 000	1.02
Hungary	10 375 300			
		Croats	30 000	0.30
		Germans	238 630	2.30
		Slovaks	103 750	1.00
		Sinti/Roma	600 000	5.78
Irish Republic	3 523 410			
		Protestants	130 365	3.70
Italy	56 400 000			
		Germans	300 000	0.53[4]
		French	200 000	0.35[5]
		Slovenes	53 000	0.09
		Ladins	30 000	0.05
		Friauls	500 000	0.88
Latvia	2 687 000			
		Russians	913 600	34.00
		Belarusians	120 900	4.50
		Ukrainians	94 450	3.50
		Poles	61 800	2.30
Lithuania	3 723 000			
		Russians	349 960	9.40
		Poles	260 600	7.00
Moldova	4 362 000			
		Ukrainians	619 400	14.20
		Russians	558 350	12.80
		Gagauz	152 670	3.50
		Bulgarians	87 250	2.00

Cont'd

Country	Total population	Minority	Minority population	Percentage
Netherlands	14 931 000			
		Friesians	500 000	3.35
Norway	4 242 000			
		Sami	40 000	0.94
		Finns	12 000	0.28
Poland	38 423 000			
		Germans	c.500 000	1.30
		Ukrainians	180 000	0.47
		Belarusians	170 000	0.44
Romania	22 760 449			
		Hungarians	1 620 000	7.10
		Sinti/Roma	410 000	1.80
		Germans	119 436	0.50
Slovakia	5 288 000			
		Hungarians	578 000	10.90
Slovenia	2 000 000			
		Hungarians	100 000	0.50
		Italians	2 000	0.01
Spain	39 433 942			
		Catalans	7 098 000	18.00
		Basques	1 842 500	4.67[6]
		Galicians	2 366 000	6.00
Sweden	8 552 000			
		Finns	30 000	0.35
		Sami	15 000	0.175
Switzerland	6 872 551[7]			
		Germans	4 204 355	74.00[8]
		French	1 136 310	20.00[8]
		Italian	284 075	5.00[8]
		Rhaeto-Romansch	56 875	1.00[8]
Ukraine	51 839 000			
		Russians	11 556 000	22.10
		Moldavians	325 000	0.60
		Tatars of the Crimea	c. 300 000	0.60
		Poles	219 000	0.40
		Hungarians	163 000	0.30

Cont'd

Country	Total population	Minority	Minority population	Percentage
United Kingdom Of Great Britain & Northern Ireland	58 400 000	Welsh	2 900 000	4.96[9]
		Scots	5 100 000	8.73[10]
		Irish (in N. Ireland)	605,000	1.03[11]
		Cornish	475 000	0.81[12]

(1) Estimates only. Figures for Balkan and East European countries should be treated with particular caution. In western Europe some states do not enquire after or differentiate between the population of a minority's homeland, those who speak and write the minority language and those who only speak it.

(2) c. 36–40,000 if the Windisch dialect is included.

(3) Figure for 1991. Now estimated at less than 1.0 per cent.

(4) Of which 287 500 in South Tyrol (1994); the remainder in Trento and Friuli-Venezia Giulia.

(5) Including Franco-Provençal and Piedmontese-Occitan.

(6) Native population, defined as born in the Basque Country of at least one Basque parent; includes the four provinces of Alava (Araba), Vizcaya (Biskaia), Guipuzcoa (Donostia), and Navarra (Nafaroa).

(7) Of which 1 190 990 (17.1%) are non-citizens, including 381 493 Italians, 84 485 Germans, 64,192 French, and 29 123 Austrians.

(8) Percentages relate to the citizen population.

(9) Of which about one-quarter speak Welsh.

(10) Of which about 5 800 speak Scots Gaelic.

(11) Based on the number of Roman Catholics in the 1991 census, and presumed to have been taught the Irish language.

(12) Resident population of Cornwall, of which up to 2 000 speak Cornish with varying degrees of fluency.

Appendix 2: Accessions to the Council of Europe's European Charter for Regional and Minority Languages (1992) and the Framework Convention for the Protection of National Minorities (1994)[1]

Member States[2]	European Charter		Framework Convention	
	Signature	*Ratification*	*Signature*	*Ratification*
Albania			Yes	
Austria	Yes		Yes	Yes
Belgium				
Bulgaria			Yes	Yes
Croatia	Yes	Yes	Yes	Yes
Cyprus	Yes		Yes	Yes
Czech Republic			Yes	Yes
Denmark	Yes		Yes	Yes
Estonia			Yes	Yes
Finland	Yes	Yes	Yes	Yes
France	Yes			
Fyrom	Yes		Yes	Yes
Georgia				
Germany	Yes	Yes	Yes	Yes
Greece			Yes	

Cont'd

Member States[2]	European Charter		Framework Convention	
	Signature	*Ratification*	*Signature*	*Ratification*
Hungary	Yes	Yes	Yes	Yes
Iceland	Yes		Yes	Yes
Ireland			Yes	Yes
Italy			Yes	Yes
Latvia			Yes	
Lithuania			Yes	
Moldova			Yes	Yes
Netherlands	Yes	Yes	Yes	
Norway	Yes	Yes	Yes	Yes
Poland			Yes	
Romania	Yes		Yes	Yes
Russia			Yes	Yes
Slovakia			Yes	Yes
Slovenia	Yes		Yes	Yes
Spain	Yes		Yes	Yes
Sweden			Yes	
Switzerland	Yes	Yes	Yes	Yes
Turkey				
Ukraine	Yes		Yes	Yes
United Kingdom			Yes	Yes
Armenia			Yes	Yes

(1) As of 31 December 1999.
(2) Only states considered in this book.

Maps of Minorities

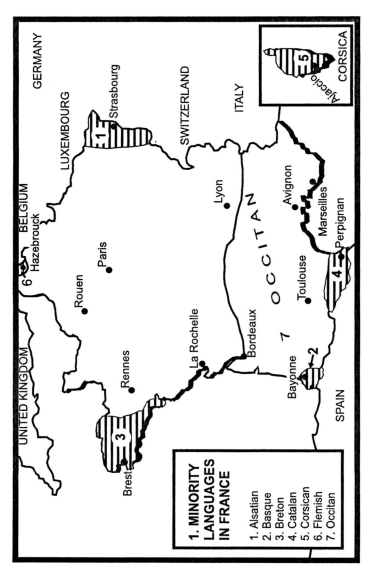

1. MINORITY LANGUAGES IN FRANCE

1. Alsatian
2. Basque
3. Breton
4. Catalan
5. Corsican
6. Flemish
7. Occitan

GERMANY

LUXEMBOURG

Strasbourg

SWITZERLAND

ITALY

CORSICA

Ajaccio

5

BELGIUM

Hazebrouck

Lyon

Avignon

Marseilles

Perpignan

Paris

Rouen

OCCITAN

7

UNITED KINGDOM

La Rochelle

Bordeaux

Toulouse

4

Rennes

Bayonne

2

SPAIN

Brest

3

6

1   Minority languages in France

225

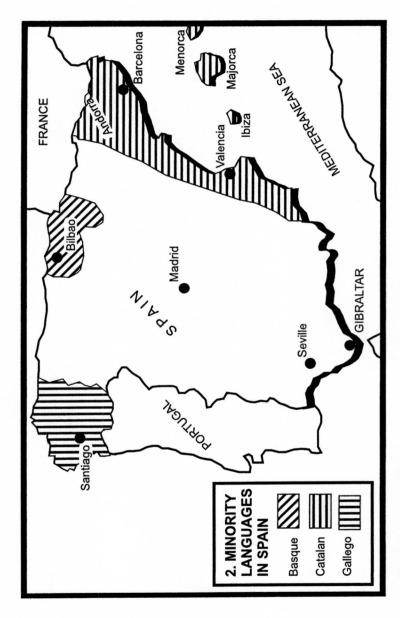

2   Minority languages in Spain

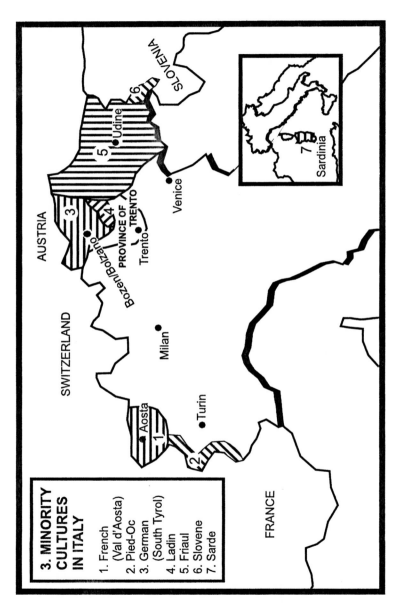

3   Minority cultures in Italy

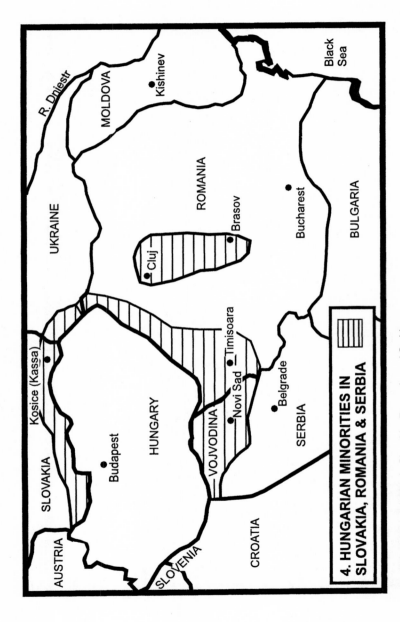

4   Hungarian minorities in Slovakia, Romania and Serbia

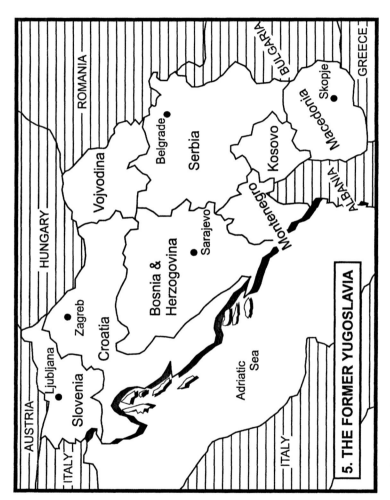

5   The former Yugoslavia

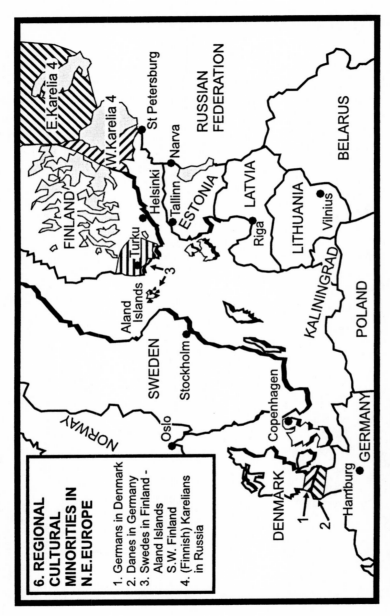

6. REGIONAL CULTURAL MINORITIES IN N.E.EUROPE

1. Germans in Denmark
2. Danes in Germany
3. Swedes in Finland - Aland Islands S.W. Finland
4. (Finnish) Karelians in Russia

6   Regional cultural minorities in NE Europe

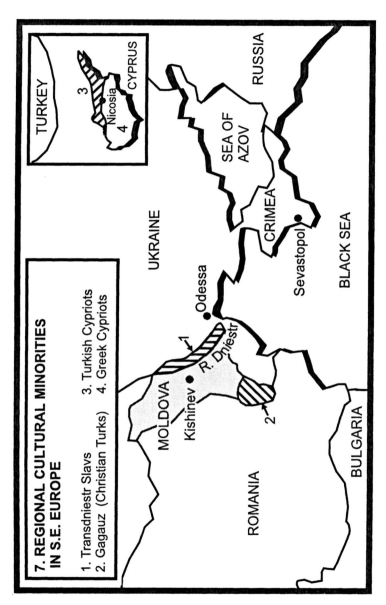

7. REGIONAL CULTURAL MINORITIES IN S.E. EUROPE

1. Transdniestr Slavs
2. Gagauz (Christian Turks)
3. Turkish Cypriots
4. Greek Cypriots

7   Regional cultural minorities in SE Europe

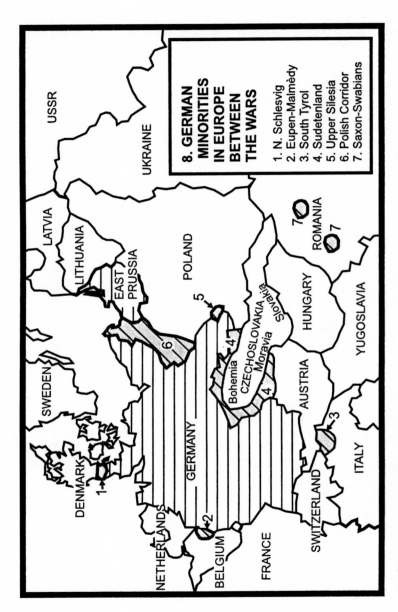

8. GERMAN MINORITIES IN EUROPE BETWEEN THE WARS

1. N. Schlesvig
2. Eupen-Malmèdy
3. South Tyrol
4. Sudetenland
5. Upper Silesia
6. Polish Corridor
7. Saxon-Swabians

8   German minorities in Europe between the wars

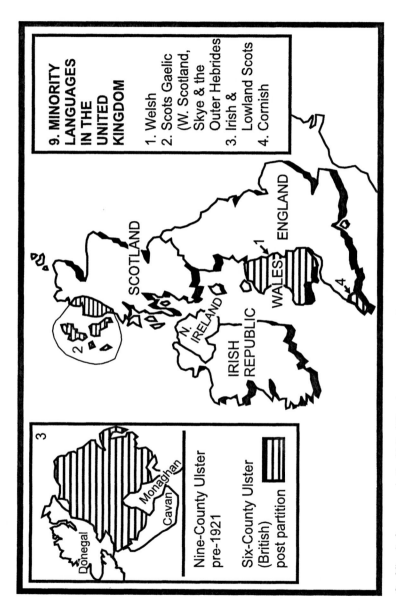

9. MINORITY LANGUAGES IN THE UNITED KINGDOM

1. Welsh
2. Scots Gaelic (W. Scotland, Skye & the Outer Hebrides
3. Irish & Lowland Scots
4. Cornish

SCOTLAND

ENGLAND

WALES

N. IRELAND

IRISH REPUBLIC

Donegal

Monaghan

Cavan

Nine-County Ulster pre-1921

Six-County Ulster (British) post partition

9   Minority languages in the United Kingdom

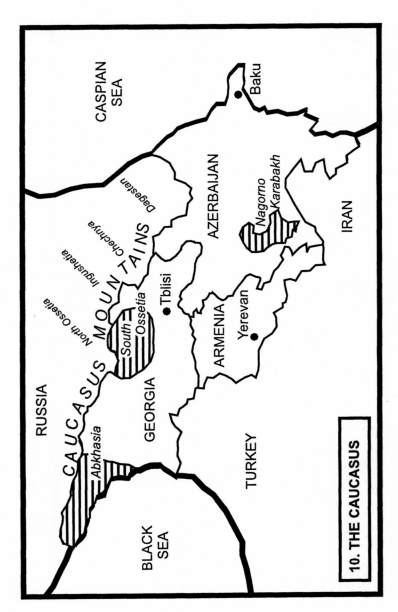

10   The Caucasus

Notes

Introduction

1 UN Doc. CCPR/C/21/Rev.1/Add.5 of 19 April 1994, para.6.2, quoted in Kristiansen, M.L., *Special Measures for the Protection of Minorities*, (Geneva: Graduate Institute of International Studies, Thesis n.556, 1997), p.36.

2 Notably those of the United Nations Sub-Committee on the Prevention of Discrimination and the Protection of Minorities in 1950, UN Doc.E/CN.4/Sub.2/85 (see below, p. 102), and of Professor Francesco Capotorti, Special Rapporteur of the United Nations Sub-Commission on Prevention of Discrimination and Protection of Minorities, who defined a 'minority' as:'A group numerically inferior to the rest of the population of a State, in a non-dominant position, whose members – being nationals of the state – possess ethnic, religious or linguistic characteristics differing from those of the rest of the population and show, if only implicitly, a sense of solidarity, directed towards preserving their culture, traditions, religion or language.'

3 Council of Europe, Parliamentary Assembly, Recommendation 1201 (1993) on an additional Protocol on the Rights of National Minorities to the European Convention on Human Rights, Article 1, Strasbourg. Text in *World Directory of Minorities*, (London: Minority Rights Group International, 1977), pp. 764–5. Note also that the Instrument for the Protection of Minority Rights adopted in November 1994 by the Countries of the Central European Initiative (Albania, Austria, Belarus, Bosnia, Bulgaria, Croatia, Czech Republic, Hungary, Italy, Macedonia, Moldova, Romania, Slovakia, Slovenia, Ukraine,) contains a very similar definition: text in European Bureau for Lesser Used Languages, *Vade Mecum*, (Dublin: 1998), p.82.

4 For example, the 1.8 million Turkish *Gastarbeiter* in Germany, 30.25 per cent of that country's 5.8 million foreigners, and the 145 000 persons from Surinam and the Dutch Antilles in the Netherlands. Figures from *Fischer Almanac, 1993*.

1 Protection of Minorities before the First World War

1 See Kohn, H., *The Modernity of Nationalism* in Tipton, C.L. (ed.), *Nationalism in the Middle Ages* (New York: Rinehart and Winston, 1972) pp.7–13.

2 The term originates from the German word *Eidgnoss* or 'confederate', and referred to Swiss Protestant reformers. McGrath, A.E., *A Life of John Calvin* (Oxford: Blackwell, 1993) p.88.

3 Elliott. J.H., *Europe Divided, 1559–98* (Glasgow: Fontana, 1974) p.103.

4 Including La Rochelle, Saumur, Montauban, Montpellier and Castres.

5 Elliott, *op.cit.*, p.364; *Cambridge Modern History, Vol.3, The Wars of Religion* (Cambridge: Cambridge University Press, 1907) p.676; other Protestant

strongholds were Alès, Millau, Nîmes, Uzès, Puylaurens, Gignac and Aigues-Mortes.

6 Bainville, J., *Histoire de France* (Paris: Fayard, 1924) p.164.
7 *Cambridge Modern History*, Vol.3, p.681.
8 Parker, D., *The Huguenots in seventeenth-century France* in Hepburn, A.C. (ed.), *Minorities in History* (London: Edward Arnold, 1978).
9 Text of the Treaty of Oliva in Parry, *Consolidated Treaty Series* (Dobbs Ferry, New York: 1969, vol.6.) pp.60–92; Haumont, E., *La Guerre du Nord et la Paix d'Olive* (Paris: Colin, 1893) p.276.
10 Text of the Treaty of Nijmegan in Parry *op.cit.*, vol.14, pp.367–97; *New Cambridge Modern History Vol. V, The Ascendancy of France 1648–88* (Cambridge: University Press, 1980) p.219.
11 Text of the Treaty of Ryswick between France and the Holy Roman Empire in Parry *op.cit.*, vol.22, pp.79–104; *New Cambridge Modern History Vol.VI, The Rise of Great Britain and Russia, 1688–1725* (Cambridge: University Press, 1970) pp.473–4.
12 Barnard, F.M., *Herder's Social and Political Thought* (Oxford: Clarendon Press, 1965), pp.xiii-xiv.
13 *ibid.*, p.16.
14 *ibid.*, pp.18, including n.58, and 29.
15 *ibid.*, p.22.
16 *ibid.*, pp.30–1.
17 *ibid.*, p.57.
18 *ibid.*, pp.57–8.
19 *ibid.*, p.58.
20 *ibid.*, pp.59, 63.
21 *ibid.*, pp.70–1.
22 *ibid.*, pp.60–2.
23 *ibid.*, p.62.
24 *ibid.*
25 Cobban, A., *National Self-Determination* (Chicago: University Press, 1951 ed.), p.5.
26 Cobban, *ibid.*
27 Le Lannou, M., *La Bretagne et les Bretons* (Paris: Presses Universitaires de France, 1978), pp.24–5.
28 Bec, P., *La Langue Occitane* (Paris: Presses Universitaires de France, 1978), p.78.
29 Cherval, A., *Histoire de la Grammaire Scolaire* (Paris: Payot, 1977), p.24, quoted in McDonald, M., *We are not French!* (London: Routledge, 1989), p.29. See also Serant, P., *La Bretagne et la France* (Paris: Fayard, 1971), p.61.
30 Le Lannou, *op.cit.*, p.33.
31 Lebesque, M., *Comment peut-on être breton* (Paris: Seuil, 1970), p.97, quoted in Esman, M.J.(ed.), *Ethnic Conflic' in the Western World* (London: Cornell University Press, 1977), p.167.
32 Stephens, M., *Linguistic Minorities in Europe* (Llandysul: Gomer Press, 1976), p.369.
33 Giordan, H., *Les Minorités en Europe* (Paris: Kimé, 1992), p.109.
34 Bec, *op.cit.*, 89ff; Mayo, P.E., *The Roots of Identity* (London: Allen Lane, 1974), p.34.

35 Ramsay, R., *The Corsican Time Bomb* (Manchester: University Press, 1983), pp.2–8.
36 Renucci, J., *La Corse* (Paris: Presses Universitaires de la France, 1982), p.18.
37 Ramsay, *op.cit.*, pp.10–11.
38 Renucci, *op.cit.*, p.28.
39 See, inter alia, Minority Rights Group Report n.46, *The Flemings and Walloons of Belgium* (London: 1980), pp.6–8.
40 For example, the case of François-Marie Laurent, a farmer from Brittany who spoke only Breton. Wounded in the trenches, he left the front in search of treatment but was arrested by a French officer who spoke no Breton. He was executed for desertion. (*The Times*, 4 July 1999).
41 Alcock, A.E., *A Short History of Europe* ((London: Macmillan, 1998), pp.205–7.
42 Mar-Molinero, C. and Smith, A., *Nationalism and Nation in the Iberian Peninsula* (Oxford: Berg, 1966), p.2
43 Mar-Molinero, *ibid.*, pp.73–4.
44 Elliott, *op.cit.*, pp.376–8.
45 Mar-Molinero, *op.cit.*, p.76
46 Mar-Molinero, *ibid.*, pp.77–8.
47 Elliott, *op.cit.*, p.378.
48 Mar-Molinero, *op.cit.*, pp.91–3.
49 Mar-Molinero, *ibid.*, pp.6, 74–8, 240.
50 This issue discussed in depth in Hooper, J., *The Spaniards* (Harmondsworth: Penguin Books, 1986), pp.216–7; Mar-Molinero, *op.cit.*, p.79.
51 Stephens, *op.cit.*, p.151.
52 Mayo, *op.cit.*, pp.64–5.
53 Mayo, *ibid.*, p.68.
54 Stephens, *op.cit.*, p.157.
55 *ibid.*, p.158.
56 *ibid.* p.159.
57 Mayo, *op.cit.*, p.68.
58 Stephens, *op.cit.*, p.160.
59 Keith, D., *A History of Scotland, Vol.2* (Edinburgh: Paterson, 1886), pp.290–307.
60 MacKinnon, K., The Lion's Tongue (Inverness: Highland Book Club, 1974), pp.16–25.
61 *ibid.*, pp.30–7.
62 *ibid.*, p.40.
63 *ibid.*, pp.54–9.
64 Gaelic in Scotland, 1979 Celtic Congress.
65 Woodham-Smith, C., *The Great Hunger* (London: Four Square Books, 1964), pp.21–2.
66 De Freine, S., *The Great Silence* (Dublin: Mercier Press, 1978), pp.6–7.
67 De Freine, *ibid.*, p.69.
68 O'Murchu, M., (ed.), *The Irish Language in Society* (Coleraine: University of Ulster, 1991), pp.5–6.
69 Hindley, R., *The Death of the Irish Language* (London: Routledge, 1990), p.12.
70 Hindley, *ibid.*, p.13; O'Murchu, *op.cit.*, p.6.

71   De Freine, *op.cit.*, p.73; O'Murchu, *op.cit.*, p.10.
72   Hindley, *op.cit.*, p.13.
73   Hindley, *ibid.*, p.14.
74   Hindley, *ibid.*, pp.15, 19.
75   O'Murchu, *op.cit.*, p.25.
76   Brown,T., *Ireland – A Social and Cultural History* (Glasgow: Fontana/Collins, 1981), pp.54–7.
77   Hufton, O., *Europe: Privilege and Protest, 1730–1789* (Glasgow: Fontana, 1980), p.143.
78   Procacci, G., *History of the Italian People* (Harmondsworth: Penguin, 1986), pp.216ff.
79   *ibid.*, pp.258–63.
80   Alcock, A.E., *A Short History of Europe*, *op.cit.*, p.176.
81   *ibid.*, p.182.
82   Kohn, H., *Prelude to Nation States* (New York: Van Nostrand, 1967), pp.170–83.
83   *ibid.*, p.226.
84   *ibid.*, p.257.
85   *ibid.*, pp.275–7.
86   Cobban, *op.cit.*, p.53.
87   Taylor, A.J.P., *The Struggle for the Mastery of Europe, 1848–1918* (Oxford: University Press, 1971) p.168 fn.1.
88   Pederson, K.C., 'The Danish-German solution to the border and minorities problem', paper presented to the Wilton Park Conference 6–10 September 1993; Tajil, S.(ed.), *Ethnicity and Nation Building in the Nordic World* (London: Hurst, 1995), p.263.
89   Bankwitz, P.C.F., *Alsatian Autonomist Leaders 1919–1947* (Kansas: Regents Press, 1978), p.7.
90   Janin, B., *Le Val d'Aoste* (Aosta: Musumeci, 1976), Table 69, p.618.
91   Lengereau, M., *La France et la Question Valdotaine au Cours et à l'Issue de la Seconde Guerre Mondiale* (Grenoble: Société d'Histoire Alpine et Italienne, 1975), p.20.
92   Fischer Almanach, 1993.
93   Straka, M., *Handbuch der Europäischen Volksgruppen* (Vienna: Braumüller, 1970), pp.200–4.
94   Text of the Protocol of 20 February 1830 in Parry, *op.cit.*, vol.80, p.333.
95   Text of the Convention in Parry, vol.119, p.358.
96   Text of the Treaty of Berlin in Parry, vol.153, pp.172–91.
97   Text of the Convention in Parry, vol.158, pp.368–76.
98   Pearson, R., *National Minorities in Eastern Europe*, 1848–1945 (London: Macmillan, 1983), pp.66–70.
99   Tajil, *op.cit.*, pp.217–22.
100 Pearson, *op.cit.*, pp.71–81.
101 Nahaylo, B., *The Ukrainian Resurgence* (London: Hurst, 1999), p.6.
102 *ibid.*, p.11.
103 Rickett, R., *A Brief Survey of Austrian History* (Vienna: Prachner, 1966), pp.100–2.
104 Hoensch, J.K., *A History of Modern Hungary*, 1867–1986 (London: Longman, 1988), pp.28–31.

105 Pearson, *op.cit.*, p.68.
106 Macartney, C.A., *National States and National Minorities* (New York: Russell & Russell, 2nd ed., 1968) pp.168–9.
107 Locke, J., (ed.) Laslett, P., *Two Treatises of Government* (London: New English Library, 1965), pp.115, 395, 402–3.
108 Bagley, T.H., *General Principles and Problems in the International Protection of Minorities* (Geneva: Imprimeries Populaires, 1950), p.11.
109 *ibid.*, p.12.
110 Hechter, M., *Internal Colonialism* (London: Routledge and Kegan Paul, 1175),
111 Hooper, *op.cit.*, pp.224, 241; Stephens, *op.cit.*, pp.160–1.
112 Hooper, *op.cit.*, pp.249–50.
113 Le Lannou, *op.cit.*, pp.35–42.
114 Ramsay, *op.cit.*, p.15.
115 Lengereau, *op.cit.*, p.20.
116 Hechter, *op.cit.*

2 Into the Night – Minorities between the Wars

1 Text in Temperley, *A History of the Peace Conference at Paris* (London: Hodder & Stoughton, 1921), vol.1, pp.431–5.
2 Text in *ibid.*, pp.435–40.
3 Sharp, A.J., *The Versailles Settlement* (Basingstoke: Macmillan, 1991), p.156.
4 'When I gave utterance to those words ('that all nations had a right to self-determination') I said them without the knowledge that nationalities existed, which are coming to us day after day...' Temperley, H.W.V., *A History of the Peace Conference of Paris*, 1969 reprint, vol.4, p.429.
5 Lyons, *Ireland Since the Famine* (Glasgow: Fontana/Collins, 1973), p.398, also quoting Macardle, D., *The Irish Republic*, American ed., New York 1965, pp.919–22.
6 Longford, Lord, *Peace by Ordeal* (London: Sidgwick & Jackson, 1972 ed.), p.31.
7 Trimble, D., *The Foundation of Northern Ireland* (Lurgan: Ulster Society, 1991), p.18.
8 Caerleon, R., *Complots pour une République Bretonne* (Paris: La Table Ronde, 1967), p.62.
9 Baker, R.S., *Woodrow Wilson and World Settlement* (London: Heinemann, 1923), vol.2, p.133.
10 Alcock, A.E., *The History of the South Tyrol Question* (London: Michael Joseph, 1970), pp.20–2, quoting Seymour, C., 'Woodrow Wilson and Self-Determination in the Tyrol' in The Virginia Quarterly Review, vol.38, n.4, 1962, p.574.
11 Carsten, F.L., *Revolution in Central Europe 1918–1919* (Aldershot: Wildwood House, 1988), p.116.
12 Raschhofer, H., and Kimminich, O., *Die Sudetenfrage* (Munich: Olzog, 1988), p.116.
13 Carsten, *op.cit.*, p.21.
14 Text of the Treaty of Versailles in Parry, vol.225, pp.189–395.

15 Texts of the Treaties of St Germain and Neuilly in Parry, vol.226, pp.9–167 and 373–435.
16 Pearson, *op.cit.,* pp.150–4.
17 Census of 1930, Pearson, *ibid.,* p.163.
18 Macartney, *op.cit.,* p.536; Pearson, *ibid.,* p.148.
19 Pearson, *ibid.,* p.173.
20 Dunn, S., and Fraser, T.G., (eds), *Europe and Ethnicity,* (London: Routledge, 1996), p.25.
21 Azcaraté, P. de, *League of Nations and National Minorities,* (New York: Kraus Reprint, 1972), pp.59–60.
22 Article 44, Treaty of Neuilly.
23 Text in Temperley, *op.cit.,* vol.5, p.470.
24 Stark, T., *Le Statut Juridique des Minorités en Pologne,* 1919–39, in *L'Encyclopédie Polonaise,* (Fribourg, 1940), pp.404–5.
25 *ibid.,* pp.403–4.
26 Macartney, *op.cit.,* pp.221–6.
27 Text of the Romanian Minority Treaty of 9 December 1919 in Parry, *op.cit.,* vol.226, pp.447–55.
28 Text of the Polish Minority Treaty in Temperley, *op.cit.,* vol.5, pp.437–42.
29 Text of the League Covenant in Northedge, F.S., *The League of Nations* (Leicester: University Press, 1988), pp.317–27. References to 'judicial settlement and decision as well as all Article 13(iii) were adopted in September 1924; Northedge, *ibid.,* p.321.
30 Bagley, T.H., *General Principles and Problems in the International Protection of Minorities* (Geneva: Imprimeries Populaires, 1950), p.79.
31 Azcaraté, op.cit., pp.102–12. The Tittoni Report is contained in Annex 115 to the Minutes of the 10th session of the League Council, adopted 22 October1920. See Bagley, *op.cit.,* p.80.
32 See above, pp.102–12.
33 Derry, T.K., *A History of Scandinavia* (Minneapolis: University of Minnesota Press, 7th ed., 1995) p.313; Temperley, *op.cit.,* vol.2, pp.203–6.
34 Wiskemann E., *Germany's Eastern Neighbours* (London: Oxford University Press, 1956) pp.15–16.
35 Horak, S., *Poland and her National Minorities* (New York: Vantage press, 1961), p.40.
36 Schlifflers, L., *Die Deutschsprachige Gemeinschaft Belgiens: ihr Legaler Status in Belgien.* Paper presented to the International Symposium on Minorities in Europe organised by the UDMR, Timisoara, 27 March 1992.
37 Unkart, R., Glantschnig, G., and Ogris, A., *Zur Lage der Slowenen in Kärnten* (Klagenfurt: Kärtner Landesarchiv, 1984), pp.265–9.
38 Azcaraté, *op.cit.,* p.137, Walters, F. P:, *A History of the League of Nations* (London: Oxford University Press, 1967), p.152–3p.
39 Venner, D., *Les Corps – francs allemands de la Baltique* (Paris: Le Livre de Poche, 1978), pp.336–7.
40 Kaeckenbeeck, *The International Experiment of Upper Silesia* (London: Oxford University Press, 1942), pp.353–5. See also German sources amalgamating the Poles and bilingual Poles as Poles in Eckert, M., *Historia Polski 1914–1939* (Warsaw: Wydawnictwa Szkolnei Pedagogiczne, 1990), p.106.

41 Text of the German-Polish Convention on Upper Silesia in Kaeckenbeeck, *op.cit.*, pp.572–822.
42 Kaeckenbeeck, *ibid.*, p.230; Azcaraté, *op.cit.*, pp.150–3.
43 Eckert, *op.cit.*, p.106.
44 *ibid.*
45 Demilitarisation Convention appendix to the Paris Peace Treaty in Parry, vol.114, pp.406–7.
46 Walters, F.P., *op.cit.*, p.104.
47 Derry, *op. cit.* p. 311.
48 Stephens, *op.cit.*, pp.275–80; see also Myntti, K., *The Protection of Persons belonging to National Minorities in Finland* (Turku; Advisory Board for International Human Rights Affairs, 1991), pp.15–17.
49 Antrim, Armagh, Down, Fermanagh, Londonderry and Tyrone.
50 Alcock, A.E., *Understanding Ulster* (Lurgan: Ulster Society, 1994),
51 Alcock, *ibid.*, p.39.
52 Treaty of 3 December 1925, in League of Nations Treaty Series, vol.44, p.263.
53 Alcock, *Understanding Ulster*, op.cit., pp.35–53, 63.
54 Alcock, *History of the South Tyrol Question*, pp.25–26
55 Alcock, *ibid.*, pp.27–32.
56 Alcock, *ibid.*, p14.
57 Alcock, *ibid.*, p.14.
58 Alcock, A.E., *Südtirol seit dem Paket* (Vienna: Braumüller, 1982), pp.74–5.
59 The Fascist denationalisation programme described in full in Alcock, *History of the South Tyrol Question*, pp.34–5.
60 The Options situation described in full in Alcock, *ibid.*, pp.45–59.
61 Raschhofer, *op.cit.*, pp.141–2.
62 Wiskemann, *Czechs and Germans* (London: Macmillan, 2 ed., 1967), p.123.
63 Pearson, *op.cit.*, p.153.
64. Mosny, P., *Notes on the Language Law of Czechoslovakia in 1918 to 1938*, in Plichtova, J. (ed.), *Minorities in Politics* (Bratislava: Czechoslovak Committee of the European Cultural Foundation, 1992), pp.125–6.
65 Wiskemann, *Czechs and Germans*, *op.cit.*, pp.147–9. A quarter of Bohemia was owned by two per cent of landowners, and a third of Moravia by less than one per cent.
66 Habel, F.P., *The Sudeten Question* (Munich: Sudeten German Council, 1984), pp.4–7.
67 Northedge, *op.cit.*, pp.78–9; Walters, *op.cit.*, pp.105–9 and 140–3.
68 Text of the Convention in League of Nations, Treaty Series, vol.48, n.1170, pp.335–79.
69 Pearson, *op.cit.*, p.168.
70 *Penguin Atlas of World History* Vol.2. p.167. Text of the Treaty of Lausanne of 24 July 1923 in League of Nations, Treaty Series, vol.28, pp.12–113.
71 Text of the Convention of Ankara, 10 June 1930, in League of Nations Treaty Series, vol.108, p.233.
72 Stephens, *op.cit.*, p.669.
73 Thomas, H., *The Spanish Civil War* (Harmondsworth: Penguin, 1965), p.80.
74 Stephens, *op.cit.*, p.615.

75 Thomas, *op.cit.*, p.83 and n.2.
76 Straka, *op.cit.* p.132.
77 Mar-Molinero, *op.cit.*, p.161.
78 *ibid.*, p.159.
79 *ibid*, p.158.
80 Stephens, *op.cit.*, p.641.
81 *ibid*, pp.619, 642.
82 *ibid.*, p.626.
83 *ibid.*, p.73.
84 Pearson, *op.cit.*, p.156.
85 *ibid*, pp.152, 157.
86 *ibid.*, p.157; *Penguin Atlas of World History*, 2, p.163.
87 Poulton, H., *The Balkans* (London: Minority Rights Group, 1991), p.29.
88 Pearson, *op.cit.*, p.159.
89 Nahaylo, *op.cit.*, p.10.
90 Derry, *op.cit.*, p.310.
91 Tajil, *op.cit.*, pp.223–4.
92 Walker, op.cit., pp.33–4; Lincoln, B., *Red Victory* (London: Sphere Books, 1991), pp.455–61.
93 The issue of the Upper Silesian dialect examined in depth in Kaeckenbeeck, *op.cit.*, pp.344–55 and Azcaraté, *op.cit.*, p.148.
94 Text of Judgement 12 of 26 April 1928 and the Dissenting Opinions in PCIJ, Series A, n.15, *Rights of Minorities in Upper Silesia* (Leyden: Sijthoff, 1928). For the documentation see PCIJ, Series C, n.14, *Rights of Minorities in Upper Silesia* (Leyden: Sijthoff, 1928). See also Hudson, M.O., *La Cour Permanente de Justice Internationale* (Paris: Pedone, 1936), pp.543–4. Text of the Advisory Opinion of 15 May 1931, *Access to German Minority Schools in Upper Silesia*, in PCIJ, Series A/B n.40 (Leyden: Sijthoff, 1931).
95 Alcock, *History of the South Tyrol Question*, p.238.
96 Text of the Advisory Opinion of 6 April 1935, documentation thereto and Dissenting Opinions in Permanent Court of International Justice, Series A/B, n.64, *Minority Schools in Albania* (Leyden: Sijthoff, 1935); (italics added).
97 Bagley, *op.cit.*, pp.89–90.
98 Macartney, *op.cit.*, p.488.
99 Azcaraté, *op.cit.*, p.26.
100 Macartney, *op.cit.*, p.292.
101 Azcaraté, *op.cit.*, p.167.
102 Claude, I.L., *National Minorities* (New York: Greenwood, 1969), pp.31–2.
103 Text of the letter in Temperley, vol.4, pp.432–7; see also Azcaraté, *op.cit.*, pp.165–7.
104 Claude, *op.cit.*, p.31.
105 Macartney, *op.cit.*, pp.327 and 390.
106 See, for example, Kaeckenbeeck, *op.cit.*, p.360; Bagley, *op.cit.*, p.121.
107 Bagley, *op.cit.*, pp.123–4.
108 See, for example, Macartney, *op.cit.*, pp.333–7.
109 *ibid.*, p.326.
110 Kaeckenbeeck, *op.cit.*, p.355; Claude, *op.cit.*, pp.36–8 and 43.

111 Macartney, *op.cit.*, pp.281–3.
112 Claude, *op.cit.*, p.37.

3 The Second World War – and After, 1939–47

1 Text of the Protocol of the Proceedings of the Potsdam Conference, and particularly Section XII, in *The Avalon Project: A Decade of American Foreign Policy*, www.yale.edu/lawweb/avalon/decade/decade17.htm
2 *Penguin Atlas of World History*, vol.2, p.221.
3 Derry, *op.cit.*, pp.333 and 344.
4 Tajil, *op.cit.*, p.232.
5 Swettenham, J.A., *The Tragedy of the Baltic States* (London: Hollis & Carter, 1952), pp.72–157.
6 Schlifflers, *op.cit.*, p.8
7 Bankwitz, *op.cit.*, pp.67–100
8 European Bureau for Lesser Used Languages, *European Language Series, n.7., Brittany – A Language in Search of a Future* (Brussels: 1998), p.26.
9 Details in Caerleon, *op.cit.*, pp.181–365.
10 Giordan, *op.cit.*, p.124.
11 Comby, *Histoire des Corses* (Paris: Nathan, 1978), pp.133–42.
12 Alcock, *History of the South Tyrol Question*, op.cit., pp.58–68 and Table D. p.496.
13 *ibid.*, pp.83–5.
14 Details in Raschhofer, *op.cit.*, pp.264–6.
15 Hoensch, *op.cit.*, p.177.
16 *ibid.*
17 *ibid.*
18 See text of the Secret Additional Protocol to the Nazi-Soviet Pact of 23 August 1939, Article 3, in Payne R., *The Rise and Fall of Stalin* (London: Pan 1968), p.549.
19 Seton-Watson, H., *From Lenin to Khrushcher* (New York: Praeger, 1960), p.208.
20 Nahaylo, *op.cit.*, p.17.
21 Penguin History, vol.2., *op.cit.*, p.203.
22 Pearson, *op.cit.*, p.196.
23 Nahaylo, *op.cit.*, pp.15–18.
24 Minority Rights Group, *Soviet Minorities* (update), 1990.
25 Magosci, R., *Carpatho-Rusyns – Their Current Status*, in Plichtova, *op.cit.*, pp.213–21.
26 Jewish statistics in Davidowicz, L., *The War against the Jews 1939–45* (Weidenfeld & Nicolson; 1975: Penguin pbk 1977), p.480. Gypsy statistics in Kenrick, D. and Puxon, M., *The Destiny of Europe's Gypsies* (London: Heinemann, 1972) pp.183–4; and in Pearson, *op.cit.* Table XII, p.200 and also p.201.
27 Claude, *op.cit.*, p.57.
28 *ibid.*, pp.55–65.
29 *ibid.*, p.78.

30 New York Times Magazine, 16 May 1948, quoted in Claude, *op.cit.*, p.81.
31 Claude, *ibid.*, pp.80–4.
32 *ibid.*, p.86.
33 *ibid.*, pp.92–105.
34 Alcock, A.E., 'La Gran Bretagna e l'Accordo De Gasperi-Gruber sul Sudtirolo del 5 settembre 1946', in Istituto Trentino di Cultura, Premesse Storiche e Quadro Internazionale dell'Accordo De Gasperi-Gruber, Trento, Supplemento n.1/1987 di ITC Informa.
35 Text of the Agreement in Alcock, *South Tyrol*, pp.473–4.
36 *ibid.*, p.144.

4 Heads (Mostly) in the Sand, 1948–72

1 Alcock, A.E., *History of the South Tyrol Question*, *op.cit.*, p.243.
2 United Nations Economic and Social Council Official Records, 3rd Year, 7th Session, Supplement n.6, Report of the *ad hoc* Committee on Genocide, 5 April–10 May 1948, pp.6–7.
3 General Assembly, Official Records, 3rd Session, 6th Committee, Summary Records, 21 September–10 December 1948, pp.193–207.
4 The full text of the definition in UN Doc. E/CN.4/Sub.2/85. Bagley, *op.cit.*, pp.180–1; (italics provided).
5 See above, p. 80–1
6 UN Doc. E/CN.4/Sub.2/40 of 7 June 1949.
7 See below, p. 122.
8 UN Doc.E/CN.4/367 of 7 April 1950. See also Feinberg, N., 'The Legal Validity of the Undertakings concerning Minorities and the Clausula Rebus sic Stantibus' in *Studies in Law*, vol.5. (Jerusalem: Hebrew Press, 1958), pp.94–131.
9 Langereau, *op.cit.*, p.76.
10 Minority Rights Group, World Directory of Minorities, *op.cit.*, p.164.
11 DL of 7 September 1945, n.545; Langereau, *op.cit.*, p.98; Weibel, E., *La Création des Régions Autonomes à Statut Spécial en Italie* (Geneva: Droz, 1971), pp.296–7.
12 *ibid.*, p.297.
13 Alcock, *History of the South Tyrol Question*, *op.cit.*, pp.91–2.
14 Ginsborg, P., *A History of Contemporary Italy* (London: Penguin, 1990), p.98.
15 Weibel, *op.cit.*, p.114.
16 *ibid.*, fns. 93 and 94.
17 Alcock, *History of the South Tyrol Question*, *op.cit.*, pp.138–41.
18 The original language of the Agreement was English. But as part of the Italian Peace Treaty the only authentic texts were the English, French and Russian. Alcock, *ibid.*, p.146.
19 The tortuous details of the 'consultation' in Alcock, *ibid.*, pp.151–68.
20 From the appeal to German unity in the Imperial German national anthem, 'Deutschland, Deutschland über alles … von der Memel bis der Etsch'.
21 Alcock, *History of the South Tyrol Question*, *op.cit.*, Table B, p.494.
22 Alcock, A.E., *Südtirol seit dem Paket*, *op.cit.*, p.174.
23 Alcock, *History of the South Tyrol Question*, *op.cit.*, pp.172–3.

24 *ibid.*, pp.276–7 and fn.24.
25 *ibid.*, p.279.
26 *ibid.*, p.276.
27 *ibid.*, pp.198–9.
28 Alcock, *Südtirol seit dem Paket, op.cit.*, pp.79–80.
29 Resolution 1497 (XV) of 31 October 1960; Alcock, *History of the South Tyrol Question, op.cit.*, p.348; (italics added).
30 Alcock, *ibid.*, p.358.
31 *ibid.*, Map3, p.512.
32 *ibid.*, p.451. For full details of the Party Congress see Alcock, *Südtirol seit dem Paket, op.cit.*, pp.20–5.
33 World Directory of Minorities, *op.cit.*, p.162.
34 Weibel, *op.cit.*, p.300 and fn.50.
35 Straka, *op.cit.*, p.321.
36 Straka, *op.cit.*, pp.275 321; World Directory of Minorities, *op.cit.*, pp.140 and 150; Ashworth, G. (ed.), *World Minorities in the Eighties* (Sunbury: Minority Rights Group,1980), vol.3, pp.32–7.
37 Pedersen, K.C., *Denmark and Germany – The German Minority in Denmark and the Danish Minority in Germany*, in *Minorities and Autonomy in Western Europe* (Minority Rights Group, 1991), p.18.
38 Tajil, *op.cit.*, pp.67–80.
39 See, for example, the Commentary by the *Rat der Kärtner Slowenen* and the *Zentralverband slowenisches Organization in Kärnten*, in Government of Austria, *Federal Government Report on the Situation of Ethnic Groups in Austria* (Vienna: Federal Press Service, c.1991), pp.57–74 (hereinafter *Report*). Text of the State Treaty in *Bundesgesetzblatt*, Vienna, n.152/1955.
40 *ibid.*, p.13–15.
41 *ibid.*
42 Austrian Ethnic Groups Centre, *Austria Ethnica – State and Perspectives, vol.7* (Vienna: AEGC, 1994), p.20.
43 *ibid.*, p.15.
44 *ibid.*, pp.26–7.
45 *ibid.*, p.28.
46 Government of Austria, *Report, op.cit.*, p.22.
47 Council of Europe, Consultative Assembly, Doc.508 of 20 April 1956.
48 *ibid.*, Doc.731, Resolution 136 of October 1957.
49 Lannung, H., 'The Rights of Minorities' in *Mélanges offerts à Polys Modinos* (Paris: Pedone, 1968), p.186, (hereinafter *Modinos*).
50 Doc.1002 of 30 April 1959.
51 Doc.999 of 24 April 1959.
52 See above p.102
53 Recommendation 285 of 28 April 1961.
54 In 1963 a linguistic frontier had been established in Belgium in which in the northern Flemish section Dutch was the official language while in the southern section French was the official language. Brussels was declared a bilingual area and children were sent to the school of the language of the father. However, around Brussels were six peripheral communes and since Brussels actually fell in the northern Flemish part of Belgium these were officially Dutch-speaking communes which, however, had sizeable French-

speaking populations but where French-speaking classes were provided at
nursery and primary level only if this was requested by 16 heads of family,
according to the cultural laws introduced in communes all-powerful in
regard to linguistic and cultural affairs.

In 1963 300 French-speaking parents, residents in some of the Flemish
Brussels-periphery communes appealed to the European Commission of
Human Rights on the grounds that they were being deprived of the right to
have their children educated in French. According to the cultural laws they
had to send their children to Flemish schools and thus be educated in a language different from their parents, or, if they wished to educate them in
French, they would have to send them – at considerable expense – to
schools some distance away. They argued on the basis of Article 8 of the
Human Rights Convention that measures in the field of education could
affect the right to respect for private and family life or derogate from it by
causing children separation from family life. The Human Rights
Commission, taking up the cudgels on behalf of the French-speaking families, asked the Court of Human Rights whether Article 8 imposed on the
Belgian government the positive obligation to establish or subsidise French-
speaking education in Flemish areas. The answer was No. There was no
guarantee of the right to be educated in the language of one's parents by
the public authorities. If parents sent their children to school in Brussels, in
Wallonia or abroad to be taught in French, this separation was imposed not
by Belgian legislation but parental choice. However, the Court held that the
law was discriminatory in that the clause granting French educational facilities at nursery and primary level in certain communes on condition that it
was requested by 16 heads of family did not apply to children whose
parents lived *outside* the communes in question, even though there were no
French-speaking schools in the commune in which they lived. What had
happened was that the Flemish communes in which these facilities in
French were available had refused to accept the French-speaking children
from other Flemish communes.

The court held this arrangement to be discriminatory since it prevented
certain children from having access to French-speaking education solely on
the place of residence of their parents, whereas Flemish-speaking schools
did accept pupils from other communes, and this situation was therefore
contrary to Article 14 of the European Convention on Human Rights.
European Court of Human Rights, Series A; Judgements and Decisions, n.6,
*Case relating to Certain Aspects of the Laws on the Use of Languages in
Education in Belgium*, Registry of the Court, Strasbourg, 1968.

55 Lannung in Modinos, *op.cit.*, p.193.
56 Benoît-Rohmer, F., *The Minority Question in Europe: Towards a Coherent
    System of Protection of National Minorities* (Strasbourg: Council of
    Europe/International Institute for Democracy, 1966), p.36.
57 *ibid.*, pp.191–2.
58 1960 census in Minority Rights Group Report No.30, *Cyprus* (London; MRG,
    1976), p.4. The 2 per cent Armenian and Maronite communities have been
    included in the Greek community.
59 *ibid.*, p.8.
60 Nejatigil, Z.M., *Our Republic in Perspective* (Nicosia: Lefkosa, 1985), p.1–3.

61 Alcock, A.E., *Protection of Minorities – Three Case Studies: South Tyrol, Cyprus and Quebec*, in Hepburn, *op.cit.*, pp.205–7; Wolfe, J.H., Heinritz, G., Hilf, R., Kellner, L., *Zypern – Macht oder Land Teilen?* (Munich: International Institute for Nationality Rights and Regionalism, 1987), pp.38–74.

62 Nejatigil, *op.cit.*, p.5.

63 Doherty, M.G., *Brittany: An Example of the Continuing Strength of French Centralism* (Coleraine: University of Ulster MA Thesis, 1990), p.67.

64 *ibid.*, pp.122–4.

65 *ibid.*, p.128.

66 *ibid.*, p.130.

67 See Giordan, H., *op.cit.*, p.109, for instances of Breton given names being rejected by the Registrar, actions upheld by the courts during the 1960s up to 1980.

68 Doherty, *op.cit.*, p.135.

69 Ramsay, *op.cit.*, pp.31–6.

70 *ibid.*, p.43.

71 *ibid.*, pp.47–9.

72 *ibid.*, pp.56–7.

73 Minority Rights Group Report n.9, *The Basques and the Catalans* (rev. 1982 ed.), p.8.

74 *ibid.*, p.7.

75 *ibid.*, p.

76 *ibid.*, p.12

77 *ibid.*, p.10

78 Mar-Molinero, *op.cit.*, p.210.

79 Alcock, *Understanding Ulster, op.cit.*, p.55

80 Lyons, *op.cit.*, p.761.

81 Alcock, *Understanding Ulster, op.cit.*, pp.55–63.

5 Renaissance in the West, 1972–99

1 Alcock, *Südtirol seit dem Paket, op.cit.*, pp.164–5.

2 Veiter, T. in *Das Menschenrecht*, Vienna, April 1970.

3 Alcock, *Südtirol seit dem Paket, op.cit.*, p.165.

4 Council of Europe, *Bordeaux Declaration* (Bordeaux: Conference of Local and Regional Authorities of Europe, 30 January–1 February 1978).

5 Esterbauer, F. (ed.), *Regionalismus* (Munich: Bayerische Landeszentrale für Politische Bildungsarbeit, 1978), pp.137 ff.

6 Text of the Madrid Convention in Pernthaler, P. and Ortino, S. (eds), *Europaregion Tirol – Euregio Tirola*, Trento, Autonome Region Trentino-Südtirol, 1997, pp.201–8.

7 Text of DPR of 13 August 1972, n.670 in Alcock, *Südtirol seit dem Paket, op.cit.*, pp.238–74.

8 Volgger, F. (ed.), *Südtirol-Themen* (Bozen-Bolzano: Südtiroler Landesregierung, Presseamt, 1995).

9 Alcock, *Südtirol seit dem Paket, op.cit.*, p.114 and fn.234.

10 DPR of 28 July 1976, n.752, Art.18.

11 *ibid.*, Art. 46.

12   Alcock, A.E., 'Italy – *The South Tyrol*', in Minority Rights Group, *Minorities and Autonomy in Western Europe* (London, 1991), p.10.
13   Volgger, *op.cit.*
14   DL of 1991, n.253.
15   *Alto Adige*, Bozen-Bolzano, 16 September 1976, quoted in Alcock, *Südtirol seit dem Paket, op.cit.*, pp.91–3.
16   Text in Penthaler and Ortino, *op.cit.*, pp.215–19.
17   Alcock, A.E., '*Trentino and Tyrol: from Austrian Crownland to European Region*', in Dunn, S., and Fraser, T.G., (eds), *op.cit.*, pp.83–4.
18   Pernthaler, P. and Ortino, S., *op.cit.*, pp.170–1, 291–2.
19   L.612 of 20 November 1991.
20   Gruppo di Studio Alpina, *1 Quattro Gruppi Nazionali del Friuli-Venezia Giulia* (Bellinzona: Salvioni, 1975), pp.5–6.
21   *Contact*, Dublin, vol.13, n.1, Spring 1996, pp.10–11.
22   *Contact*, vol.14, n.3, June 1998, p.9.
23   Hooper, *op.cit.*, pp.255–6.
24   *Times*, London, 13 November 1992.
25   Minority Rights Group, *World Directory of Minorities, op.cit.*, p.175.
26   Donaghy, P.J. and Newton, M.T., *Spain – A Guide to Political and Economic Institutions* (Cambridge: University Press, 1987), p.105.
27   Hooper, J., *The New Spaniards* (London: Penguin, 1995), p.436.
28   Xunta di Galicia, *The History of the Galician Language, op.cit.*, p.43.
29   Fitzmaurice, J., '*Federalism by Stealth: The Reform of the Belgian State*', in *Dutch Crossing*, London, Centre for Low Countries Studies, n.37, April 1989, pp.92–106.
30   *ibid.*
31   *Financial Times*, London, 16–17 January 1999.
32   Peeters, Y., *The Dutch Language Union* in *Contact*, Dublin, 1988, n.1.
33   European Community, *Official Journal*, n.C224, vol.35 of 31 August 1992.
34   Ingelaere, F., '*The New Legislation on The International Relations of the Belgian Communities and Regions*', in *Studia Diplomatica*, Brussels, 1994, n.1, pp.25–49.
35   cf. Doherty, *op.cit.*, pp.69–75.
36   *ibid.*, p.78.
37   *ibid.*, pp.79–81.
38   Wangermée, R., and Bernard, G., '*Programme Européen d'Evaluation: La Politique Culturelle de la France*', in *La Documentation Française*, Paris, 1988, p.217, quoted in Giordan, *op.cit.*, p.139.
39   Giordan, *ibid.*, p.143.
40   *I'Independent*, Carcassonne, 24 June 1999.
41   *Le Figaro*, Paris, 24 June 1999.
42   *Le Figaro*, 18 June 1999; *Le Monde*, Paris, 25 June 1999.
43   Le Monde, *ibid.*
44   Breton Prisoners Solidarity Committee, *Where Does the Responsibility Lie for Violence in Brittany?*(Dublin, 1978).
45   *European*, London, 7–13 March 1996.
46   Doherty, *op.cit.*, pp.87–92.
47   *ibid.*, pp.76–83.
48   *European*, London, 26–29 August, 1993.

49 *European*, London, 20–26 July 1998.
50 Loughlin, J.P., *Regionalism and Ethnic Nationalism in France: A Case Study of Corsica*, Florence, European University Institute Ph.D. Thesis, 1987, pp.295–301.
51 Savigear, P., 'Corsica: Regional Autonomy or Violence', in *Conflict Studies*, London, Institute for the Study of Conflict, n.149, 1990, p.12.
52 Heraud, G., in *Europa Ethnica*, Vienna, 1991, n.4.
53 *European*, London, 6–12 February 1997.
54 *ibid.*, 11–14 July 1992.
55 *Daily Telegraph*, London, 4 January 1991; Savigear, op.cit., p.10.
56 *European*, London, 11–14 June 1992 and 18–24 July 1996; Savigear, *op.cit.*, p.10.
57 Stephens, *op.cit.*, p.325.
58 *Le Soir*, Paris, 31 January 1974.
59 *Sunday Telegraph*, London, 23 July 1978.
60 Synak and Wicherkiewicz, *Language Minorities and Minority Languages in the Changing Europe* (Gdansk: Wydawnictwo Univwersytetu Gdanskiego, 1997). pp.229–37.
61 Symptomatic of this attitude were the remarks of the Conservative Secretary of State for Northern Ireland, Sir Patrick Mayhew, in an interview with *Die Zeit*, 16 April 1993: 'Viele Leute glauben, wir wollten NordIrland nicht aus dem Königreich entlassen. Wenn ich ganz ehrlich bin: Mit Handkuss! – Nein, den Handkuss nehme ich zurück', quoted in Alcock, A.E., *Understanding Ulster, op.cit.*, p.87 and fn.22, p.157. This contemptible attitude has been confirmed by the revelations from Cabinet Papers released at the end of 1999: expelling Northern Ireland from the United Kingdom was indeed an option considered by London in 1969 (*Sunday Times*, 1 January 2000).
62 Maginnis, K., *McGimpsey & McGimpsey v. Ireland* (Dungannon, 1990), pp.3–10.
63 Alcock, *Understanding Ulster, op.cit.*, p.70.
64 *ibid.*, pp.66–70.
65 *Newsletter*, Belfast, 25 May 1993.
66 See above, p.68.
67 Text of the Agreement in TSO, London, Cmd 3883, April 1998.
68 Fay, M.T., Morrissey, M., Smyth, M. and Wang, T., *The Cost of the Troubles Study, Final Report* (Belfast: April 1999), Appendix 1, p.57.
69 *Newsletter*, Belfast, 9 June 1999.
70 Gallagher T., (ed.), *Nationalism in the Nineties* (Edinburgh: Polygon, 1991), p.9.
71 Levy, R., *Scottish Nationalism at the Crossroads* (Edinburgh: Scottish Academic Press, 1990), pp.42–3.
72 Mitchell, J., *Conservatives and the Union* (Edinburgh: University Press, 1990), p.95.
73 Gallagher, *op.cit.*, p.12.
74 *ibid.*, p.17.
75 *ibid.*, p.63.
76 *ibid.*, pp.87–8.
77 The Scotland Act 1998, ch.46, London, TSO, November 1998.
78 *Daily Telegraph*, London, 1 September 1994.

79 *ibid.*, 30 April 1994..
80 *ibid.*, 23 December 1996.
81 Foulkes, D., Jones, J.B., and Wilford, R.A., *The Welsh Veto* (Cardiff: University of Wales Press, 1982), p.13.
82 Jones, A.R. and Thomas, G., *Presenting Saunders Lewis* (Cardiff: University of Wales Press, 1983), pp.127–141; Williams, C.H., *'Non-Violence and the Development of the Welsh Language Society'*, in *The Welsh History Review*, vol.8, n.4, 1977, p.429.
83 Foulkes, *op.cit.*, pp.22–9.
84 Stephens, M., *The Welsh Language Today* (Llandysul: Gower Press, 1973), p.100.
85 Williams, *op.cit.*, p.440.
86 *Daily Telegraph*, London, 17 and 19 November 1976, 5 August 1986 and 8 November 1988.
87 Foulkes, *op.cit.*, pp.22–9.
88 *ibid.*, pp.118–38.
89 *Daily Telegraph*, 31 December 1990; *Sunday Telegraph*, 1 September 1996.
90 *Daily Telegraph*, 13 September 1985.
91 *ibid.*, 19 December 1992 and 20 January 1993.
92 Text of the Government of Wales Act in TSO, London, ch.38, August 1998.
93 Rennwald, J.C., *La Question Jurassienne* (Paris: Editions Entente, 1984), p.36.
94 Jenkins, J.R.G., *Jura Separatism in Switzerland* (Oxford: Clarendon, 1986), p.13.
95 For the details see Rennwald, *op.cit.*, p.45.
96 Jenkins, *op.cit.*, p.26.
97 *ibid.*, p.91.
98 Rennwald, *op.cit.*, p.73; Jenkins, *op.cit.*, p.100.
99 Jenkins, *ibid.*, pp.86–7.
100 Rennwald, *op.cit.*, p.75.
101 *ibid.*, p.77.
102 *ibid.*, p.78.
103 *ibid.*, pp.84–90.
104 Jenkins, *op.cit.*, p.4.
105 Rennwald, *op.cit.*, pp.70, 145–6.
106 Lia Rumantscha, *Rhaeto-Romansch – Facts and Figures* (Chur: Lia Rumantscha, 1996), pp.20–2.
107 Rennwald, *op.cit.*, pp.107–9; Decurtins, A., *Il Romantsch – In Model per la Sort da Minoritads Linguisticas e Culturales?* (Chur: Ligia Romontscha, 1976.
108 Lia Rumantscha, *op.cit.*, pp.28–49.
109 Provincial Government of Friesland, *The Frisian Language* (Leeuwarden: 1987); MRG, *World Directory of Minorities*, p.168.
110 Tajil, *op.cit.*, pp.116–175; MRG, *World Directory of Minorities*, pp.143, 170–1, 179–80.
111 European Parliament, *Resolution on a Community Charter of Regional Languages and Cultures and on a Charter of Rights for Ethnic Minorities*, October 1981, OJC 287, p.57.

112 For example, *The Kuijpers Resolution on the Languages and Cultures of Regional and Ethnic Minorities in the European Community*, adopted on 30 October 1987, OJC 310, p.144; *Killilea Resolution on Linguistic and Cultural Minorities in the European Community*, adopted on 9 February 1994, OJC 061 p.110.

113 Ermacora, F., and Pan, C., *Volksgruppenschutz in Europa* (Vienna: Braumüller, 1992, 1993 eds.)

114 Senator Friedl Volgger (SVP), Senator Karl Mitterdorfer (SVP), Professor Christopher Pan (University of Innsbruck).

115 Ermacora and Pan, *op.cit.*, 1993, p.105.

116 English text in Ermacora and Pan, *op.cit.*, 1992, pp.63–98.

117 Text of Recommendation 1201 (1193) and draft Additional Protocol in Minority Rights Group, *World Directory of Minorities, op.cit.*, pp.764–66.

118 Wright, J., 'The Protection of Minority Rights in Europe: From Conference to Implementation', in *The International Journal of Human Rights*, vol.2, n.1 (Spring 1998), p.6.

119 Benoît-Rohmer, *op.cit.*, p.37.

120 See below, pp.194 and 196.

121 Text of the Charter in Council of Europe, *Treaty Series*, n.148, Strasbourg, 5 November 1192. See also comments on the Charter in Kristianssen, *op.cit.*, p.473.

122 See Appendix 2, pp.223–4

123 Text of the Convention in Council of Europe, *Treaty Series*, n.157, Strasbourg, 1 February 1995.

124 See Appendix 2, pp.223–4

6 Eastern Europe

1 Liebich, A., *Ethnic Minorities and Long-Term Implications of EU Enlargement* (Badia Fiesolana: European University Institute, 1998), p.5.

2 Roessingh, M.A., *Ethnonationalism and Political Systems in Europe* (Amsterdam: University Press, 1996), pp.89–91.

3 There seems to be great uncertainty as to the true figure. Liebich gives 300–800 000, *op.cit.*, p.20; the *Fischer Almanach, 1990*, gives 100 000 but according to Polish sources, 200 000, while the 1993 version, i.e. after the fall of communism, gives 0.5 to 1 million.

4 Minority Rights Group, *Romania's Ethnic Hungarians*, 1980, pp.12–17.

5 *ibid.*, p.18; Fischer Almanac, *op.cit.*, 1993.

6 Bloed, A., *The Conference on Security and Co-operation in Europe, Analysis and Basic Documents, 1972–1993* (Dordrecht: Kluwer, 1993), p.5.

7 Text of the Helsinki Agreement in Keesing *Contemporary Archives*, 1975, vol.21, pp.27301ff.

8 Alcock, *Understanding Ulster, op.cit.*, pp.110–13.

9 Kristiansen, *op.cit.*, p.460.

10 Schachter, O., 'The Twilight Existence of Non-Binding International Agreements', in *American Journal of International Law*, vol.71, 1997, p.300, quoted in Kristiansen, *op.cit.*, p.214 and fn.334.

11 Bloed, *op.cit.*, p.22, quoting Van Dijk, P., in *Netherlands Yearbook of International Law*, 1980, p.10.
12 Kristiansen, *op.cit.*, pp.216–20.
13 Text of Part IV in Minority Rights Group, *World Directory of Minorities*, *op.cit.*, pp.771–2; for the whole text see Bloed, *op.cit.*, pp.439–65.
14 Text of the Vienna Mechanism in Bloed, *op.cit.*, pp.367–9.
15 *ibid.*, pp.460–1.
16 Kristiansen, *op.cit.*, p.461.
17 Packer, J., 'The Role of the OSCE High Commissioner on National Minorities, in *Cambridge Review of International Affairs*', vol.12, n.2, 1999, p.169; see also Kristiansen, *op.cit.*, p.461.
18 The text of the Mandate of the High Commissioner in The Foundation on Inter-Ethnic Relations (hereinafter FIER) '*The Role of the High Commissioner on National Minorities in OSCE Conflict Prevention* (The Hague: 1997), pp.85–92 (hereinafter, *High Commissioner*).
19 Bloed, *op.cit.*, pp.893–4.
20 Text of the Convention in Bloed, *ibid.*, pp.1008–15.
21 FIER, *The Hague Recommendations regarding the Educational Rights of National Minorities*, The Hague, 1996.
22 FIER, *The Oslo Recommendations Regarding the Linguistic Rights of National Minorities*, The Hague, 1998.
23 Packer, *op.cit.*, p.179; Liebich, *op.cit.*, p.5.
24 Liebich, *op.cit.*, p.5, fns.9 and 10, pp.22–3, gives a number of authors and publications in which these interpretations are analysed.
25 Keesing, vol.42, n.12, pp.41417–8.
26 *Sunday Telegraph*, London, 24 January 1999.
27 Synak and Wicherkiewicz, *op.cit.* pp.330–4.
28 *ibid.*, pp.337–44.
29 *Eagle Street*, n.11, January 1999.
30 Tajil, *op.cit.*, pp.240–2.
31 Keesing, vol.38, n.1, p.38737.
32 Figures in Brunner, G., *Nationality Problems and Minority Conflicts in Eastern Europe* (Gütersloh: Bertelsmann Foundation, 1996), pp.176–7.
33 'Every citizen shall have the right ... without any of the distinctions mentioned in Article 2 ... (a) To take part in the conduct of public affairs, directly or through freely chosen representatives.' Article 2 specifically mentions language as a distinction.
34 Brunner, *op.cit.*, p.68 fn.90.
35 See in particular Gabzdilova, S., '*Schools in the Slovak Republic with instruction in the Hungarian language*', in Plichtova, J. (ed), *Minorities in Politics*, The Bratislava Symposium II/1991, Bratislava, Czechoslovak Committee of the European Cultural Foundation, 1992, pp.164–71.
36 FIER, *The Role of the High Commissioner on National Minorities in OSCE Conflict Prevention* (The Hague:1997), pp.59,72.
37 Wright, *op.cit.*, p.10.
38 Wright, *op.cit.*, pp.8–26.
39 Magyar Koalicio Partja, *A Short Analysis of the Law on the Use of the Languages of National Minorities*, Bratislava: n.d. (c. July/August 1999).

40 HCNM press release, The Hague, 19 July 1999.
41 FIER, *High Commissioner*, pp.70–1.
42 Law LXXVII of 7 July 1993.
43 Wright, *op.cit.*, pp.25–26.
44 Minority Rights Group, *Romania's Ethnic Hungarians*, p.21.
45 Brenner, *op.cit.*, p.53.
46 For this overview of Ukrainian-Crimean relations see Packer, J., '*Autonomy within the OSCE: The Case of Crimea*', in Suksi, M. (ed.), *Autonomy: Applications and Implications* (Dordrecht: Kluwer, 1998), pp.295–312.
47 *ibid.*, pp.312–15.
48 Keesing, vol.43, 1997, n.6, p.41710; n.9, pp.41835–6; n.10, p.41878; vol.44, n.11, p.42636.

7 No Lessons Learned

1 *European Commission v. Belgium*, Case 149/79, Judgement of 17 December 1980 (Luxembourg: European Court Reports, 1980), pp.3886–7.
2 *Official Journal*, C72, vol.31, 18 March 1988, p.2.
3 *European Commission v. Belgium*, Case 149/79, Judgement of 17 December 1980, *op.cit.*, p.3882.
4 *ibid.*, p.3886.
5 *European Commission v. France*, case 307/84, Judgement of 3 June 1986 (Luxembourg: European Court Reports, 1986), pp.1731–2; 1739–40.
6 *Official Journal*, C72, vol.31, 18 March 1988, p.3.
7 These issues explored in depth in Alcock, A.E., '*The Protection of Regional Cultural Minorities and the Process of European Integration: the Example of South Tyrol*', in *International Relations*, London, David Davies Institute, vol.xi, n.1, April 1992, pp.17–36.
8 *Groener v. the Minister for Education and the City of Dublin Vocational Educational Committee*, Case, 379/87, Judgement of 28 November 1989 (Luxembourg: European Court Reports,1989), p.3993 (hereinafter *Groener*.)
9 See above, pp.111–2
10 Groener, *op.cit.*, p.3982.
11 Alcock, *Südtirol seit dem Paket*, *op.cit.*, p.32.
12 Doc.Conf.-UP-UEM 2008/91, Luxembourg, 18 June 1991.
13 Text of the Maastricht Treaty in OJC224, vol.35, 31 August 1992.
14 For fuller details see Jansson, R., *The Aland Islands* in European Institute of Public Administration, EIPASCOPE, 1997, n.2, pp.32–3.
15 *Daily Telegraph*, 14 July 1998; *Guardian*, 20 July 1998.
16 *European*, 5–8 August, 1993.
17 Sunday Times, 9 May 1999.
18 International Association for the Protection of Human Rights in Cyprus, *Violations of Human Rights by Turkey in Cyprus* (Nicosia: 1991); Government of Cyprus, *The Cyprus Refugee Problem – Humanitarian Aspects* (Nicosia: Press and Information Office, 1989).
19 *Cyprus Bulletin*, vol.35, n.17, 23 September 1998.
20 *Cyprus Bulletin*, vol.35, n.14, 12 August 1998; *Times*, 27 August 1998.
21 Brunner, *op.cit.*, pp.170–73.

22 Details of the Dayton Accords in Keesing, November 1995, pp.40830 ff.
23 Pearson, *op.cit.*, p.152; Brunner, *ibid.*, pp.170 and 172.
24 Poulton, op.cit., pp.15 and 57.
25 Poulton, *ibid.*, p.60.
26 Poulton, *ibid.*, pp.68–9.
27 Keesing, August 1998, p.42459.
28 *Times*, 18 August 1998.
29 Keesing, March 1999, pp.42845–8.
30 FIER, *High Commissioner op.cit.*, pp.58–9.

Conclusions

1 In an interview with *L'Adige*, 8 March 1979, quoted in Alcock, *Südtirol seit dem Paket, op.cit.*, p.56.
2 Alcock, *History of the South Tyrol Question, op.cit.*, p.230.
3 Packer, J., 'The OSCE and International Guarantees of Local Self-Government', in European Commission for Democracy through Law, *Local Self-Government, Territorial Integrity and Protection of Minorities*, Council of Europe, Strasbourg, 1996, p.271.

Bibliography

Official texts

General

Parry, C., *Consolidated Treaty Series*, Dobbs Ferry, New York: Oceana Publications, 1969.

Governments

Austria

Bundesgesetzblatt n.152/1955, State Treaty of 15 May 1955.
Federal Government General Report on the Situation of Ethnic Groups in Austria, Vienna: Federal Press Service, 1991.

Cyprus

Cyprus Bulletin, Government of Cyprus, Press and Information Office, Nicosia, Series.
The Cyprus Refugee Problem – Humanitarian Aspects, Press and Information Office, Nicosia, 1989.

Hungary

Declaration on the Principles of Co-operation Between Hungary and the Ukrainian SSR in Guaranteeing the Rights of National Minorities, Budapest, 31 May 1991.
Convention on Providing Special Rights for the Slovenian Minority living in Hungary and for the Hungarian Minority in Slovenia, Ljubljana, 6 November 1992.
Declaration on the Principles guiding Co-operation between Hungary and the Russian Federation regarding the Guarantee of the Rights of National Minorities, Budapest, 11 November 1992.
Treaty on Good Neighbourly Relations and Friendly Co-operation Between Hungary and Slovakia, Budapest/Bratislava, 19 March 1995.
Convention between Hungary and Croatia on the Protection of the Hungarian Minority in Croatia and the Croatian Minority in Hungary, Osijek, 5 April 1995.
Treaty between Hungary and Romania on Understanding, Co-operation and Good Neighbourliness, Timisoara, 16 September 1996.
Law LXXVII of 7 July 1993 on the Protection of the Rights of National and Ethnic Minorities.

Ireland

Agreement between the Government of the United Kingdom of Great Britain and Northern Ireland and the Government of Ireland, 15 November 1985, *Ireland Today*, Dublin, Department of Foreign Affairs, Special Issue, November 1985.

Italy

DLL of 7 September 1945, n.545 on the Administrative Organisation of the Aosta Valley.
Constitutional Law of 26 February 1948, n.3 (Special Statute for Sardinia).
Constitutional Law of 26 February 1948, n.4 (Special Statute for the Aosta Valley).
Constitutional Law of 26 February 1948, n.5 (Special Statute for Trentino-Alto Adige) revised by DPR of 31 August 1972, n.670.
Constitutional Law of 31 January 1963 (Special Statute for Friuli-Venezia Giulia).
Law 612 of 15 November 1991 on Protection of Minority Languages and Cultures in Italy.

Slovakia

Act on the State Language of the Slovak Republic, dated 15 November 1995.
Act on the Use of National Minority Languages, adopted 10 July 1999.

United Kingdom of Great Britain and Northern Ireland

The Agreement reached in Multi-Party Negotiations, TSO, London, Cmd 3883, April 1998.
The Government of Wales Act 1998, ch.38, London, TSO, August 1998.
The Scotland Act 1998, ch.46, London, TSO, November, 1998.

International Organisations

Council of Europe

Committee of Ministers.
Resolution 10(97) *on Rules adopted by the Committee of Ministers on the Monitoring Arrangements under Arts. 24–26 of the Framework Convention on the Protection of National Minorities,* adopted on 17 September 1997 (601st meeting of the Ministers' Deputies).
Conference of Local and Regional Authorities of Europe, *Bordeaux Declaration*, 1 February 1978.

Consultative (later Parliamentary) Assembly.
Doc.508, 20 April 1956.
Doc.1002, 30 April 1959: Report on the Position of National Minorities in Europe (P. Struye).
Recommendation 1201 (1993) on an Additional Protocol on the Rights on National Minorities to the European Convention of Human Rights, 1 February 1993.
Order 484 (1993) on an Additional Protocol on the Rights of National Minorities to the European Convention on Human Rights, Appendix 6, adopted 1 February 1993.

European Court of Human Rights.
Doc.731, Resolution 136 of October 1957.
Doc.999, 24 April 1959.
Publications of the European Courts of Human Rights, Series A: Judgements and Decisions, n.6., *Case Relating to Certain Aspects of the Laws on the Use of Languages in Education in Belgium*, Registry of the Court, Strasbourg, 1968.

Treaty Series.
n.5. *European Convention for the Protection of Human Rights and Fundamental Freedoms*, 4 November 1950.
n.106. *Madrid Outline Convention on Transfrontier Co-operation between Territorial Communities or Authorities*, 21 May 1980.
n.148. *European Charter for Regional or Minority Languages*, 5 November 1992.
n.157. *Framework Convention for the Protection of National Minorities*, 1 February 1995.

European Community
European Court of Justice.
Court Reports, Luxembourg.

Official Journal.
Luxembourg, Office for Official Publications of the European Community.

European Parliament
Doc.1-965/80 – *Arfé Report on a Charter for Ethnic Minorities.*
Resolution by Gaetano Arfé on a Community Charter of Regional Languages and Cultures and on a Charter of Rights of Ethnic Minorities, adopted 16 October 1981, OJC 287 p.57.
Resolution by Gaetano Arfé on Measures in Favour of Minority Languages and Cultures, adopted 11 February 1983, OJC 68 (14.03.93), p.104.
Resolution by Willy Kuijpers on the Languages and Cultures of Regional and Ethnic Minorities in the European Community, adopted 30 October 1987, OJC 318 (30.11.87), p.144.
Resolution by Mark Killilea on Linguistic and Cultural Minorities in the European Community, adopted on 9 February 1994, OJC 861, p.110.

League of Nations
Treaty Series.

Permanent Court of International Justice
Series A; Series C; Series A/B, Leyden, Sijthoff.

OSCE, High Commissioner on National Minorities
Report on the Linguistic Rights of Persons Belonging to National Minorities in the OSCE Area, The Hague, March 1999.

United Nations

General Assembly.
Genocide Convention (Resolution 260 III) of 9 December 1948.
Universal Declaration of Human Rights, (Resolution 217 III A), 10 December 1948.
Resolution 217 III C, 10 December 1948 (authorising a study of the problems of minorities in order to take measures for their protection).
*Covenant on Civil and Political Rights and Optional Protocol, (Resolution 2200 A XXI),*16 December 1966.

Sub-Commission on the Prevention of Discrimination and Protection of Minorities:
Doc.E/CN.4/Sub.2/40, 7 June 1949: *Report on the Prevention of Discrimination.*
Doc.E/CN.4/Sub.2/85, December 1949: *Definition and Classification of Minorities.*
Doc.E/CN.4/Sub.2/384/rev.1, 1979: *Study on the Rights of Persons Belonging to Ethnic, Religious and Linguistic Minorities* (F.Capotorti).

Unpublished Sources

Doherty, M.G., *'Brittany: An Example of the Continuing Strength of French Centralism',* Coleraine: University of Ulster MA Thesis, 1990.
Kristiansen, M.L., *'Special Measures for the Protection of Minorities',* Thesis n.556, Geneva: Graduate Institute of International Studies, 1997.
Loughlin, J.P., *'Regionalism and Ethnic Nationalism in France: A Case Study of Corsica',* Ph.D. Thesis, Florence: European University Institute,1987.
Pederson, K.C., *'The Danish-German Solution to the Border and Minorities Problem.'* Paper presented to the Wilton Park Conference on Redrawing the Map of Europe, 6–10 September, 1993.
Schlifflers, L., *'Die Deutschsprachige Gemeinschaft Belgiens: ihr legaler Status in Belgien.'* Paper presented to the International Symposium on Minorities in Europe organised by the UDMR (Hungarian Democratic Party in Romania), Timisoara, 27 March 1992.

Secondary Sources

Books

Albrecht-Carrié, R., *Italy at the Peace Conference,* New York: Columbia, 1938.
Alcock, A.E., *The History of the South Tyrol Question,* London: Michael Joseph, 1970.
Alcock, A.E., Protection of Minorities – *Three Case Studies: South Tyrol, Cyprus, Quebec,* Belfast, Northern Ireland Constitutional Convention, 1975.
Alcock, A.E., Taylor, B.K., and Welton, J., *The Future of Cultural Minorities,* London: Macmillan, 1979.
Alcock, A.E., *Geschichte der Südtirolfrage – Südtirol seit dem Paket* 1970–80, Vienna: Braumüller, 1982.
Alcock, A.E., *Understanding Ulster,* Lurgan, The Ulster Society, 1994.
Alcock, A.E., *A Short History of Europe – from the Greeks and the Romans to the Present Day,* Basingstoke, Macmillan, 1998.

Alcock, A.E., and O'Brien, T., *Policies to Support Radio and Television Broadcasting in the Lesser Used Languages of the European Community*, Coleraine, New University of Ulster, 1980.

Ashworth, G., *World Minorities*, 3 vols., Sunbury: Minority Rights Group, Quartermaine House, 1977–80.

Azcaraté, P. de, *League of Nations and National Minorities*, Washington, Carnegie, 1945 (Kraus reprint, New York, 1972).

Bagley, T.H., *General Principles and Problems in the International Protection of Minorities*, Geneva: Imprimeries Populaires, 1950.

Bainville, J., *Histoire de France*, Paris: Fayard, 1924.

Baker, R.S., *Woodrow Wilson and World Settlement*, 3 vols., London: Heinemann, 1923.

Bankwitz, P.C.F., *Alsatian Autonomist Leaders 1919–1947*, Kansas: Regents Press, 1978.

Barnard, F.M., *Herder's Social and Political Thought*, Oxford, Clarendon Press, 1965.

Bec, P., *La Langue Occitane*, Paris, Presses Universitaires de France, 1978.

Benoît-Rohmer, F., *The Minority Question in Europe: Towards a Coherent System of Protection for National Minorities*, Strasbourg: Council of Europe, International Institute for Democracy, 1996.

Bloed, A., (ed.), *The Conference on Security and Co-operation in Europe, Analysis and Basic Documents*, Dordrecht: Kluwer, 1993.

Brown, T., *Ireland – A Social and Cultural History 1922–79*, Glasgow: Fontana/Collins, 1981.

Brunner, G., *Nationality Problems and Minority Conflicts in Eastern Europe*, Gütersloh, Bertelsmann Foundation, 1996.

Cambridge Modern History, vol.III., *The Wars of Religion*, Cambridge: University Press, 1907.

Caerleon, R., *Complots pour une République Bretonne*, Paris: La Table Ronde, 1967.

Carsten, F.L., *Revolution in Central Europe 1918–1919*, Aldershot: Wildwood House, 1988.

Claude, I.L., *National Minorities*, New York: Greenwood, 1969.

Claude, I.L., *Swords into Ploughshares* (4th ed.), New York: Random House, 1971.

Cobban, A., *National Self-Determination*, Chicago: University of Chicago Press, 1951.

Comby, L., *Histoire des Corses*, Paris: Nathan, 1978.

Davidowicz, L., *The War against the Jews 1939–45*, Weidenfeld & Nicolson, 1975, Penguin pbk 1977.

De Freine, S., *The Great Silence*, Dublin: Mercier Press, 1978.

Derry, T.K., *A History of Scandinavia* (7th ed.), Minneapolis: University of Minnesota Press, 1995.

Donaghy, P.J., and Newton, M.T., *Spain – A Guide to Political and Economic Institutions*, Cambridge: University Press, 1987.

Drobizheva, L., Gottemoeller, R., Kelleher, C.M., and Walker, L., *Ethnic Conflict in the Post-Soviet World*, London: Sharpe, 1996.

Dunn, S., and Fraser, T.G., (eds), *Europe and Ethnicity*, London: Routledge, 1996.

Eckert, M., *Historia Polski 1914–1939*, Warsaw: Wydawnictwa Szkolne i Pedagogiczne, 1990.

Elliott, J.H., *Imperial Spain 1469–1716*, Harmondsworth: Penguin Books, 1970.

Elliott, J.H., *Europe Divided, 1559–98*, Glasgow: Fontana, 1974.

Ermacora, F., and Pan, C., *Grundrechte der europäischen Volksgruppen, (Fundamental Rights of Ethnic Groups in Europe)* Vienna: Braumüller (Ethnos, n.42) 1993.

Ermacora, F., and Pan, C., *Volksgruppenschutz in Europa (Protection of Ethnic Groups in Europe)*, Vienna: Braumüller (Ethnos n.46), 1995.

Esman, M.J. (ed.), *Ethnic Conflict in the Western World*, London: Cornell University Press, 1977.

Esterbauer, F., *Regionalismus*, Munich: Bayerische Landeszentrale für Politisches Bildungsarbeit, 1978.

European Commission for Democracy Through Law, *Local Self-Government, Territorial Integrity and Protection of Minorities*, Science and Technique of Democracy Series, n.16. Strasbourg: Council of Europe, 1996.

Fenet, A., *La Question du Tyrol du Sud*, Paris: Pichon & Durand-Auzias, 1968.

Foulkes, D., Jones, J.B., and Wilford, R.A., *The Welsh Veto*, Cardiff: University of Wales Press, 1982.

Gallagher, T., (ed.), *Nationalism in the Nineties*, Edinburgh: Polygon, 1991.

Gillett, N., *The Swiss Constitution – Can it be Exported?* Bristol: YES Publications, 1989.

Ginsborg, P., *A History of Contemporary Italy*, London: Penguin, 1990.

Giordan, H., *Les Minorités en Europe*, Paris: Kimé, 1992.

Habel, F.P., *The Sudeten Question*, Munich: Sudeten German Council, 1984.

Haumont, E., *La Guerre du Nord et la Paix d'Olive*, Paris: Colin, 1893.

Hechter, M., *Internal Colonialism*, London: Routledge & Kegan Paul, 1975.

Hepburn, A.C., *Minorities in History*, London: Edward Arnold, 1978.

Heraud, G., *L'Europe des Ethnies*, Brussels: Bruylant, 1993.

Hindley, R., *The Death of the Irish Language*, London: Routledge, 1990.

Hoensch, J.K., *A History of Modern Hungary 1867–1986*, London: Longman, 1988.

Hooper, J., *The Spaniards*, Harmondsworth: Penguin Books, 1986; revised edition, *The New Spaniards*, Penguin, 1995.

Horak, S., *Poland and her National Minorities*, New York: Vantage Press, 1961.

Horne, A., *The Fall of Paris*, London: Pan Books, 1968.

Hufton, O., Europe: *Privilege and Protest 1730–1789*, Glasgow: Fontana, 1980.

Hudson, M.O., *La Cour Permanante de Justice Internationale*, Paris: Pedone, 1936.

Janin, B., *Le Val D'Aoste – Tradition et Renouveau*, Aosta: Musemeci, 1976.

Jenkins, J.R.G., *Jura Separatism in Switzerland*, Oxford, Clarendon, 1986.

Jenkins, R., *Rethinking Ethnicity*, London: Sage, 1997.

Jones, A.R., and Thomas, G., *Presenting Saunders Lewis*, Cardiff: University of Wales Press, 1983.

Kaeckenbeeck, G., *The International Experiment of Upper Silesia*, London: Oxford University Press, 1942.

Keith, D., *A History of Scotland*, 2 vols., Edinburgh: Paterson, 1886.

Kemp, W.A., *Nationalism and Communism in Eastern Europe and the Soviet Union: A Basic Contradiction?* Basingstoke: Macmillan, 1999.

Kohn, H., *Prelude to Nation States*, New York: Van Nostrand, 1967.

Kenrick, D. and Puxon, M., *The Destiny of Europe's Gypsies*, London: Heinemann, 1972.

Le Galès, P., and Lequesne, C., *Regions in Europe*, London: Routledge, 1998.

Le Lannou, M., *La Bretagne et les Bretons*, Paris: Presses Universitaires de France, 1978.

Lengereau, M., *La France et la Question Valdotaine au Cours et à l'Issue de la Seconde Guerre Mondiale*, Grenoble: Société d'Histoire Alpine et Italienne, 1975.

Levy, C., (ed.), *Italian Regionalism*, Oxford: Berg, 1996.

Levy, R., *Scottish Nationalism at the Crossroads*, Edinburgh: Scottish Academic Press, 1990.

Lincoln, B., *Red Victory*, London: Sphere Books, 1991.

Locke, J., ed. Laslett, P., *Two Treatises of Government*, London: New English Library, 1965.

Longford, Lord, *Peace by Ordeal*, London: Sidgwick & Jackson, 1972 ed.

Lynch, P., *Minority Nationalism and European Integration*, Cardiff: University of Wales Press, 1996.

Lyons, F.S., *Ireland Since the Famine*, Glasgow: Fontana/Collins, 1973.

Macartney, C.A., *National States and National Minorities*, 2nd ed., New York: Russell & Russell, 1968.

Mackinnon, K., *The Lion's Tongue*, Inverness: Highland Book Club, 1974.

McDonald, M., *We are not French!* London: Routledge, 1989.

McGrath, A.E., *A Life of John Calvin*, Oxford: Blackwell, 1993.

Mar-Molinero, C., and Smith, A., *Nationalism and the Nation in the Iberian Peninsula*, Oxford: Berg, 1966.

Mayo, P.E., *The Roots of Identity*, London: Allen Lane, 1974.

Mitchell, J., *Conservatives and the Union*, Edinburgh: University Press, 1990.

Mousnier, R., *The Assassination of Henry IV*, London: Faber, 1973.

Minority Rights Group, *World Directory of Minorities*, London: MRG, 1997.

Myntti, K., *The Protection of Persons belonging to National Minorities in Finland*, Turku: Advisory Board for International Human Rights Affairs, 1991.

Nahaylo, B., *The Ukrainian Resurgence*, London: Hurst, 1999.

Nejatigil, Z.M., *Our Republic in Perspective*, Nicosia: Lefkosa, 1985.

New Cambridge Modern History vol.5, *The Ascendency of France 1648–88*, Cambridge: University Press, 1980 ed.

New Cambridge Modern History vol.6, *The Rise of Great Britain and Russia 1688–1725*, Cambridge: University Press, 1970.

Northedge, F.S., *The League of Nations – its Life and Times 1920–1946*, Leicester, University Press, 1988.

O'Murchu, M., (ed.), *The Irish Language in Society* (based on papers by C. O'Huallachain, OFM), Coleraine: University of Ulster, 1991.

Ortino, S., and Pernthaler, P., (eds), *La Riforma Costituzionale in Senso Federale*, Trento: Regione Autonoma Trentino-Alto Adige, 1997.

Packer, J., and Myntti, K., (eds), *The Protection of Ethnic and Linguistic Minorities in Europe*, Abo/Turku: Institute for Human Rights, 1993.

Payne, R., *The Rise and Fall of Stalin*, London: Pan, 1968.

Pearson, R., *National Minorities in Eastern Europe 1848–1945*, London: Macmillan, 1983.

Penguin Atlas of World History (2 vols.), Harmondsworth: Penguin, 1978.

Pernthaler, P., and Ortino, S., *Europaregion Tirol – Euregio Tirolo*, Trento: Autonome Region Trentino-Südtirol, 1997.

Pizzorusso, A., *Il Pluralismo Linguistico tra Stato Nazionale e Autonomie Regionali*, Pisa: Pacini, 1975.

Plichtova, J., (ed.), *Minorities in Politics*, Proceedings of the II (1991) Bratislava Symposium, Bratislava: Czechoslovak Committee of the European Cultural Foundation, 1992.

Poulton, H., *The Balkans*, London: Minority Rights Group, 1991.

Prebble, J., *The Highland Clearances*, Harmondsworth: Penguin, 1972 ed.

Procacci, G., *History of the Italian People*, Harmondsworth: Penguin, 1986.

Ramsay, R., *The Corsican Time Bomb*, Manchester: University Press, 1983.

Raschhofer, H., and Kimminich, O., *Die Sudetenfrage*, Munich: Olzog, 1988.

Rennwald, J.C., *La Question Jurassiènne*, Paris: Editions Entente, 1984.

Renucci, J., *La Corse*, Paris: Presses Universitaires de France, 1982.

Rickett, R., *A Brief Survey of Austrian History*, Vienna: Prachner, 1966.

Roessingh, M.A., *Ethnonationalism and Political Systems in Europe*, Amsterdam: University Press, 1996.

Salvemini, G., *Mussolini Diplomatico*, Bari: Laterza, 1952.

Santarelli, E., *Dossier sulle Regioni*, Bari: De Donato, 1970.

Scott, P.H., *Towards Independence*, Edinburgh: Polygon, 1991.

Serant, P., *La Bretagne et la France*, Paris: Fayard, 1971.

Seton-Watson, H., *From Lenin to Khrushchev*, New York: Praeger, 1960.

Seymour, C., (ed.), *The Intimate Papers of Colonel House*, vol.3, London: Benn, 1928.

Sharp, A., *The Versailles Settlement*, Basingstoke: Macmillan, 1991.

Smelser, R.M., *The Sudeten Problem, 1933–1938, Volkstumspolitik and the Formulation of Nazi Foreign Policy*, Folkestone: Dawson, 1975.

Stephens, M., *Linguistic Minorities in Western Europe*, Llandysul: Gomer Press, 1976.

Stephens, M., (ed.), The *Welsh Language Today*, Llandysul: Gomer Press, 1973.

Straka, M., *Handbuch der Europäischen Volksgruppen*, Vienna: Braumüller, 1970.

Swettenham, J.A., *The Tragedy of the Baltic States*, London: Hollis & Carter, 1952.

Synak. B., and Wicherkiewicz, T., *Language Minorities and Minority Languages in the Changing Europe*, Gdansk: Wydawnictwo Univwersytetu Gdanskiego, 1997.

Tajil, S:, *Ethnicity and Nation Building in the Nordic World*, London: Hurst, 1995.

Taylor, A.J.P., *The Struggle for the Mastery of Europe, 1848–1918*, Oxford: University Press, 1971.

Temperley, H.W.V., *A History of the Peace Conference of Paris*, 5 vols., London: Hodder & Stoughton, 1921 (reprinted 1969).

Thomas, H., *The Spanish Civil War*, Harmondsworth: Penguin, 1965.

Tipton, C.L., (ed.), *Nationalism in the Middle Ages*, New York: Rhinehart & Winston, 1972.

Trimble, D., *The Foundation of Northern Ireland*, Lurgan: Ulster Society, 1991.

Unkart, R., Glantschnig, G., and Ogris, A., *Zur Lage der Slowenen in Kärnten*, Klagenfurt: Kärntner Landesarchiv, 1984.

Veiter, T., *Das Recht der Volksgruppen und Sprachminderheiten in Österreich*, Vienna: Braumüller, 1966.

Venner, D., *Les Corps–francs allemands de la Baltique*, Paris: Le Livre de Poche, 1978.

Walker, C.J., (ed.), *Armenia and Karabagh*, London: Minority Rights Group, 1991.

Walters, F.P., *A History of the League of Nations*, London: Oxford University Press, 1967 ed.

Watt, R.M., *The Kings Depart*, Harmondsworth: Penguin, 1973.

Weibel, E., *La Création des Régions Autonomes à Statut Spécial en Italie*, Geneva: Droz, 1971.
Wiskemann, E., *Germany's Eastern Neighbours*, London: Oxford University Press, 1956.
Wiskemann, E., *Czechs and Germans*, 2nd ed., London: Macmillan, 1967.
Woodham-Smith, C., *The Great Hunger*, London: Four Square Books, 1964.

Articles in journals/chapters in books

Alcock, A.E., 'La Gran Bretagna e l'Accordo De Gasperi-Gruber sul Sudtirolo del 5 Settembre 1946', in *ITC Informa*, Atti della Tavola Ronda su Premesse Storiche e Quadro Internazionale dell'Accordo De Gasperi-Gruber, 12 Dicembre 1986, Istituto Trentino di Cultura, Supplemento al n.1/1987, pp.9–11.
Alcock, A.E., 'Proportional Representation in Public Employment as a Technique for Diminishing Conflict in Culturally Divided Communities: The Case of South Tyrol', in *Regional Politics and Policy*, London: Cass, vol.1, n.1, 1991, pp.74–86.
Alcock, A.E., 'The Protection of Regional Cultural Minorities and the Process of European Integration: the Example of South Tyrol' in *International Relations*, London: David Davies Memorial Institute, vol.xi, 1992, n.1, pp.17–36.
Bilder, R.B., 'Can Minority Treaties Work?' in Dinstein, Y., and Tabory, M., *The Protection of Minorities and Human Rights*, Tel Aviv, 1992.
Feinberg, N., 'The Legal Validity of the Undertakings Concerning Minorities and the Clausula Rebus Sic Stantibus', in *Studies in Law*, Jerusalem: Hebrew University, vol.5, 1958, pp.94–131.
Fitzmaurice, J., 'Federalism by Stealth: The Reform of the Belgian State', in *Dutch Crossing*, London: Centre for Low Countries Studies, n.37, April 1989, pp.92–106.
Gabzidilova, S. 'Schools in the Slovak Republic with instruction in the Hungarian Language,' in Plichtova, J. (ed.) *Minorities in Politics*, Bratislava, Czechoslovak Committee of the European Cultural Foundation, 1992.
Guillen, P., 'La Francia e la Questione dell'Alto Adige (Sudtirolo) 1945–1946', in *ITC Informa*, Atti della Tavola Ronda su Premesse Storiche e Quadro Internazionale dell'Accordo De Gasperi-Gruber, 12 Dicembre 1986, Istituto Trentino di Cultura, Supplemento al n.1/1987, pp.12–16.
Heraud, G., 'La Décision du Conseil Constitutionnel du 9 mai 1991 niant l'existence d'un peuple corse', in *Europa Ethnica*, Vienna: Braumüller, n.4, 1991, pp.183–5.
Ingelaere, F., 'The New Legislation on the International Relations of the Belgian Communities and Regions', in *Studia Diplomatica*, Brussels, 1994, n.1, pp.25–49.
International Journal of the Sociology of Language, *Language Death*, Paris: Mouton, n.12, 1977.
Keating, M., 'Regional Autonomy in the Changing State Order: A Framework of Analysis', in *Regional Politics and Policy*, London: Cass, vol.2, n.3, 1992.
Kimminich, O., 'A Federal Right of Self-Determination', in Tomuschat, C., (ed.), *Modern Law of Self-Determination*, Dordrecht, Nijhoff, 1993.

Lannung, K., 'The Rights of Minorities', in *Mélanges Offert à Polys Modinos*, Paris: Pedone, 1968, pp.181–95.

Das Menschenrecht, (T. Veiter), Vienna, April 1970.

Morrow, D., 'Regional Policy as Foreign Policy: The Austrian Experience', in *Regional Politics and Policy*, London: Cass, vol.2, n.3, 1992, pp.27–44.

Packer, J., 'Autonomy within the OSCE: The Case of Crimea', in Sutsi, M. (ed.), *Autonomy: Applications and Implications*, Dordrecht: Kluwer, 1998.

Packer, J., 'The Role of the OSCE High Commissioner on National Minorities in the Former Yugoslavia', in *Cambridge Review of Current Affairs*, vol.12, n.2, 1999.

Savigear, P., 'Corsica: Regional Autonomy or Violence', in *Conflict Studies*, n.149, London: Institute for the Study of Conflict, 1990.

Schachter, O., 'The Twilight Existence of Non-Binding International Ageements', in *The American Journal of International Law*, vol.71, Washington, DC: Society of International Law, 1977.

Seymour, C., 'Woodrow Wilson and Self-Determination in the Tyrol', in *The Virginia Quarterly Review*, vol.38, n.4, Richmond, 1962.

Stark, T., 'Le Statut Juridique des Minorités en Pologne 1919–39', in *L'Encyclopédie Polonaise*, Fribourg, 1940.

Williams, C.H., 'Non-Violence and the Development of the Welsh Language Society, 1962–74', in *The Welsh History Review*, vol.8, n.4, 1977, pp.426–55.

Wright, J., 'The Protection of Minority Rights in Europe: From Conference to Implementation', in *International Journal of Human Rights*, vol.2, n.1, (Spring 1998), London: Cass, pp.1–31.

Reports, documentation, information

European Bureau for Lesser Used Languages, *Contact*, Dublin.

1988/1 *Schleswig.*

Dutch Language Union (Yvo Peeters).

1996/1 *New Language Law for Friulan; Focus on Friuli–Venezia Giulia for Regional or Minority Languages.*

1998 vol.14 n.3, *European Charter.*

Sardinia.

1998 vol.15, n.1, *UK and Charter for Regional and Minority Languages.*

Report on Regional Languages in France.

OSCE – Oslo Recommendations on Linguistic Rights of Minorities.

Bilingual Radio Stations in Austria.

Vade Mecum – A Guide to the Legal, Political and other Documents Pertaining to the Lesser Used Languages of Europe.

European Languages Series

1. *The Valley d'Aosta.*

7. *Brittany – A Language in Search of Future*, Brussels, 1998.

8. *Irish – Facing the Future*, Dublin, 1999.

Fay, M.T., Morrissey, M., Smyth, M., and Wong, T., *The Cost of the Troubles Study*, Belfast, 1999.

Fay, M.T., Morrissey, M., Smyth, M., and Wong, T., *Final Report*, Belfast 1999.

Der Fischer Welt Almanach, Frankfurt am Main: Fischer Taschenbuch Verlag, 1990–93.

Jansson, R., *The Aland Islands*, European Institute of Public Administration. Eipascope, Series Maastricht,1997/2, pp.30–3.

Foundation on Interethnic Relations (FIER).
The Hague Recommendations Regarding the Education Rights of National Minorities and Explanatory Note, The Hague, October 1996.
Bibliography on the OSCE High Commissioner on National Minorities, The Hague, March 1997.
The Role of the High Commissioner on National Minorities in OSCE Conflict Prevention, An Introduction, The Hague, June 1997.
The Oslo Recommendations Regarding the Linguistic Rights of National Minorities and Explanatory Note, The Hague, February 1998.

Keesing's Contemporary Archives /(after 1986) Record of World Events, London: Longmans, Series.

Lia Rumantscha.
Rhaeto-Romansch – Facts and Figures, Chur: Lia Rumantscha, 1996.
Minority Rights Group International, Reports.
n.2, 1972, *The Two Irelands*, (revised 1982).
n.9, 1977, *The Basques and Catalans*, (revised 1982).
n.30, 1976, *Cyprus*.
n.32, *The Armenians*.
n.37, 1978, *The Hungarians of Romania* (reissued April 1990 as 'Romania's Ethnic Hungarians'.)
n.46, *The Flemings and Walloons of Belgium*.
n.50, *The Ukrainians and Georgians*.
n.55, *The Sami of Lapland*.
n.72, *Co-existence in some Plural European Societies* (reissued 1991 as 'Minorities and Autonomy in Western Europe').
n.82, 1989, *Minorities in the Balkans*.
1990, *Soviet Minorities Update*.
1993, *Minorities in Central and Eastern Europe*.

Xunta de Galicia.
The History of the Galician Language, Santiago de Compostela, n.d.
Estatuto de Autonomia de Galicia, Milladoiro, Santiago de Compostela, n.d.

Yale Law School, *The Avalon project: A Decade of American Foreign Policy*, www.yale.edu/lawweb/avalon/decade/decade17.htm

Monographs, brochures and pamphlets

Albion, A.S., and Lampe, J.R., *Strains of Economic Transition and Ethnic Conflict*, Washington: Woodrow Wilson International Center, 1994.
'Alpina' Gruppo di Studio (Alpina), *I Quattro Gruppi Nazionali del Friuli-Venezia Giulia*, Bellinzona: Salvioni, 1975.
Austrian Ethnic Groups Centre, Austria Ethnica, vol.7, State and Perspectives, Vienna: AEGG, 1994.
Boelens, K., *The Friesian Language*, Leeuwarden: Provincial Government of Friesland, 1987.
Breton Prisoners' Solidarity Committee, *Where does the Responsibility Lie for Violence in Brittany?* Dublin: BPSC, 1978.
Decurtins, A., *Il Romanstch – in Model per la Sort Minoritads Linguisticas e Culturales?*, Chur: Ligia Romontsche, 1976.

Eagle Street, Newsletter of the Finnish Institute in London.
International Association for the Protection of Human Rights in Cyprus, *Violations of Human Rights in Cyprus*, Nicosia, 1991.
Liebich, A., *Ethnic Minorities and Long-term Implications of EU Enlargement*, Badia Fiesolana, European University Institute, 1998.
Maginnis, K., *McGimpsey & McGimpsey v. Ireland*, Dungannon, 1990.
Magyar Koalicio Partja, *A Short Analysis of the Law on the Use of the Languages of National Minorities*, Bratislava, c.July/August 1999.
Volgger, F., *Südtirol-Themen*, Bozen/Bolzano, Südtiroler Landesregierung, Presseamt, 1995.
Wolfe, J.H., Heinritz, G., Hilf, R., and Kellner, L., *Zypern – Macht oder Land Teilen?* Munich: International Institute for Nationality Rights and Regionalism, 1987.
Zaagman, R., *Conflict Prevention in the Baltic States: the OSCE High Commissioner on National Minorities in Estonia, Latvia and Lithuania*, Flensburg: European Centre for Minority Issues (ECMI), Monograph n.1, April 1999.

Newspapers

L'Adige, Trento.
Alto Adige, Bolzano-Bozen.
Daily Telegraph, London.
The European, London.
Le Figaro, Paris.
Financial Times, London.
Guardian, London.
L'Independant, Carcassonne.
Le Soir, Paris.
Le Monde, Paris.
Newsletter, Belfast.
Sunday Telegraph, London.
Sunday Times, London.

Index

270 *Index*

Printed in the United States
1318500001B/23